Fem

Legal Strategy

Edited by
Anne Bottomley
and
Joanne Conaghan

Blackwell Publishers

Copyright © Basil Blackwell Ltd.

ISBN 0-631-18787-1

First published 1993

Published simultaneously as Vol. 20, No. 1
of Journal of Law and Society ISSN 0263-323X

Blackwell Publishers
108 Cowley Road, Oxford, OX4 1JF, UK
and
238 Main Street, Cambridge, MA 02142, USA.

British Library Cataloguing in Publication Data
A CIP Catalogue record for this book is available from the British Library

Library of Congress Cataloging in Publication Data
Feminist theory and legal strategy / edited by Anne Bottomley and
Joanne Conaghan.
 p. cm.
 "Published simultaneously as vol. 20, no. 1 of Journal of law and society, ISSN
0263–323X"–T.p. verso.
 Includes bibliographical references.
 ISBN 0–631–18787–1 (pbk. : alk. paper) : $19.95
 1. Women–Legal status, laws, etc.—Great Britain. 2. Feminist
theory. I. Bottomley, Anne. II. Conaghan, Joanne.
KD734.F46 1993   93–9867
305.42'01—dc20   CIP

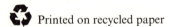 Printed on recycled paper

Typeset by Megaron, Cardiff, Wales.
Printed and bound in Great Britain by Whitstable Litho, Whitstable, Kent.

Contents

Feminist Theory and Legal Strategy

ANNE BOTTOMLEY and JOANNE CONAGHAN*

We have entitled this collection feminist theory and legal strategy. At one level, this could be read as no more than an attempt to bracket together themes and issues developed in theoretical debate with concrete, specific examples by way of application. Indeed some of the papers may be read this way: such a project has a recognized academic history with which we have all engaged at some stage in our own work. Equally, the move from particularities to more general principles has frequently been employed in (feminist) academic work; locating strategies within a broader theoretical context is a common approach and one which allows us to continually remind ourselves of the potential ramifications of our immediate project. Again, there are aspects of this in some of the papers which follow.[1]

Feminist work within law has been characterized by both of these trajectories; it is in the very mode of our operation as lawyers that we are continually faced with specific instances. It is also in our lives as women that our feminism is informed by the particular operations and instances of our engagement with law. This collection, however, is premised on a rather different base. It is a base which we would assert has been the particular strength of feminist work within and on law; it is that our work is not so much concerned with the application of 'theory' to 'law' or vice versa, but rather that it is the interface between the two which is the very site of our theoretical work.

What we are posing here is twofold. On the one hand, it is a model of theory which sees theory as simply that – a model; one which offers us ideas which we return to and use as a series of tools to raise questions, test insights, and find a language to bring together and communicate our ideas. It does not exist in and for itself, but only in relation to the use to which it is put. For this reason, the strength of feminist jurisprudence is tested not by claims to internal coherence[2] but rather by an ability to deliver. This may sound harshly pragmatic but we

* Kent Law School, University of Kent, Canterbury, Kent CT2 2NY, England

We are grateful to Andy Dart and Belinda Meteyard for their comments on an earlier draft of this paper. The views expressed herein do not necessarily reflect the views of all the contributors to the collection. In putting together this volume, we would particularly like to thank Paddy Ireland (not least for his invaluable courier services) and Nick Jackson (for his instant computer advice). The collection has taken form along with new lives (birth, pregnancy, birth); we thank all those who sustained us and our children in a difficult but exciting year.

1

firmly believe that those aspects of theoretical work which have proven of value to us over the years are those which have enabled us to develop and access concrete material gains in our work.

There are undoubtedly those who would read this as an anti-theoretical stance. Carol Smart might, for instance, identify us with what she terms as 'resistance to theory':

> . . . based on the argument that, because law is a practice which has actual material consequences for women, what is needed in response is counterpractice not theory. This constituency demands 'practical engagement' and continually renders (mere?) theoretical practice inadequate. This argument comes from certain feminist constituencies which may define 'doing' theory as male. These . . . elements present a major obstacle to proponents of feminist legal theory as they (we) meet with the frustrations of being ignored or seen as outmoded in and by law and are simultaneously moved to renounce theory by the moral imperative of doing something through or in law.[3]

In our view, it is not a question of whether different forms of theoretical practice are seen as male or not. Equally, it is not a question of demanding practical engagement at the expense of theory. It is rather that the mode and strength of feminist theory in law has been the interface between the use of abstract models and ideas to interrogate the practices of law.[4] It may not have been articulated in quite this way before – in that sense it has not yet been 'theorized' – but if we examine our feminist academic heritage, it is the one point which consistently characterizes the work, in all its rich plurality and diverse perspectives. Thus, our stance is not anti-theory, neither is it concerned simply with the application of theory. It is theory, but it is not one which traditionalists would recognize in their limited use of the term. If the counterpoint to our approach is the idea that theory stands for theory's sake, then certainly our notion of theory will be too radical. If we need (and we are not convinced that we do need) to find parallels in the work of 'theorists' who would exemplify a similar approach it would be with, for instance, Braidotti[5] or Deleuze.[6] They exemplify a theoretical stance based on engagement, on what used to be called 'praxis'. It is not so much a question of application but rather of movement between 'theory' and 'practice'.

This theoretical stance allows, perhaps reflects, a pluralism within which there can be no *one* analytical model deployed but rather a series of engagements and incursions. In a legal context, this precludes seeing 'law' as a closed model but rather recognizes it as a series of ideas, practices, and engagements, all of which are loosely held together under the rubric of the term 'law'. We would be the first to acknowledge the experience of any marginal or disadvantaged group within our society which has (rightly) felt, and continues to feel, in many ways and in many instances, the oppressive (or in terms of their own needs, unresponsive) operation of law.[7] But to then characterize law *simply* in these terms is to fly in the face of our experience of law in other ways.

One of the most important insights to emerge from the critical legal studies movement has been to highlight the internal inconsistencies in law, the paradoxes, silences, and contingencies. This matches our experiences as women and feminists engaged with law. It is not an internally coherent system which operates smoothly to oppress us at all times and in all ways. The 'power' of law is certainly present but not undifferentiated. It is uneven and it allows us space: space to argue, to engage, and (in the active sense of the word) to 'resist'.[8]

We have only to listen to our sisters in practice to learn this lesson in a very pragmatic way. The operation of law involves a continual use of strategies, in which one is constantly balancing the possibilities against the probabilities.[9] Again, let us be clear – in general, it is a more than uneven fight. As law is constituted in a society which still privileges sections of that society in terms of gender, race, class, and socially defined standards of ability, so it is by no means a 'free space' for equal engagement. But neither is it closed space which we must continually struggle *against* rather than *within*. When Smart states that 'the entry of feminists into law has turned law into a *site* of struggle rather than being taken only as a *tool* of struggle'[10] we would agree, but we would add that it is a site within which we find tools; it was never a tool because it is not a single entity or practice. Indeed, one of our problems has been that (ironically) the sense of this is far more available in the practice of law than in the academy. It is in the academy that law has been (partly under the influence of the social sciences) most frequently presented as an internally coherent, undifferentiated model which leaves one only with the choice of submission or resistance in the narrow sense of the word. In practice we experience law as more complex and hence more open to incursions.

The problem is that this experience of law must not only be placed against a context of generally negative expectations and experiences (in other words, we must keep a perspective), but also that it is difficult to record. We mean this in two ways. First, there is still (properly) a tendency to focus on those areas of law which operate most to women's detriment. This necessarily reinforces our sense of neglect and exclusion. Secondly, the interstices of practice – not merely the operation of substantive law but the elements of process in bargaining and negotiation – are less visible than the record of judgments in the higher courts or the passing of legislation. Small (but significant) developments which we could characterize as victories go unnoticed but radically improve the position of particular women in particular ways. We might think here of developments requiring the sharp thinking of women solicitors and barristers in helping to devise means by which rape victims might receive representation in criminal cases or strategies to protect the claims to ownership made by women who do not hold legal title to property. This low-profile lawyering, reflected neither in case material nor academic texts, is a rich tapestry of strategies which often cross conventional legal categories.[11] Of course this must be read against a generally negative background but, importantly, it leads us to dismiss an entirely negative stance towards the tools of lawyering, whether in practice or within the academy. Our stance then is a politics of engagement, informed and considered, moving continually between the abstract and the specific.[12]

3

The overwhelming tone of this particular collection is with the problems we encounter when we engage in this way, problems which go beyond substantive law, to issues of procedure and process and beyond that to the very languages with which we engage.[13] They also reflect issues relating to the diversity of women's position and needs,[14] and to the general problems encountered by taking abstract stances, reliant upon concepts such as equality or rights.[15] In this sense, read as a whole, the collection reflects the *modus operandi* of our claim to a particular type of theoretical work – the interface between the particular, concrete circumstance, and the general, abstract model. It is that interface that we understand as 'strategy'.

NOTES AND REFERENCES

1 See, for example, Conaghan, De Gama, and Lacey. Although this is not the place to pursue the particular problems of choosing different modes of entry to work (indeed some may see the choice simply as an heuristic decision, a question of which entry point is most likely to carry a readership into the argument), we should record that we are only too aware of the pitfalls of both modes of operation outlined above. Indeed this is one of our reasons for arguing (below) that what should be highlighted is the broader frame of the continuing relations of moves between the more abstract and the more concrete.

2 This should not be read as an argument against the need for clear and rigorous thinking; it is simply another way of asserting that canons of 'grand theory' are of no use to us so long as they continue to remain concerned with internal proofs of coherence as their source of validity.

3 C. Smart, 'The Woman of Legal Discourse' (1992) 1 *Social and Legal Studies* 29. Smart does not give examples of the type of work to which she is referring here. Her characterizations of 'three voices' of resistance to theory (of which this is the third) seem to us to be overdrawn to the point of caricature. They may be useful polemically but read more like a misreading of feminist work within law counterposed to her espousal of feminist socio-legal theory, with which she identifies at the beginning of her article. If this is a misreading of her argument, we apologize; we have used her article to show how this introduction might be read as 'anti-theory', when we see it as, importantly, a mode (and a radical mode) of theoretical work.

4 We have used the word 'interface' to try and convey the inter-relational aspect of the work. However, this is only a way of representing the *modus operandi*. It could equally be tackled by arguing that there is no real, final, distinction between theoretical and practical work. Theoretical work, following this analysis, is practical. Equally, practical work is necessarily theoretical. This disruption of the binary follows the patterns developed by Gilles Deleuze, particularly in his reading of and discussions with Michel Foucault. See *Language, Countermemory, Practice* (1977).

   However, the initial positing of a binary is useful. It not only locates us within the traditional language of division which is our academic heritage, but it also serves to activate the interface as the site of relations which then becomes the focus. The problem is that many (especially Anglo-American) academics still operate as if models, particularly binary models, are the final 'truth' around which we have to organize choice or privilege, rather than devices by which to organize our thinking. Thus, orthodox scholars might accuse us of conflation or elision, rather than accepting that the point is to open up space by rejecting the closures of oppositional (binary) thinking. The binary model is a useful tool, and one which we will continually and necessarily return to, but it is not a final analysis. As an example of the constructive use of this tension, see Lacey below.

5 R. Braidotti, *Patterns of Dissonance* (1991). See also I. M. Young, *Justice and the Politics of Difference* (1990).

4

6 op. cit., n. 4, and in *Foucault* (1988) Deleuze presents a very different reading of Foucault from that traditionally offered by English academics, particularly in the social sciences. We are grateful to Andy Dart for drawing this parallel to our attention. It is of interest to us that although the genealogy of the work is so different from feminism, the parallels now become so close and the archaeology so similar. It is also interesting that Braidotti (op. cit., n. 4) derives more from Deleuze than from any of the other major French (male) theorists whom she examines in her book.

7 See, for example, Cheney below.

8 We refer here to the more Nieztschian use of the term, expressing the continual tension between referents, not simply (as is often the case) a resistance to power which is perceived as one-directional.

9 We are indebted here to the insights we have gained from the women practitioners with whom we have worked closely, particularly Catherine Carpenter, Jane Hinde, and Susan Olley. At the same time we are not privileging their experience of the operation of law in practice over our experience of the operation of law within the academy as somehow 'more real' – we are simply recognizing that through many practices (including this very project), one experience is recorded far more frequently than the other. This has sometimes led, in our opinion, to a very partial image of law which has rendered or portrayed it as more coherent and powerful (more 'closed') than the broader experience of law teaches us. This does not seem to have been understood by some feminist writers who in our view take law too seriously, almost accepting an academic version of law, current in the late nineteenth century, which attempted to construct law as a coherent and internally rational system, projecting 'Law' with a capital 'L'. Law has never been that simple.

10 Smart, op. cit., n. 3, p. 30.

11 For examples of litigation strategies, see Olsen and Twomey below.

12 Including, where appropriate, arguments for not using particular legal strategies – for example, see Lacey below.

13 See, for example, Bottomley below.

14 See, for example, Cheney and Bunting below. We believe that the need to move between an acknowledgement of the specificity and diversity of women's lives and the patterns which impinge upon all women is central to the argument we are making. In contemporary terms, 'situationalism' is simply another indicator of the need to be constantly vigilant of the diversity of experience and practice. Hence the focus on strategy. At another level, a constant theme of this volume is the construction of images of women through presence (for example, 'wives' in Bottomley and Cheney) or absence (as with 'pregnant women' in Conaghan and De Gama). The use of narratives of women's lives (which at best are only ever partial representations) in debates over law reform is interestingly examined by Sally Sheldon in 'Who is the Mother to make the Judgement? The Constructions of Women in English Abortion Law' (1993) 1 *Feminist Legal Studies* 3. On the Woman/women distinction, see for example, Teresa de Lauretis, *Technologies of Gender* (1987).

15 See, for example, Conaghan (equality); De Gama and Bunting (rights). Many of the essays also point to the dangers of wielding what may turn out to be a double-edged sword.

Theorizing Women's Cultural Diversity in Feminist International Human Rights Strategies

ANNIE BUNTING *

INTRODUCTION

In this article I want to explore how international human rights strategies can be more responsive to the needs of women in diverse cultural settings. While there has been an increasing amount of feminist legal writing which has examined the cultural assumptions that often lie within the category of 'women', feminist scholarship concerning international human rights protections has been dismissive of culturally relative positions and therefore has implicitly maintained universalistic and essentialist norms. Feminists fear that challenging the artificial cultural unity of women's experience will hinder the project of prioritizing women's concerns in the international sphere. My argument is that cultural and gender critiques of the dominant discourse are interrelated and necessary aspects of a project for women's empowerment. It is my contention that international women's rights will not have the support of diverse women worldwide until the cultural assumptions within international human rights norms are interrogated along with the gendered premises of those norms. To ignore the importance of culture, race, class, sexuality, and history ends up leaving feminist theory within international human rights theoretically impoverished and strategically weak.

In many ways the cultural critiques of the dominant human rights discourse echo the critiques of the dominant feminist discourse and yet neither of the critiques has been adequately merged in feminist international scholarship. The prevailing tendency for feminists is to address cultural relativism only when evaluating strategies for the implementation of international human rights standards. I know of no attempts to evaluate systematically the appropriateness of those universalist standards for women in varying cultures, nor to problematize the internationalist feminist project. The general

**Legal Consultant and Researcher, 132 Albany Ave., Toronto, Ontario, M5R 3C4, Canada*

I would like to thank Michael Anderson, Susan Boyd, Brenda Cossman, and Tim Murphy for their helpful comments on earlier drafts of this article. Special thanks to Bruce Ryder for his support and critical editorial eye. An earlier version of this paper was presented to a Faculty of Law seminar, University of British Columbia, December 1991.

inclination in cultural critiques of human rights, on the other hand, has been to ignore questions of gender oppression. As a result, the feminist and non-Western analyses of international human rights bypass each other's insights, and neither concerns itself with the contemporary debate in feminist theory with respect to its own universalism.

I will attempt to draw on both cultural relativism and feminist theories of anti-essentialism to unite the strengths of each (in what I call asymmetrical anti-essentialism) and suggest ways in which projects and writing in this area could better address cultural diversity. To introduce these themes and contextualize the current international writing, I will briefly outline the features of international human rights discourse. Cultural critiques of the dominant discourse and responses of feminist scholars to cultural relativism will then be discussed. Internal feminist critiques of universalism and essentialism will then be introduced, with the implications of both cultural relativism and anti-essentialism taking shape in the final section.

CULTURAL RELATIVISM AND FEMINIST RESPONSES IN INTERNATIONAL HUMAN RIGHTS DISCOURSE

The contemporary international human rights rhetoric is characterized by political, philosophical, and historical universality, gender neutrality, and cross-cultural applicability. This dominant discourse has been criticized from a number of different perspectives which have revealed that the universal pretensions hide the fact that it is a predominantly male,[1] Western,[2] liberal human rights discourse which has evolved in a particular historical and philosophical context.[3] Critics of the dominant discourse usually attack its purported universality from one perspective, and, as we shall see, rarely incorporate the insights of work in other disciplines. This section will survey the critiques made by feminist and non-Western scholars, and attempt to show the prevailing tendencies in these works: feminists largely reject cultural critiques of human rights discourse (broadly called cultural relativism) and non-Western scholars who are not working within the feminist tradition generally overlook the gendered nature of human rights discourse.

1. Dominant Discourse

The general features of the dominant discourse define the parameters of the feminist and cultural debates. I want to emphasize two themes: the universalistic assumptions of the discourse and the exclusion or marginalization of women's concerns.

The moral theories of the self encoded in the United Nations documents can be described as consonant with classical liberalism:

> The liberal conception of self is individualistic and atomistic. The self is posited as a separate, autonomous unit capable of free choice. The voluntaristic self exists prior to its aims and attachments – it is a self unconstituted by its relationships with others.[4]

7

It is within the modern Western tradition of contract theories that the self is 'disembedded and disembodied'.[5] Interestingly, the autonomous individual of contract theories, as Carole Pateman argues, is clearly located in patriarchal social relations: 'the meaning of the individual and the social contract depend on women and the sexual contract'.[6]

Consistent with expressions of liberal individualism, United Nations' human rights documents and theories place priority on the individual over society or community; rights are considered immutable; and they are universal for all human beings. The rhetoric holds that the 'human condition' is 'gender-free'.[7] There is no need to articulate specific gender dimensions of rights violations, because human rights discourse is said to be gender-neutral.

Feminists, however, see 'universality' as deeply gendered and women's concerns as largely marginalized in the international human rights community.[8] While there has been some progress in bringing women to the centre of the discourse and institutional framework, the struggle continues. Many, mostly Western, feminists have seen cultural critiques as antagonistic to this strategy, however, and therefore their scholarship and strategies remain situated within the mainstream discourse's claim to universal, cross-cultural applicability.

2. Cultural Relativism

As with concepts in other social sciences, human rights concepts in law are being challenged as culturally-specific. While there are many understandings of 'cultural relativism', in human rights scholarship, the relativists' challenge can be summarized as follows: norms of morality are relative to a given society; the ethical basis for international human rights is Western; therefore international norms should not be the basis of value judgements in other cultural contexts. In other words, contrary to the claim to universality that human rights discourse makes, the genesis of notions of human rights is historically and philosophically Western. Cultural relativism therefore undermines one of the fundamental tenets of international human rights discourse.

Numerous writers on international human rights have debated the cross-cultural applicability of codified norms.[9] Authors from various traditions note that the standards in international human rights law reflect a specific moral philosophy which is not consistent with many non-Western value systems: '[w]hereas Western conceptions are based on the autonomous individual, African conceptions do not know such individualism.'[10]

What Third World conceptions of human rights might be, though, is far from a resolved issue. Some theorists argue that conceptions of human rights similar to those in international documents can indeed be found in contemporary Third World societies[11] while others maintain that the dominant Western discourse is antithetical to the norms in many societies.[12]

There are aspects of cultural relativism in human rights which are important to incorporate into our analyses;[13] however, some of the assertions are reductionist. First, norms in societies are presumed to be ascertainable and

8

cohesive; the multiply-constituted nature and competing understandings of any given culture are rarely discussed, and the tensions and contradictions within a society go unmentioned. Secondly, the notion of 'Western' is rarely problematized by critics; while culture is seen as differentiated along the Western/non-Western lines, Western culture itself is not seen as heterogeneous. Norms of morality within the West may be as diverse as norms found in non-Western contexts. Thirdly, while human rights language may derive from Western sources, its present currency is not unproblematically and solely Western. Many in the West are critical of liberal individualism and Enlightenment universalism and many in the 'East' and 'South' have endorsed the ethical basis of international human rights law. Further, cultural relativists presume that all members of society will benefit equally from society and are often blind to gender oppression. In particular, questions of the power to constitute dominant cultural norms are never raised and the gendered nature of society is rarely explored.[14]

3. Feminist Responses to Cultural Relativism

According to some commentators, the 'challenge from relativism is increasing'.[15] Certainly it seems that the legitimacy of positions based on anti-colonialism and cultural integrity is increasing. How serious a challenge these arguments can make to the mainstream discourse is yet to be determined. Theorists who defend universal human rights rely upon natural law, positivism, or modernizing arguments. Some assert that since the international documents have been ratified by most countries, their universal applicability and validity is proven. Others assert that, since societies are no longer isolated entities and are influenced by a wide variety of external forces,[16] the cultural relativists are misrepresenting or idealizing 'traditional' society. Another position is that international human rights norms in fact can be found in indigenous concepts of justice and, therefore, are appropriate. Yet another position leaves universalism unexamined by simply holding that the standards articulated in the international documents are the best way to protect individual rights against violation and hence ought to be complied with.[17] Most universalists also express dismay at the apparent critical paralysis and international impotence which relativism is said to imply.[18]

Feminists writing about women's international human rights express concern that relativism will only prolong the inattentiveness of the world community to the needs of women and often rely upon one of these above defences when considering cultural relativism. The prevailing tendency in writing on women's international human rights is to strongly oppose cultural relativism,[19] largely I would think because most authors perceive these arguments as being the defence of a sexist, not the deliberation of a sister. Ashworth states, for example, that:

> The cry against 'interference in culture' is used as a defense of men's rights, not of women's; it is used to avoid creating a 'national shame' over the behaviour of one sex toward the other, at the expense of the second sex.[20]

9

Even when radically criticizing the dominant discourse as encoding 'androcentric' notions, Western feminists are not apt to include the cultural specificity of rights discourse in their critique. Custom is seen as something which perpetuates the subordination of women to men.[21] Culture is seen as an impediment to the implementation of universal laws. For feminists who 'claim universal rights in the face of a world that does not universally agree, they are plagued by the counter-claim of cultural relativism'.[22]

I would argue that strategic implementation of universal rights suppresses and devalues cultural diversity. Fundamental cultural conflicts are left unresolved, buried beneath presumptively universal norms. Simply to dismiss cultural relativism and resist engaging with other critiques of international human rights discourse can lead to a strategy which is only relevant to a minority of women in the world. We Western feminists could do more to interrogate the universalism of human rights discourse by questioning its cultural as well as its gender biases.

It is interesting to note that the cultural relativistic critiques of the dominant discourse in many ways mirror the feminist critiques, with clear parallels with the most radical feminist arguments. Both see the dominant discourse as based on individualistic and particular moral philosophies which serve to exclude the perspectives of 'others'. Both see the dominant discourse as founded on liberal notions of the self and on liberal prioritization of civil and political rights. Both critiques are looking at the centre from different places on the margin. These critical schools of thought, however, have passed each other by.

PROBLEMATIZING UNIVERSALISM AND ESSENTIALISM: ANTI-ESSENTIALIST FEMINIST THEORIES

Much of feminist scholarship attempting to expose the fallacy of universalism in international human rights law is premised upon questioning the assumption of objectivity inherent in human rights discourse. Whether through an analysis of the exclusion of women's concerns, institutional bias, or the gendered nature of the language being deployed, the aim is to show that universalistic norms have yet to be universally applied; the discourse, it is argued, has gender dimensions which serve to silence and/or marginalize women's experience. This is very much the international dimension of a (Western) feminist project to unsettle the claims of objectivity and gender neutrality made in many disciplines, including law. This project, however, has itself been subjected to criticism for conflating the experience of white Western middle-class women with experience of all women. In many ways, feminist theories grow from and reflect upon other feminist thought,[23] with the process of internal critique creating new ground for feminist theorizing and strategizing. Recent examples of internal reflection and critique are the focus here.

10

1. Anti-Essentialist Approaches

While more contemporary feminist social theorists have tended to focus less on an all-encompassing explanation of sex discrimination and a totalizing theory of sexism, Fraser and Nicholson note that, 'essentialist vestiges persist in the continued use of ahistorical categories like gender identity'.[24] Women's essence is a particular premise for international feminism found in some, though not all, explanations of a universal women's subordination.

Elizabeth Grosz defines essentialism in the following manner:

> The term usually entails biologism and naturalism. . . . Essentialism entails that those characteristics defined as women's essence are shared in common by all women at all times: it implies a limit on the variation and possibilities of change.[25]

The anti-essentialist critique, like those relying on women's essence, has come from diverse positions: materialist, social constructionist, deconstructionist, postmodern, and poststructuralist. One common thread running through these feminist theories, though, is the rejection of a (universal) unified or non-contingent female subject. Moreover, unlike the 'empirical' critique of women's essence, experience is seen as a problematic basis for theorizing.

Within the feminist poststructuralist tradition, deconstruction has been methodologically significant. Deconstructionism seeks to displace all categories of language and to show the shifting nature or contingency of concepts and consciousness. Deconstruction 'as reversal-displacement . . . teaches one to question all transcendental idealism'.[26] Feminist literary theorists like Gayatri Chakravorty Spivak and Toril Moi oppose binary oppositions and fixed categories in writing and meaning. Deconstruction clearly rejects any essential category of woman. As Spivak states:

> It is . . . the deconstructive view which keeps me resisting an essentialist freezing of the concepts of gender, race, and class. I look rather at the repeated agenda of the situational production of those concepts and our complicity in such production. This aspect of deconstruction will not allow the establishment of a hegemonic 'global theory' of feminism.[27]

The implications for feminist theory, therefore, are a radical subversion not only of masculinist language but also the work of feminists ourselves.

2. Asymmetrical Anti-essentialism

From a deconstructionist, materialist, or social constructionist point of view, positing an essential nature of women is seen as ahistorical and a reinscription of socially constructed gender roles. However, we should be wary of theorizing on the basis of the rigid binary opposition of essentialism and constructionism. Diana Fuss in her impressive reading of the essentialist/social constructionist debate[28] argues that 'essentialism underwrites theories of constructionism and constructionism operates as a more sophisticated essentialism.'[29] She argues that to see essentialism as inherently reactionary 'is to act as if essentialism has an essence';[30] moreover, to substitute the social for the biological is to essentialize subject-positions.[31] Fuss maintains that the deployment of experience and essence can have disruptive effects on dominant discourses which oppress on the basis of these identities.

An evaluation of essentialism should take into account by whom and in what context identity politics based on essence are being deployed. There may be strong reasons to heed Spivak's call for 'strategic positivist essentialism'[32] or to follow Fuss in 'risking essentialism'.[33] Fuss states that:

> [i]n the hands of a hegemonic group, essentialism can be employed as a powerful tool of ideological domination; in the hands of the subaltern, the use of humanism to mime . . . humanism can represent a power displacing repetition.[34]

In other words, rather than decrying all theories based on essential differences, an asymmetrical approach would seek to understand the context of (essential) identity politics: essentialism from a dominant position can perpetuate oppression while, as a means of challenging dominant ideologies, it can be necessary and persuasive.

Strategic essentialism is nothing if not employed self-consciously: there must be a constant critical deconstruction of categories and identity since essentialism can reinforce both stereotypes and exclusions. Fuss argues for an 'understanding of identity as alienated and fictitious . . . all representations of identity as simultaneously possible and impossible'.[35]

In Spivak's reading of the work of the Subaltern Studies group,[36] she evaluates their reliance on a homogeneous subject of historiography, the subaltern, and the idea of a unified subaltern consciousness. She concludes that their methodology is counterhegemonic and 'strategically adhering to the essentialist notion of consciousness'[37] for it subverts colonial history and aims to recover a buried subaltern consciousness. She also emphasises that:

> [t]he discourse of the unified consciousness of the subaltern must inhabit the strategy of these historians, even as the discourse of the micrologized or 'situated' subject must mark that of anti-humanists on the other side of the international division of labour.[38]

By both deconstructing received categories and contextualizing the politics of essence, Spivak and Fuss have developed analyses that are powerful tools for feminist theory and practice. From this position we can open spaces for 'marginalized knowledges' in feminist theory while maintaining the theoretical and political rigour necessary for feminist engagement with other disciplines and discourses. The 'asymmetry' of essentialism and deconstructionism involved in this analysis is consonant with the work of many feminists writing from non-mainstream positions; echoes can be heard, for example, in the search by Awa Thiam,[39] Patricia Collins[40] and others for spaces for black feminist epistemologies and voices. bell hooks puts it this way:

> Abandoning essentialist notions would be a serious challenge to racism. . . . This critique should not be made synonymous with a dismissal of the struggle of the oppressed and exploited peoples to make ourselves subjects.[41]

Engaging with anti-essentialism as Western feminists, therefore, is imperative to a theory which will embrace women's cultural diversity. At the same time, this anti-essentialist posture cannot be over-simplified to disempower non-Western, non-white women from articulating identity politics: thus, the asymmetry that anti-essentialists must adopt.

Some feminists respond to the 'post-modern challenge' or 'turn' with concerns about the political and theoretical consequences for feminism. Sandra Harding and Seyla Benhabib, for example, caution that post-modern theory can lead to epistemological relativism and incoherent politics.[42] These concerns mirror those of international human rights scholars who fear that relativism and its accompanying abandonment of grand theory implies critical paralysis or contradiction. Brenda Cossman disagrees:

> If the postmodern project is understood as an attempt to recognize the multiplicity of perspectives and stories, then it would seem perfectly consistent with the project to bring forth women's experiences and perspectives as one which has been silenced and excluded from the official story.[43]

While the internal critiques within feminist theory come from divergent and even antagonistic positions, they represent incisive critiques of unified categories such as sisterhood, gender, women, and, even, woman. They offer from their different perspectives methods of theorizing difference and contradiction between women, between women and men, and within women's subjectivity and experiences of difference.

IMPLICATIONS OF CULTURAL RELATIVISM AND ANTI-ESSENTIALISM FOR INTERNATIONAL HUMAN RIGHTS STRATEGIES FOR WOMEN

Both cultural relativism in human rights scholarship and anti-essentialism in feminist theory have posed challenges to the assumptions that dominate the respective discourses. While the two counterclaims rarely meet in feminist human rights scholarship, this interface can produce constructive insights for the project of using international human rights protections for women. I will argue that cultural relativism should not be dismissed outright and that post-structuralist theory does not imply political paralysis. I will use three examples to show that, by rejecting culturally-based arguments about human rights norms, Western feminists can effectively silence Third World women's concerns and overlook important aspects of human rights struggles in non-Western contexts. Further, I will argue that an asymmetrical deployment of anti-essentialist theory can mediate the apparent tension between universalistic norms and culturally specific practices of concern to women.

Clitoridectomies and excision of women have been studied by anthropologists and feminists for decades. Mary Daly calls these practices torture;[44] Charlotte Bunch and others label them 'genital mutilation'.[45] Georgina Ashworth says that 'female circumcision' 'is intended to prepare the female sex for a life of suffering; to state that her identity is pain and powerlessness, unquestioning submission to social norms defined by men'.[46] Terms such as barbaric, uncivilized, and inhuman are often used in discussions about the

13

practices amongst Western feminists and human rights officials. Defences of the practices on the grounds of race, culture, or tradition are vehemently rejected as patriarchal rationalizations.

African feminists disagree with Western feminists both about the characterization of these practices and how to address them using human rights language. As Boulware-Miller discusses, when feminists advocate that such practices constitute mutilation and violate women's right to sexual and corporal integrity, 'in so describing an important part of African women's cultural identity, they offend all Africans'.[47] Awa Thiam reiterates:

> [p]eople who understand nothing of ritual practices must beware of attacking them, especially when they base their judgement on criteria which bear no relationship to the mentalities of people under consideration.
>
> The women of Black Africa have suffered enough from these colonial and neo-colonial attitudes.[48]

There are many women's organizations in Africa actively opposing the practices, but they are doing so with language and strategies that differ from their Western sisters.[49] African women's movements are proceeding in a manner attuned to the socio-political cultures of their communities. Rather than arguing that these practices constitute mutilation and barbarism, some African opponents highlight the health risks involved for girls and women. They are actively engaged in struggles to define the meaning of their cultural heritages and futures.

Muslim women are also involved in a dynamic and creative process of effecting change in many Arab countries and Muslim communities internationally. However, when Western feminists protest the lack of civil rights of women 'under Islam' the tendency is to see them as inescapably oppressed by a sexist religion and culture. Marnia Lazreg argues, in her critique of feminist scholarship on Algeria and North Africa, that the 'religious paradigm' which dominates the social science and feminist approaches to women in the Middle East and North Africa effectively silences Muslim women from expressing their own identity. Further, it leaves unexamined questions of the meaning (in other than fundamentalist terms) of Islam for women:

> The overall effect of this paradigm is to deprive women of self-presence, of being. Because women are subsumed under religion presented in fundamental terms, they are inevitably seen as evolving in nonhistorical time. They have virtually no history. Any analysis of change is therefore foreclosed.[50]

Islam as a religion, and not the interpretations and discursive uses of Islam, is seen as fundamentalist. The religion is also seen as a complete picture of the social system as opposed to a component of a Muslim culture.[51] Islamic respect for women's rights and Muslim feminists are seen as oxymorons.[52]

Lazreg goes on to say that 'Western gynocentrism has led to an essentialism of otherhood'.[53] Western feminists must dispense with the stereotypical images and paradigms of Third World women and must be 'willing to think differently about the variety of modes of being female, including their own'.[54] Ifi Amadiume makes a similar point in her critique of the rigid use by Western

14

feminists of the public/private model to analyze the status of women in Africa.[55] Lazreg concludes that 'Eastern' feminists 'must shoulder a double burden, namely, to work toward an epistemological break with the prevailing paradigm *and* to re-evaluate the structure of gender relations in their own societies.'[56]

Violence against women in societies has also been an issue which has highlighted the methodological and strategic tropes of feminists using international human rights discourse. To see the issue of rape in singularly gender terms negates the experiences of many women who are assaulted by officers of an occupying army, state prison authorities, or domestic employers.[57] Rape in these situations is inextricably linked to other political and historical factors. To understand the meaning of violence against women often demands an understanding of its race, class, and historical dimensions. For example, a Kashmir woman along the border with Pakistan,[58] a Tamil woman in Sri Lanka, a dissident activist in Guatemala, are at greater risk of rape for reasons which are intertwined with, but not encapsulated by, gender. To ignore these interactions and to subsume the experiences within gender constructs alone tells a partial and skewed story.[59]

To reject a culturally relative approach to violence against women denies the simultaneity of oppressions which may be implicated in the acts of violence women experience. Cultural relativism does not necessarily imply condoning the violence. Attention to culture and history, on the other hand, invites a richer analysis of rape, wife battery, sexual harassment, and assault.

A common theme in the writings of Thiam, Lazreg, Amadiume, and other Third World feminist scholars is the tendency of Western feminists to proceed on false assumptions about other cultural contexts, assumptions which show their reluctance to evaluate these contexts within non-Western paradigms. The approach of many mainstream feminists can perpetuate stereotypical, racist, and neo-colonial perspectives on African, Muslim, Asian, and other, peoples. Indeed, as Spivak says, 'varieties of feminist theory and practice must reckon with the possibility that, like any other discursive practice, they are marked and constituted by, and even as they constitute, the field of their production'.[60] These stereotypical paradigms silence women in non-Western communities.

Like Third World feminists, cultural relativists recognize the need for critical interrogation of Western analytical assumptions and respect for non-Western structures of interpretation and understanding. Marilyn Strathern's approach to her study of gender relations in Melanesia, contextualizing both Western and Melanesian metaphors of understanding sociality, points in this direction:

> It is important to show that inapplicability [of Western concepts] is not just a result of poor translation. Our own metaphors reflect a deeply rooted metaphysics with manifestations that surface in all kinds of analyses. The question is how to displace them most effectively.[61]

Talal Asad similarly challenges anthropologists to subject their language of translation to scrutiny and expansion. In his discussion of the inequality of languages between dominant and dominated societies, Asad states that:

> The relevant question therefore is not how tolerant an *attitude* the translator ought to display toward the original author . . . but how she can test the tolerance of her own language for assuming unaccustomed forms.[62]

This methodological perspective goes farther than simply rejecting a certain tool of analysis because of its historical and social specificity; it provides a means by which the historical determinants of both 'tool and object' can be contextualized and the interests at stake exposed.

In undertaking critical cultural examinations, it is crucial that one's own constructs, assumptions, and preoccupations be understood before one ventures to understand those of others. Moreover, Strathern cautions that 'one has to understand the Melanesian constructs first before taking *them* apart'.[63] She goes on to say that '[o]f course "we" may still wish to make up our own minds'[64] when observing cultural constructs. The stamp of our own cultural traditions, nevertheless, will always remain:

> I do not imagine, however, that I can extract myself from this mode [of knowledge and explanation]: I can only make its workings visible. To this end, I exploit its own reflexive potential.[65]

It is important to reiterate at this point that 'Western' society is not homogeneous and unitary. There are multifarious cultural 'realities' in the West, each with its own set of precepts and customs. One need only look at the relatively distinct communities making up Canada, England, or the United States of America to query whether the term 'Western culture' can accurately be said to have common constituent parts. Clearly, as Strathern notes, 'there are only generalizations'[66] of Western society, as there are only generalizations of other broadly categorized cultures.

The above approach to cultural interpretation is consonant with the anti-essentialist/post-structuralist feminist theories which seek to displace categories of knowledge and language. They, too, hold that universal understandings cannot exist, but only partial, contingent insights. The projects are similar in their aim to deconstruct the taken-for-granted assumptions of dominant discourses, such as that of the rational individual. Yet, simultaneously, there is a complicity, a participation, in those discourses.

Such an approach to cultural interpretation is also, broadly speaking, within the relativist tradition, given the recognition of historically and culturally constituted subjectivities and metaphysics. In the context of international human rights discourse, this perspective is found in the work of some African and Asian human rights scholars. Commentators have specifically noted the tendency among Western scholars 'to pay lip service' to alternative conceptions of human rights 'without substantially modifying their own Western positions and perspectives'.[67] However, not many authors within the cultural relativist school in human rights complicate their analysis with a deconstruction of the notion of 'Western' or Western notions.

Within the relativist tradition in human rights scholarship, the dominant discourse has been critiqued using essentialist notions of cultural difference; this places it at odds with postmodern or anti-essentialist theories. Some African scholars assert, for example, that traditional African social understandings are based on the notion of community and, therefore, individualistic Western human rights conceptions are ill-placed in Africa. Attempts have been made to codify specifically African human rights ideas in documents such as the Algiers Declaration and the African Charter of Human and Peoples' Rights. Third World feminists have similarly sought a distinct perspective premised upon the history of colonialism, cultural heritage, and contemporary socio-economic struggles. This is parallelled in work towards a black feminist epistemology or Asian-American identity as a ground of critique of mainstream tendencies in feminist theory. All of these challenges are grounded in an essential, unifying experience defined by race or culture.

The reliance on essentialist notions, just as with universalistic notions, cannot be dismissed categorically in human rights as reactionary, imperialist, and culturally colonial. This is a reductionist argument which does not recognize the complexity of interests in the debate. The key questions are by whom and in whose interests the rhetoric or discourse is being deployed. I believe these questions will lead us to adopt a strategic, asymmetrical anti-essentialism as our theoretical posture.

In the above cases where African, Muslim, and other Third World feminist and human rights scholars assert culturally based arguments, they do so to critique the dominant discourses in question. In addition, these perspectives may be a retrieval of formerly 'subjugated knowledges',[68] marginalized through the historical production of legitimate truth claims. This is precisely the task that the Subaltern group of historians set themselves, one of simultaneous critique and construction. And while the reliance on a coherent, essential subject can be criticized from a post-structuralist or anti-essentialist perspective:

> [O]ur own transactional reading of them is enhanced if we see them as *strategically* adhering to the essentialist notions of consciousness . . . within a historiographic practice that draws many of its strengths from that [anti-essentialist] critique.[69]

Human rights struggles can also draw many of their strengths from dominant language and the legitimacy of that discourse.[70] This is the position that many feminists have taken in national and international struggles as well: while the law and legal system is critiqued as being predominantly masculinist and for perpetuating gender oppression, rights discourse is still appropriated given its rhetorical and discursive power. Since there is always the risk that the deployment of the discourse buttresses its power, this strategy is combined with other critical practices to challenge and de-centre the discourse.[71]

Reliance on essentialist notions from dominant subject positions must be evaluated differently. Mainstream discourses which essentialize difference, or essentialize categories which negate difference, ought to be interrogated from a critical perspective. To leave the claims to universal truth unsettled in Western

17

scholarship will perpetuate the marginalization of the voices of Third World feminist and human rights scholars. In particular, to maintain the claim of universal applicability and validity of international human rights norms will further close off the possibility of creative expansion in this discipline. Theoretical critique will necessarily undermine the rhetorical power of human rights discourse as it is constituted by claims of universalism. However, a recognition that international norms can be filled with local contextual meaning will enhance the use of international human rights. To some extent this process is taking place as national constitutions (which incorporate international instruments) are interpreted in light of the indigenous situation. However, little change has occurred in the mainstream international human rights forum.

CONCLUSIONS

This leads me back to feminist international human rights scholarship. Western feminists have to be 'cautious and contingent'[72] in our prescription of strategies to address issues for Third World women. We ought to be careful in our assumptions, critical of our paradigms of analysis, and aware of our position in the debate. Asymmetry would require a systematic interrogation of the terms of international instruments and feminist theories being utilized. In addition, we should be wary of speaking *for* women whose culture is the object of scrutiny.

As Awa Thiam says, alliance and solidarity are the keys to feminist politics; this is quite different from imposition of politics.[73] bell hooks also cautions white feminists about the difference between solidarity and 'solipsism'. She stresses, along with Fuss and Spivak, the importance of distinguishing the self-aggrandizing essentialism of dominant groups in society from the essentialist foundations of identity politics of oppressed groups. This means that the critique of essentialist notions of difference:

> . . . should not become a means to dismiss differences or an excuse for ignoring the authority of experience. . . . This way of thinking threatens the very foundation that makes resistance to domination possible.[74]

In looking at examples such as violence against women and clitori-dectomies, then, asymmetrical anti-essentialism means recognizing that these experiences of oppression may be intertwined with the history of colonialism, racism, and neo-imperialism and not a simple equation of gender oppression; it means speaking with a recognition of our privileged voice; making room to hear the voices of Third World women who, as Thiam states, have different priorities and are in the process of articulating these issues.[75] It is an asymmetrical and contradictory politic at every turn. It involves more than an attempt at successful implementation of international human rights norms; it is also a displacement and fracturing of the dominant norms through a critique of their premises and an evaluation of their deployment.

18

NOTES AND REFERENCES

1 Charlesworth argues that international law 'is in fact constructed on the silence of women':
   H. Charlesworth, 'The Public/Private Distinction and the Right to Development in
   International Law' (1992) 12 *Australian Yearbook of International Law* 190 at p. 230; H.
   Charlesworth, C. Chinkin, and S. Wright, 'Feminist Approaches to International Law'
   (1991) 85 *American J. International Law* 613.

2 For a list of selected articles from non-Western perspectives, see A. Dundes Renteln,
   International Human Rights: Universalism Versus Relativism (1990) 55–56.

3 I. G. Shivji describes the dominant discourse as 'within an idealist philosophical world
   outlook' and 'within imperialist domination of Africa' in I. G. Shivji, *The Concept of Human
   Rights in Africa* (1989) pp. 43 and 52 respectively.

4 B. Cossman, 'A Matter of Difference: Domestic Contracts and Gender Equality' (1990) 28
   Osgoode Hall Law J. 303 at p. 332 (footnote omitted).

5 S. Benhabib, 'The Generalized and the Concrete Other: The Kohlberg-Gilligan Controversy
   and Feminist Theory' in *Feminism As Critique: On the Politics of Gender*, eds. S Benhabib
   and D. Cornell (1987) 77 at p. 85.

6 C. Pateman, *The Sexual Contract* (1988) 221.

7 G. Ashworth, *Of Violence and Violation: Women and Human Rights* (1986) 221.

8 It is beyond the scope of this paper to detail all the criticisms made of human rights
   machinery by feminists. See R. Cook, 'Women's International Human Rights: A Bibliography' (1992) 24 *New York Univ. J. of International Law and Politics* 857, and 'The
   International Right to Nondiscrimination on the Basis of Sex: A Bibliography' (1989) 14
   Yale J. of International Law 161.

9 Some works on this topic include: A. An-Na'im, 'Religious Minorities Under Islamic Law
   and the Limits of Cultural Relativism' (1987) 9 *Human Rights Q.* and 'The Rights of Women
   and International Law in the Muslim Context' (1987) 9 *Whittier L. Rev.* 491; J. Donnelly,
   'Cultural Relativism and Universal Human Rights' (1984) 6 *Human Rights Q.* 400 and *The
   Concept of Human Rights* (1985); R. Howard, 'The Full-Belly Thesis: Should Economic
   Rights Take Priority Over Civil and Political Rights? Evidence from Sub-Saharan Africa'
   (1983) 4 *Human Rights Q.* 467; A Pollis and P. Schwab, 'Human Rights: A Western
   Construct with Limited Applicability' in *Human Rights: Cultural and Ideological Perspect-
   ives*, eds. A. Pollis and P. Schwab (1979); A Dundes Renteln, op. cit., n. 2, and 'Relativism
   and the Search for Human Rights' (1988) 90 *American Anthropologist* 56 and 'The
   Unanswered Challenge of Relativism and the Consequences for Human Rights' (1985) 7
   Human Rights Q. 514; Shivji, op. cit., n. 3; and C. E. Welch Jr. and V. Leary (eds.), *Asian
   Perspectives on Human Rights* (1990).

10 Shivji, op. cit., n. 3, p. 12.

11 See R. Howard, *Human Rights in Commonwealth Africa* (1986) and K. M'Baye and B.
   Ndiaye, 'The Organizations of African Unity' in *The International Dimensions of Human
   Rights*, ed. P. Alston (1982) 583, both cited in Shivji, op. cit., n. 3, pp. 12 and 13 respectively.

12 J. A. M. Cobbah, 'African Values and the Human Rights Debate: An African Perspctive'
   (1987) 9 *Human Rights Q.* 309, cited in Shivji, op. cit., n. 3, p. 14; Donnelly, op. cit., n. 9.

13 See text accompanying notes 61 to 69 below.

14 Shivji, for example, only makes incidental mention of women at the end of his purportedly
   contextualized critique of the dominant human rights discourse (op. cit., n. 3, p. 89).

15 Renteln, 'Unanswered Challenge', op. cit., n. 9, p. 520: 'Despite the absolutist language in
   which the Charter is framed, the need to quell relativism remains.'

16 See R. Howard, 'Evaluating Human Rights in Africa: Some Problems of Implicit
   Comparisons' (1984) 6 *Human Rights Q.* 164.

17 J. Donnelly, 'Human Rights and Human Dignity: An Analytical Critique of Non-Western
   Human Rights Conceptions' (1982) 76 *American Political Science Rev.* 303, discussed and
   critiqued in Dundes Renteln, op. cit., n. 9, pp. 525–531.

18 Renteln, op. cit., n. 2, p. 67.

19 I am not aware of any feminist writing in this discipline which has attempted to explicitly

combine theories of cultural relativism and gender oppression. Perhaps this should not be surprising since, by definition, the work in this area centres on the implementation of human rights standards for women world-wide. An-Na'im is one author writing on women's rights who does accept a variation of cultural relativism and also supports respect for the rights of women as broadly articulated in international law.

20 Ashworth, op. cit., n. 7, p. 8.
21 id., and see R. Howard, 'Women's Rights in English-Speaking Sub-Saharan Africa' in *Human Rights and Development in Africa*, ed. C. E. Wright (1984) 46.
22 K. Engle, 'International Human Rights and Feminism: When Discourses Meet' 13 *Mich. J. International Law* 517 at p. 545.
23 M. Strathern calls feminist discourse one of 'internal pluralism' and says that in feminist scholarship 'One position evokes others. Yet the manner in which these multiple positions are constantly recalled has a further effect. They do not come together as parts of a whole but are held as coeval presences within discussion. Each bears its proximity to experience.' M. Strathern, *The Gender of the Gift* (1988) 23.
24 N. Fraser and L. J. Nicholson, 'Social Criticism without Philosophy: An Encounter between Feminism and Postmodernism' in *Feminism/Postmodernism*, ed. L. J. Nicholson (1990) 33.
25 E. Grosz, 'Conclusion; A Note on Essentialism and Difference' in *Feminist Knowledge: Critique and Construct*, ed. S. Gunew (1990) 332, at p. 334.
26 C. Spivak, 'Explanation and Culture: Marginalia' in *In Other Worlds: Essays in Cultural Politics* (1987) 103.
27 id., p. 84; and see T. Moi, *Sexual/Textual Politics: Feminist Literary Theory* (1985).
28 This debate in feminism can be summarized as follows: the essentialist school maintains a biological determinism for sexual difference while the constructionist theory argues that there is nothing innate to sexual difference, only that which is constructed in society. Thus, for an essentialist, 'woman is born not made; for an anti-essentialist like Simone de Beauvoir, woman is made not born': see D. Fuss, *Essentially Speaking: Feminism, Nature, and Difference* (1989) 3.
29 id., p. 119.
30 id., p. 21.
31 id., p. 32.
32 Spivak, op. cit., n. 26, pp. 179 and 210.
33 Fuss, op. cit., n. 28, pp. 19–20 and 40.
34 id., p. 32.
35 id., p. 102.
36 Ranajit Guha (ed.), *Subaltern Studies III: Writings on South Asian History and Society* (1984). The Subaltern Studies group seeks to retrieve the history of colonized peoples in India and to make 'a theory of consciousness or culture rather than specifically a theory of change': Spivak, 'Subaltern Studies: Deconstructing Historiography' in op. cit., n. 26, 197 at p. 198. The term 'subaltern' refers to silenced, subjugated, colonized, or oppressed groups.
37 id., pp. 206–7.
38 id., p. 210.
39 A. Thiam, *Black Sisters, Speak Out: Feminism and Oppression in Black Africa* (1986) 113–4. Translation by Dorothy S. Blair.
40 P. H. Collins, *Black Feminist Thought: Knowledge, Consciousness, and the Politics of Empowerment* (1990).
41 b. hooks, 'Postmodern Blackness' in *Yearning: Race, Gender, and Cultural Politics* (1990) 29.
42 op. cit., n. 5.
43 Cossman, op. cit., n. 4, p. 353.
44 M. Daly, *Gyn/Ecology* (1979) 157 and 154.
45 C. Bunch, 'Women's Rights as Human Rights' (1990) 12 *Human Rights Q*. 487 at p. 489.
46 Ashworth, op. cit., n. 7, p. 12.
47 K. Boulware-Miller, 'Female Circumcision: Challenges to the Practice as a Human Rights Violation' (1985) 8 *Harvard Women's Law J*. 155 at p. 170. And see K. Engle, 'Female Subjects of Public International Law: Human Rights and the Exotic Other Female' (1992) 26 *New England Law Rev*. 1509.

48 Thiam, op. cit., n. 39, p. 80.
49 See 'Report of the Workshop: African Women Speak on Female Circumcision' (1985) 11
    Women's International Network News 27; 'Meeting at Mid-Decade Forum, Copenhagen
    1980' (1980) 6 *Women's International Network News* 43; R. Saurel, *L'Enterée Vive* (1981)
    260–62.
50 M. Lazreg, 'Feminism and Difference: The Perils of Writing as a Woman on Women in
    Algeria' in *Conflicts in Feminism*, eds. M. Hirsch and E. Fox Keller (1990) 326, at p. 330.
51 I am indebted to Shama Nijabat who made this point to me in the context of a discussion of
    the English media portrayal of violence against women in Muslim societies. She argues, as a
    Muslim feminist, that it is those who control the dominant interpretation of the original
    texts, such as the Koran, and those who perpetuate a static view of Islam outside Muslim
    communities who are guilty of discrimination on the basis of sex and religion respectively.
    She went on to say that Islam is only one part of the culture. See M. Anderson, 'Islamic Law
    and the Colonial Encounter in British India' in *Islamic Family Law*, eds. C. Mallat and J.
    Connors (1990).
52 Lazreg notes that 'Although US feminists have attempted to accommodate Christianity and
    feminism and Judaism and feminism, Islam is inevitably presented as antifeminist. . . . Like
    tradition, religion must be abandoned if Middle Eastern women are to be like Western
    women. As the logic of the argument requires, there can be no change without reference to an
    external standard deemed to be perfect.' (Lazreg, op. cit., n. 50, p. 329.
53 id., p. 338.
54 id., p. 341.
55 I. Amadiume, *Male Daughters, Female Husbands: Gender and Sex in an African Society*
    (1987).
56 Lazreg, op. cit., n. 7, p. 341.
57 Amnesty International, *Women in the Front Line* (1990).
58 R. McCullagh and A. Wood, 'Shame of a Kashmiri Village' *Observer Magazine*, 1 June 1991,
    pp. 30–32, reported the mass rapes of over 50 women in Kunan Poshpura perpetuated by
    Indian army soldiers on 23 February 1991.
59 Black feminists have pointed out the colour-blind aspect of many feminist theories of rape: in
    their discussions, white feminists disregard the historical importance of slavery and its
    implications for black women and men in the United States of America. A. Harris, 'Race and
    Essentialism in Feminist Legal Theory' (1990) 42 *Stanford Law Rev.* 581 at pp. 598 and 601.
60 G. C. Spivak, 'Imperialism and Sexual Difference' (1986) 8 *Oxford Literary Rev.* 225.
61 Strathern, op. cit., n. 23, p. 12.
62 T. Asad, 'The Concept of Cultural Translation in British Social Anthropology' in *Writing
    Culture: The Poetics and Politics of Ethnography*, eds. J. Clifford and G. E. Marcus (1986)
    157.
63 Strathern, op. cit., n. 23, p. 326.
64 id., p. 326.
65 id., p. 7.
66 id., p. 343.
67 id., p. 15.
68 M. Foucault, 'Two Lectures' in *Power/Knowledge: Selected Interviews and Other Writings,
    1972–77*, ed. C. Gordon (1980) 82.
69 G. C. Spivak, 'Subaltern Studies' in *In Other Worlds*, op. cit., n. 26, pp. 206–7.
70 Shivji says that 'Human rights talk constitutes one of the main elements in the ideological
    armoury of imperialism. Yet from the view of African people, human rights struggles
    constitute the stuff of their daily lives.' Shivji, op. cit., n. 3, p. vii.
71 Perhaps feminists should take more seriously, though, Carol Smart's suggestion that 'the concept
    of rights has severe limitations, and may even be detrimental to the development of progressive
    policies of the Women's Movement' in C. Smart, *Feminism and the Power of Law* (1989) 158.
72 Cossman, op. cit., n. 4, p. 353.
73 Thiam says that 'any external action must be undertaken in alliance with that of the women
    most affected, or with the movement which represents them' (op. cit., n. 39, p. 87).

74 b. hooks, 'Culture to Culture: Ethnography and Cultural Studies as Critical Intervention' in *Yearning*, op. cit., n. 41, p. 130. Nancy Hartsock also queries '[w]hy is it, exactly at the moment when so many of us who have been silenced begin to demand the rights to name ourselves, to act as subjects rather than objects of history, that just then the concept of subjecthood becomes problematic?' N. Hartsock, 'Rethinking Modernism: Minority vs. Majority Theories' (1987) 7 *Cultural Critique* 196.

75 Thiam, op. cit., n. 39, p. 113.

Valued Judgments?: A Reading of Immigration Cases

DEBORAH CHENEY *

> I was very sad leaving my kids behind, very sad. But y'know since I had that plan to send for them, I knew it wouldn't be too long before I see them again.[1]

This reading of immigration cases does not profess to be a 'black letter law' analysis designed to advance cases as worthy to be read for their precedent import. Rather, those very cases which have been elevated to precedent status by reaching the dizzy heights of being 'reported', are approached in a different manner. I ask the reader to invest them less with a status born of and legitimized by their position within an institutional culture, than to be valued as accounts of how people are seen and families conceptualized; to see those party to the cases less as mere ciphers of legal watersheds than as individuals; to regard the tenor of reports less as objective accounts of two sides within a legally boundaried reasoned debate than as emotionally complex human beings trapped and manipulated within the pressures of a wider socio-political framework.

How these cases are to be read here is in or of itself part of the message the paper seeks to advance. Drawing upon a range of different areas before approaching the textuality of the cases is to truly 'read' them in hearing the voices of those who are their subject. Drawing upon diverse materials to supplement the 'word' of the law within which parties are embroiled becomes a means to render visible issues of gender and race which are otherwise marginalized. In the day-to-day operation of the immigration laws there is little acknowledgement either that valid argument can advance from other than strictly delineated areas, or that considerations outside the parameters of the drafters and operatives of the rules can be deemed pertinent 'knowledge'. This paper is thus a reading which acknowledges the complexity of the law, seeing it not as an entity 'out there', pristine and inviolate in the face of such considerations as racial and sexual stereotypes or categorizations, but as informed by and informing these very issues.

By highlighting how whiteness can effectively become the premise from which others are inscribed and marginalized, there can be an acknowledgement of the very position I as a writer seek to avoid – namely the

* University of Kent, Keynes College, Canterbury CT2 7NX, England

Thanks to Delia Jarrett-Macauley for her faith.

23

continual re-centring of a white supremacy within very particular 'spaces' of everyday life. To adopt such re-centring is to re-inscribe racist domination. In the same manner that white Western intellectual traditions embrace a specific political discourse by seeking to interpret the reality of others, the content and mode of operation of the Immigration Rules interlocks with systems of domination. It is the very specific spell of the law that renders the latter association an apparent impossibility, it is the very specific alchemy of learning to speak the language of law in another register that makes that impossible thought a very real possibility.

THE POWER: IMMIGRATION LAW

The Hydra which is immigration law, like the monster of Greek myth, turns a number of faces toward those who come before it. When legislative amendments strike off one of the heads new heads replace it, making the character of the whole eternally tinged with ambiguity. Immigration law is less an entity in or of itself that can be fixed and 'read' than a shifting array of expressions which confuse and disorientate, which have the character to turn a gaze fixedly upon one group and then upon another as socio-political forces demand.

Whilst the primary legislation is contained in general terms in the Immigration Act 1971, the fleshing out of these terms and the practice to be followed in their administration are embodied in the Statement of Changes in Immigration Rules[2] enacted under s.3(2) of the Immigration Act 1971. The transmutation of the primary legislation through the alchemy of the non-statutory Immigration Rules renders 'the word of the law' which is immigration law, a combination of legal rules and administrative practice.

Those invested with administrative duties are equally variously empowered. The immigration officers, who must apply the rules, have a status recognized by the Immigration Act; entry clearance officers, who issue or refuse applications abroad on the basis of the rules controlling entry, are not mentioned in the primary legislation. Both are persons 'lawfully acting in execution of the Act';[3] both act in accordance with the Immigration Rules and instructions issued to them by the Secretary of State.

THE SPACE: IMMIGRATION CONTROL

The world of immigration control is a space between formality and informality, between the public and the private. The Immigration Rules which emerge into the light of the public domain do so from shadows wherein lie their unpublished sub-texts, each with their own conceptual frameworks – appeal cases, unpublished instructions to immigration officers, the very training of the executives themselves. Into this twilight space are drawn men and women whose lives and very identities are subjected to scrutiny, the

24

scrutiny of the powerful over the powerless, the voiced over the voiceless. The matter of seeking entry becomes the manner of individuals facing each other in an interview process as two constructed entities. One is product and producer of an 'institutional culture', a public servant legitimated by a combined persona and disclaimer with which the Immigration Rules open, namely that: 'Immigration Officers will carry out their duties without regard to the race, colour and religion of people seeking to enter the UK'.[4] The other in the equation, the applicant, is forced to construct an identity in the image that very culture demands by qualifying under a category within the Immigration Rules. From this disparate base, justice is expected.

The mechanics of immigration control are premised in an androcentric and eurocentric base of ideology, theory, and method. This is revealed in the categories encompassed within the immigration rules. It is also revealed in the conceptual frameworks born of and contributing to these rules – in terms not only of what is regarded as 'knowledge' within the testimony given by those seeking to qualify, but also in the questions posed, language used, and interpretations made to elicit this knowledge. The tool used to extract this knowledge embraces a paradigm of traditional interviewing practice which prioritizes value-free objectivity and detachment, establishing a subject-object hierarchy between interviewer and interviewee. Whether it be undertaken at a port of entry or an overseas post, the professionally correct interview is regarded as a one-way instrument of data collection where the interviewer is assumed to be able to stand back from objects in the world to be investigated. Transcribed upon refusal into an 'explanatory statement' which will become the focal document at any appeal against refusal – compiled by either the interviewer or a third party – the words of interviewees become downgraded by objectification, their experiences given neither validity nor integrity in their own right. Revolving around a power relationship, with dichotomies of 'official/supplicant' and 'passive/active' participants, the system functions to enable imposition of one person's definition of reality upon another.

That there is an interaction affecting both parties, that wider socio-political issues feed into the interaction, is rarely – if ever – acknowledged. Any such suggestion is countered, not least by the opening exoneration of those involved in the decision-making process. Yet such subtleties do fuel the quality of the interaction, acting as an effective sub-text of control. Relationships entered into in the interview situation are structured equally by elements which exist within underlying social relations outside that situation, and which therefore affect the discourse itself. In an arena characterized by cross-cultural communication, the dominant power relations of race in society itself are reproduced. The difficulties inherent in an interview engagement *per se* are thus problematized, acting to disadvantage applicants to a further degree. Compounding this is the factor that the territory of immigration control itself is one in which the interviewer's claim to an 'innocence' which stands as objectivity is blurred – by socio-historical factors in which control is grounded. The objectivity of the interviewer is of a particular kind, in essence an 'objectification of subjectivities', a claim to objectivity wherein what has been objectified is a mythologized image of the applicant born of ethnocentric and androcentric assumptions, stereotypes, and expectations. This gives rise to a double jeopardy for those applying: in the inherently unequal power relationship of the legislator and legislated against; in the need to create themselves in the image in which they are seen. There can be no escape from the latter without failure of the application, in that with a eurocentric model as a 'given', the evidence selected for success is governed by this. In effect, what is eventually 'proven' as a reality will be a reality already pre-supposed. It is a pre-supposed reality defined by rules which carry no requirement in or of themselves to be non-discriminatory; only the operatives are required to act in a non-discriminatory manner. The innocence of the former is pre-supposed as a 'given', as being a characteristic of law itself.

THE RULE: SOLE RESPONSIBILITY

How women fare under the operation of immigration control is illustrative of these highlighted problems. What 'kind of woman' someone is becomes interlocked with cultural heritage in that 'having a particular "racial" identity is a necessary condition of having any gender identity at all'.[5] This paper will concentrate upon one facet of immigration control which affects women in order to elaborate upon this thesis: the instance where children of single-parent families apply to join mothers in the United Kingdom.

Choice of this particular focus is many-faceted. It allows examination of how women settled in the United Kingdom, whilst themselves not the applicant, are equally vulnerable to 'judgment' being made upon *them* in the terms I have outlined. Further, it is an area which highlights how the androcentric and ethnocentric practices central to the practical operation of control are mirrored in the word of the law itself – in the assumptions that underlie the 'categories' into which mother and child must fit. It is also an area of control in which is clearly demonstrated the wider socio-political factors that feed into the operation of the rules, there being a demonstrable tension between the facilitation of family unity and a desire to curb secondary immigration.

The rule governing the admission of unmarried children under eighteen years of age joining a mother in the United Kingdom establishes the criteria for successful application as:

> if one parent is settled in the UK or is on the same occasion admitted for settlement and has had sole responsibility for the child's upbringing;
> or
> if one parent or a relative other than a parent is settled or accepted for settlement in the United Kingdom and there are serious and compelling family or other considerations which make exclusion undesirable – for example, where the other parent is physically or mentally incapable of looking after the child – and suitable arrangements have been made for the child's care.[6]

Applicants in these cases, left in the care of a relative when their mothers have travelled to the United Kingdom, are quite clearly unable to meet the strictest literal interpretation of 'sole responsibility', a state distinct from legal custody. The criterion thus becomes one of proving fine distinctions: whether a mother has delegated responsibility in her absence or abdicated responsibility; whether she has been the source of financial support; whether there is demonstrable emotional commitment in the mother's interest in, and affection for, the child. In 1985, the Commission for Racial Equality (CRE), reporting upon immigration control procedures, quoted guidance given to entry clearance officers (ECOs) upon circumstances to be taken into account in reaching decisions in such cases. These included the length of separation; arrangements made for the child's care prior to the separation, and who decided these; source and proportion of maintenance; source of important decisions in the child's upbringing; part played by the parent in the United Kingdom; relationship of the parent in the United Kingdom to the child.[7] The same report expressed concern at the lack of consistency in criteria adopted by ECOs determining these cases.[8]

When decisions are taken in such cases there are a number of assumptions in operation: what a mother is; how a mother/child relationship is characterized; what stand as 'important decisions' in a child's upbringing. These issues are premised in how a 'family' is seen. Viewing matters in a historical framework, Cohen[9] posits the construct of the 'family' as an integral part of the theme of 'nation' which underpins immigration control. The hurdles within the rules that must be faced by families, 'deviant' in the eyes of a considered universal and preferred norm, certainly support such a position. The 'sole responsibility' rule is but one of these hurdles and directs itself particularly toward the family and migration patterns of the West Indies. In a report by two immigration appeal adjudicators who had visited the Caribbean, the criteria appeared as 'a monstrous injustice, a rule which apparently applies British standards of morality to a West Indian society which is totally different'.[10] This was in 1974. The rule remains.

That the 'difference' of these families is posed as a 'problem to be dealt with' by being legislated against is seen in what has been and continues to be a pathologizing of the West Indian family. Littlewood and Lipsedge[11] point to how criticism of the matricentral family as matriarchal rests on confusion between 'household' and 'family'. They refer also to the tendency for West Indian families to be regarded at a further remove from the 'nuclear' ideal than Asian families, and thereby more dysfunctional. Both Carby[12] and the Black Health Workers and Patients Group[13] criticize what has become in a number of areas of life the evaluation of the 'black family' against an image and ideology of a universal norm premised in a 'progressive' white nuclear family. Kline[14] forges these issues into a chain with links which are both historical and proactive. It is her view that the disparity between what has been the construction of ideologies of black and white domesticity and motherhood has led to a situation where the role of the former as mothers often goes unrecognized, a situation attested to by the difficulty these women face when they wish their children to join them in the United Kingdom.[15]

27

Certainly Kline's view is demonstrable. Elements of how black women are seen today can be regarded as an example of the 'naturalization' of myth, myth which is the legacy of colonial slavery. Medical attitudes to black women in the fields of abortion and use of Depo-Provera in Third World countries, their commodification as the 'exotic' in advertising, are as much testament to a persistently insidious image of the 'black woman' as is their experience of the application of the immigration rules with regard to marriage, children, and extended families. It is an image which renders them subject to injustice, not least the injustice of circumscribing their identity through a dual oppression of sexism and racism. The roots of this very particular image lie within the era of the slave trade, a construction born of plantocratic dogma and anti-slavery literature; of their passivity and their resistance; of the physical characteristics of slavery itself and tribal traditions supplanted and transformed. It was product of and contributor to a construction of white women, each in their turn serving a particular construction of 'man', both black and white.

Well-researched material stands far better as comment upon this 'construct' than the necessarily brief mention which must be made here.[16] Rather, my own brief confines itself to how a chasm existed between, on the one hand, how women represented *themselves* in early slave narratives, and on the other, the conceptualization of black women in such works as those of Edward Long. The latter's *History of Jamaica* became common currency in 1774 and the ideas therein have been demonstrated by Fryer[17] to have been perpetuated for centuries after. Not least of these relevant to the debate at hand was the interpretation of wide kinship groups as characteristic of disintegrating families and indifferent parentage – a myth underscored by how views of black women as sexually voracious and prone to practices of abortion and infanticide (regarded as merely to facilitate periods of prostitution) itself underlay how they were seen as wives and mothers. The matrifocal legislative approach of the plantocracy which rendered children 'of their mother's status' at birth, made their maternity inseparable from slavery and thus denied them the respectability of conventional motherhood; black women were 'breeders', not 'mothers'. But even in their mode of motherhood, when understandably transmitting survivalist behaviour to children, they were regarded as harsh – contributing to claims such as the late eighteenth-century account from Barbadian planters of 'a severity toward them . . . even at the expense of the parental affections'.[18] In sum, slavery provided a catalytic arena in which the elements of exploitation, degradation, judgement, and contempt could combine to present a fundamental image of black women. Their denigration, through the exploitation of existing currency of myth, was a pragmatic direction for the plantocracy to take in order to meet the axiom of slavery itself – the exploitation of the greatest labour potential of their workforce. Only through the 'annulment' of female slaves as 'women' could the plantocracy justify equality of enforced labour and equality of punishment with male slaves – as one Barbadian plantocratic defence of flogging women put it in

1823, the presence of an 'Amazonian cast of character' rather than 'femininity' was justification enough.[19] Yet the crucial point is that these women were consistently denied the opportunity to be seen in other than the terms in which their masters had cast them – the system which 'legislated' their existence denied them the opportunity.

Such a historical perspective brings valuable insights to the debate at hand in terms of parallels to be drawn with the 'categories' that constitute immigration legislation – not least the position of the mother of the twentieth century, seeking to be reunited with her child. The strategies of immigration control operate within a structure which recognizes a hegemony of knowledges of the mother/child relationship, yet places the evidence of the mother below that of the knowledge held by officialdom. The mother's claimed lived experience of having had 'sole responsibility' for her child is rendered mere rhetoric in the face of an official version of what sole responsibility is. The latter has been fixed in no small part by the courts, in their processing of appeals against refusal of such applications. It is to a number of examples of these instances that I now turn to explore this fixity of meaning.

THE WORD OF THE LAW: THE CASES

Twenty years ago determination in the case of *McGillivary* v *Secretary of State for the Home Department*[20] focused upon whether the term 'responsibility' within the word of the law, then embodied in departmental paper Cmnd. 4298 paragraph 39, meant more than legal responsibility. *McGillivary* held that the term embraced a wider meaning virtually by default, in that if it did not:

> It would follow that all illegitimate children would, prima facie, be able to join their mothers in the UK, and if this were to be the effect of para. 39 one would expect the Secretary of State to say so instead of speaking about 'responsibility'.[21]

Determining precision of meaning was quite another matter, leading to very particular attention being paid in this case to what the Secretary of State actually said in the published rules. The adjudicator's finding unearthed an interesting conundrum in that detailed attention to vocabulary suggested:

> ... that there is and has been one person responsible for the child. If the phrase were 'some responsibility' or (as in earlier Instructions) simple 'sole responsibility', this could be interpreted as meaning responsibility at some time or another, in other words, one of several responsibilities by several people for the same child. The definite article 'the' indicates 'one thing only' and excludes the possibility of one, or some, of many.[22]

However, establishing this clearly posed less a clarification than an unavoidable paradox, namely that children for whom the rule was clearly designated (those left in the care of relatives and called subsequently to join a parent in the United Kingdom) could not, by the very definition of their circumstances, hope to be able to demonstrate this strictly construed meaning of the term. The adjudicator nonetheless sought a logic in the rule, believing:

> ... this conclusion must be avoided, for I assume that the Secretary of State does nothing in vain and has not issued Instructions which are of no effect from the outset. Obviously we have to look for a broader interpretation of 'the sole responsibility' or perhaps avoid interpreting it in detail.[23]

Guidance was sought through comparison of the term with the phrase 'continuously in the care and possession', embodied in the Adoption Act 1958. Admitting the more stringent tenor of the latter requirement, it was felt that given potential successful qualification under that rule by a child in temporary custody of another, it was reasonable to hold that a child left in the care of a relative abroad was safe from immediate disqualification for consideration within the 'sole responsibility' category. In effect, this positioned the definition of 'sole responsibility' upon a subjective pivot, the finding being:

> ... that to attempt a precise definition of the phrase in question would be unwise. As soon as one draws up a list of precise requirements to be fulfilled before the parent can be said to have sole responsibility, one has to begin making exceptions to the general rules in order to accommodate individual cases. Each case must be decided separately, and although this may mean that one adjudicator would decide a particular case differently from another adjudicator because they have no precise definition to guide them, I think that this is the preferable alternative.[24]

How then did Mrs Green fare in this case in her attempt to be reunited with her fifteen year old daughter, Rita McGillivary? She had left Rita in the care of her own step-mother some ten years earlier, and had seen her daughter once since that time during a trip to Grenada in 1969. The adjudicator dismissed the appeal against refusal of entry clearance. In sum, he felt he would have been prepared to accept sole responsibility as demonstrated had there been evidence that Mrs Green had made every possible effort to bring the child to the United Kingdom as soon as possible, finding: 'The longer the separation between mother and daughter, the more difficult it becomes to justify such separation in terms of economic necessity.'[25] Mrs Green had offered an explanation for the length of separation in stating her accommodation was initially insecure and later amounted to an inadequate one room. The adjudicator countered this claim by reference to her husband's employment, initially with London Transport and later with the Post Office in holding that:

> Neither of these organizations pay such low wages that it is entirely necessary to live in one room. .... Furthermore, Mrs Green was able to afford the round trip from the United Kingdom to the West Indies and back in 1969 and had she wished to bring Rita to the United Kingdom she could presumably have paid Rita's single fare instead of going to Grenada.[26]

A number of points are raised by this case. Clearly, a series of assumptions are made regarding the intent of the Secretary of State in the drafting of the Immigration Rules. Yet, why was the wording of the rule changed from terms which had held implicit (in the adjudicator's assessment) 'responsibility at some time or another ... one of several responsibilities' to a term, '*the* sole responsibility', where the strict definition could not possibly be fulfilled by those it applied to? Does the resultant elusive criteria of such cases act to effectively place sponsors in a 'Catch 22' situation, where facts of the case can be interchangeable in working both 'for and against' as the situation desires? Certainly, the visit Mrs Green made to her child was not only discounted in terms of demonstrable contact but in fact counted against her, yet without it the lack of evidence of maintaining contact would surely have been a matter for comment. The adjudicator found that the determination of sole responsibility was a question of fact to be decided in each case, but is this in effect the nature of the appeal beast or rather a carte blanche authorization of potentially dangerous subjectivity of judgment? In the case under discussion, the adjudicator assumed 'knowledge' of the personal finances and budget of the sponsor, of her ability to secure accommodation, and implied a lack of effort upon her part in the latter respect. This rendered a lie the sponsor's claim that one-room living made earlier application impossible. Finally, is it in fact an acceptable price to pay in the pursuit of family unity, a 'preferable alternative' as this adjudicator suggested, that one adjudicator may decide cases differently to another?

In *Emmanuel* v *Secretary of State for Home Office*,[27] the principle which the adjudicator raised in *McGillivary* regarding the scope of the term 'sole responsibility' was consolidated. The tribunal acknowledged the inevitable presence of some responsibility on the part of the relative with whom a child lived, such as that pertaining to ensuring school attendance, feeding and clothing the child, and held: 'We do not therefore think that literal or absolute responsibility of the parent in the United Kingdom could ever be established.'[28] In so doing they overturned a decision by an adjudicator who, in dismissing an appeal, had interpreted what the appellant's representative termed 'the customary delegation of responsibility by mother to grandmother which is part of the accepted way of life in the West Indies' as an 'abdication', rather than a 'delegation' of responsibility.[29] It was a decision taken notwithstanding acknowledgement within the determination of the mother's 'close interest and affection for her daughter'.[30]

Given the shifting sands of the elements that make up 'sole responsibility', providing 'evidence' has proven crucial to the success of many cases. *Sloley* v *Entry Clearance Officer, Kingston, Jamaica*[31] fulfilled this in the submission of sixteen letters between the mother of the overseas appellant and her mother in Jamaica, to whom she had entrusted the care of her child on travelling to the United Kingdom. The tribunal finding, again overturning an adjudicator's decision to dismiss the appeal, considered:

> These letters present a picture of Mrs Taylor continuously consulting and seeking the advice and approval of Mrs Buchanan regarding the appellant's upbringing and activities . . . demonstrated a continuing and positive concern on the part of the sponsor in the welfare and upbringing of the appellant.[32]

Yet such letters are not in themselves a key to success, as the decisions in *Sugara Ramos* v *Immigration Appeal Tribunal*,[33] *Secretary of State* v *Pusey*,[34] and *Entry Clearance Officer, Kingston, Jamaica* v *Martin*[35] demonstrate. Fine distinctions are made in respect of such evidence.

Ramos took the form of an appeal against a decision in the Divisional Court to refuse judicial review of a decision by the tribunal. The tribunal had dismissed an appeal against an adjudicator's decision to dismiss an appeal against a refusal by the Home Office of Sugara Ramos's application to join her mother in the United Kingdom. Sugara was born in 1969 and her application for entry clearance was refused in 1984, in subsequent appeals against this decision before adjudicators and tribunals, and in application for judicial review, proceeding to the Court of Appeal in 1988. Concentrating for the purposes of this discussion upon the matter of letters submitted in evidence, nine personal letters were submitted to an adjudicator at the initial hearing and thirty-one at the time of referral of the case by the tribunal to a different adjudicator (with reference to additional letters available untranslated). In the final dismissal of the appeal by the Court of Appeal in 1988, their lordships took account of a number of factors which weighed against a decision in favour of the appellant:

> ... despite the obvious continuous financial support being provided by this mother and despite also her obvious continuing concern as to her child's welfare and upbringing and the equally obvious genuine interest and affection which she has displayed towards her.[36]

The appellant in *Pusey* sought to join his father in Britain. The adjudicator recorded the sponsor impressed him as a 'truthful and reliable witness' and, in attending to whether he had demonstrated 'sole responsibility', stated:

> It is quite clear to me that he genuinely believes he has had and continues to have such a responsibility. But such a subjective belief is not sufficient to show a compliance with the rule. There must be some objective evidence of it.[37]

Turning to correspondence submitted as evidence, he remarked:

> This in my view confirms in fact and independently Mr Pusey's feeling and belief that he has had sole responsibility for the appellant . . . there is no reason for the maternal grandmother to have maintained this kind of correspondence with Mr Pusey unless she was answerable to him. I regard the correspondence as evidence of a state of affairs in which the grandmother is Mr Pusey's delegate and no more in the upbringing of his daughter.[38]

The Secretary of State appealed to the tribunal against the decision of the adjudicator allowing this appeal, at which time the contact between the child and her mother residing in Jamaica overrode the weight the adjudicator gave to the letters in evidence. In allowing the Secretary of State's appeal and thereby overturning the decision of the adjudicator, the decision was taken that:

> It may well be that as between the father and the grandmother the father has shouldered the main responsibility for the respondent but in our view the position of the mother must be taken into consideration . . . there has been a sharing of responsibility.[39]

The case was deemed distinct from *Emmanuel* where a principle of the inevitability of a shared responsibility was established, in that in *Emmanuel*, the in-country parent (the father) had taken no interest in his daughter. Considered together with *Martin*, the two cases show how, in the same tenor that presence of a parent within the ambit of the applicant's world can be detrimental to an application, so too can the presence of the applicant's siblings. *Martin* involved a seventeen-year-old girl in Jamaica seeking to join her mother in the United Kingdom. Left in the care of relatives for twelve years, Sybil shared accommodation with (amongst others) her siblings. The adjudicator at the initial appeal considered the correspondence annexed to the entry clearance officer's statement to show that the mother exercised 'guidance at a distance' and this, together with other factors, led him to allow the appeal against refusal. Before the tribunal, upon the appeal of the entry clearance officer against this decision, the case was rendered distinct from that of *Sloley* wherein letters had stood as evidence of continuous consultation between guardian and sponsor. Instead the tribunal made the distinction that:

> ... though of course Mrs White was always interested in Sybil's academic progress and general welfare, but she also was as regards Daisy to whom she wrote, and her other children.[40]

In effect, demonstration through letters of interest and affection, the giving of advice and approval to *all* her children, diminished the claim to 'sole responsibility' made in respect of one.

The cases of *Sloley*, *Pusey*, *Martin*, and *Emmanuel*, regarded in the light of weight given in each to correspondence and both parental and sibling contact, raise a number of problematic issues. Not least of these is consideration of how documentary evidence, in this case personal letters, fluctuates in value as 'evidence' between cases. Equally there is a paradoxical state of affairs in regarding occasional contact with a parent in-country as sufficient to demonstrate a responsibility which can devalue or cancel out a sponsor's claimed responsibility, when the comparable intermittent contact between sponsor and child (occasioned by distance) invariably detracts from the claim by the sponsoring parent to both responsibility taken and affection held. The very claims, which avow the justice of treating each case individually, in practice function to render the criteria to be met all the more difficult to pin down in its complexity – and thereby render justice more elusive.

Turning towards how the rules might be interpreted to render justice more readily, consider first how the tribunal regard the proper approach to the construction of the Immigration Rules. This is encapsulated in the case of *R* v *Immigration Appeal Tribunal ex parte Sajid Mahmood*, a judicial review case.[41] It followed a determination of the tribunal allowing the appeal of the visa officer in Islamabad against the determination of an adjudicator. The adjudicator had allowed the appeal of the parent of Sajid Mahmood, finding he had demonstrated sole responsibility for the child's upbringing.

The determination of the Tribunal records that:

> [the] Home Office representative accepted the proper approach to the construction of the Immigration Rules is that laid down in *R* v *Immigration Appeals Tribunal ex parte Alexander* [1982] 1 W.L.R. 1076, where, at page 1080, Lord Roskill said:
> 'These rules are not to be construed with all the strictness applicable to the construction of a statute or a statutory instrument. They must be construed sensibly according to the natural meaning of the language which is employed. The rules give guidance to the various officers concerned and contain statements of general policy regarding the operation of the relevant immigration legislation.'[42]

Are the rules then construed 'sensibly according to the natural meaning of the language which is employed'? In *Sajid Mahmood*, Roch J. held that in dealing with such cases:

> The natural concern of a caring parent for his or her child falls short of the exercise of the 'sole responsibility for the child's upbringing' required by the rule.[43]

In the same case the Home Office representative made reference to how the very inclusion within a sub-heading of para. 50 H.C.169 (the rules then in force) of a provision for admission where there are 'serious or compelling family or other considerations' which make exclusion undesirable, allowed a stricter interpretation of the sole responsibility criterion than if the reference had not been included. Clearly a very high standard of proof is required under a rule which not only gives no pointers toward criteria, but which under adjudication compounds the already elusive criteria. On the one hand it has been held unhelpful:

> ... to make a check-list of particular aspects which have to be considered in the decisions on the other cases and then, as it were, allocate so many points to the applicant against each item that has been put on the check-list.[44]

On the other hand, instructions are issued to entry clearance officers giving guidance on how the rule is to be interpreted and, in the findings of the Commission for Racial Equality:

> A great deal of discretion was available to entry clearance officers in how they arrived at their judgments and conclusions on such matters, and the criteria they used tended to vary.[45]

In sum, given that the individual opinion and attitudes of issuing officers is relied upon to such a great degree, qualifying under the rule is in effect a lottery. That it is a lottery for only a section of applicants has been identified by the CRE, pointing out:

> ... we see no good reason in principle why the rules should discriminate as they do between children joining two parents and children joining one parent as far as previous support and responsibility are concerned. As we have pointed out, the present rule has had its major impact on women from the West Indies who have found themselves unable to secure admission for their children not because of inability or lack of intention to care for them in the future but because they had not exercised sole responsibility, as interpreted by immigration officials, in the past.[46]

A relevant consideration in looking at why applications meet with such difficulty might be found in the fact that the 'sole responsibility' criterion was introduced into the Immigration Rules in 1969 as a measure of exclusion. It was designed to stem the arrival of Pakistani boys seeking to join their fathers in the United Kingdom, whilst their mothers remained in Pakistan.[47] In effect, it continues to operate as a measure of exclusion despite the legitimation of continuing use in subsequent years under an apparent philosophy of enabling 'family unity'.

STRATEGIES: ALL FOR ONE OR ONE FOR ALL?

Wherein lies the proactive strategy to combat this exclusion? There are two strands of debate to review. The first respects women as distinguished by difference, the second essentializes womanhood. These polarities of objectified fixed identity versus subjectivity parallel the fixed criteria of the category 'sole responsibility' and the exhortation of executives and adjudication machinery alike to decide each case individually.

Are we forced into a choice between two perspectives? That is to say, that either one accepts cultural differences in perception of gender roles and definitions of motherhood or one operates a dominant ideology of mother-hood. One can argue, in the context of immigration laws, that the latter perspective prevails in the form of a white ideology setting a standard against which other mothers are measured. But either position has faults and pitfalls. In the former, there is potential to embrace myths in the perception of mothers from specific cultural backgrounds, an outcome demonstrated by the currency of such stereotypes of Asian women and myths of Afro-Caribbean mothers.[48] In the latter there is potential to deny the reality of another by mere blindness to cultural practices.

Given the problems inherent in both of these perspectives the remedy lies less in the 'matter', than the 'manner' of operation of the immigration laws. 'Sole responsibility' is decided either at initial interview of the applicant (together with possibly parent or relatives) by an entry clearance officer or in an appeal context before adjudicator or tribunal. Each of the decision-makers at these crucial points is born of a specific institutional culture and bound at the time by a specific format of operation. This has a bearing upon what is regarded as relevant knowledge and how it is sought, thereby directing the quality of the decision taken. Debate upon the strictures of these considerations is of the complexity to warrant exploration in or of itself and thus necessitates acknowledgement rather than elaborate expansion here. Suffice for the purposes of this work to suggest such debate revolves around factors such as training procedures, internal reports and instructions, and the contexts of operation of control. If each case is to be considered upon individual merits in such a climate, as indeed the precedent cases extol, it is surely fundamental to the just operation of the rule that the utmost is capitalized upon within these frameworks of operation. The question is – how to do so?

One possible answer to this lies within feminist debate. Is there a unique feminist method of inquiry wherein contradictions between researcher and researched are removed, that could be utilized by legislator and those legislated against? Advocates of feminist research lay claim to a methodology that is premised in interaction devoid of a subject/object split. A view with much currency, acknowledging that knowledge creation means power, advocates a feminist perspective developing new criteria for what counts as 'knowledge'. This construct poses feminist research as completely reconcept-ualizing traditional research paradigms from a feminist perspective; trans-forming not only 'knowledge' but its means of production.[49] The practical manifestation of this stance is the interviewing process as a non-hierarchical relationship, where the researched are transformed from being objects of scrutiny and manipulation; where personal investment by the interviewer introduces a subjective element claimed to increase objectivity.[50] This accommodates feminist traditions of centralizing the 'personal', sharing, self-examination, so that in prioritizing women's experiences theory itself becomes situated in that experience. Thus what in traditional paradigms of sociological research remain the unexamined beliefs, feelings, and behaviour of social scientists become included through a conscious subjectivity to provide an evaluation of the research process *per se*. This co-operative interactive/reflexive framework in which research subjects themselves become knowers and actors stands as a 'shared vulnerability' which contributes to altering what is otherwise an imbalance of power between researcher and researched.[51]

Yet these tenets are predicated upon the positing of an 'essential womaness' traversing race and class differences. I question whether it is in fact an achievable state in that 'feminist knowledge and skills' can be considered as part of that theory which is the product of a small number of women enjoying political, social, and economic privilege as white Western feminists. The 'womaness' that is essentialized in such debate is itself eurocentric and if such a stance provides the conceptual framework for research, it will infect method – how then will the research process validate the experiences of non-white women? Is there not a danger that a eurocentric model as a 'given' will direct that the evidence selected is likely to be governed by this – that what is 'proven' as a reality will be a reality pre-supposed. Talking about differences becomes problematic within a premise which assumes commonality, yet it is only through acknowledgement of differences that any commonality can be understood. If there is no such area of 'innocence' in which to delve, is it the case that no valid alternative can be posed to the procedures of immigration control which marginalize and silence, define and thus 'speak for'.

It is my view that a recognition of these problematics of a cross-cultural research situation premised in feminism can in fact offer an insight into the areas of control to be criticized. It is a recognition that can become a facet of theoretical argument and therefrom a strategy with which to challenge the basis of control. Both the shortcomings of the traditional interview paradigm identified by feminist debate, and the criticisms I level at the 'feminist interview' in cross-cultural research are consistent with the criticisms I level at control procedures within the immigration context. If the immigration rule which is the subject of this debate is to remain unchanged within the legislation, although I feel strongly it should not, it is the manner of decision-making under that rule which must be highlighted for review. This can only be remedied by a fuller opportunity allowing the sponsoring parent to be 'given voice', a stance which includes investing their own 'knowledge' of events with the weight it deserves rather than assessing this as a shadow of 'official knowledge' premised in the legitimating light of statutory procedures and courtrooms. In the same way that the 'legislative systems' of plantocratic masters and British colonial administrators are culpable in denying women

36

the opportunity to be seen in other than the terms in which they deemed it suitable they be cast, and did so as a means to an end, the immigration conceptualization is culpable.

If both executives operating control procedures and the adjudicatory bodies are proffered the tool of subjectivity with which to make a decision, then it is not equitable to dismiss the demonstrable belief of a parent as 'a subjective belief [is] not sufficient to show a compliance with the rule' as seen earlier in the case of *Pusey*. If the subjectivity of the operatives and appeal courts is to be the safeguard of justice, providing the means to ensure each case is considered upon its merits, then it must be of the purest kind unfettered by prejudices. If the objectivity of these parties is the sentinel of justice, it too must be of an order wherein the external phenomena it presupposes is not born of stereotypical assumptions. In this difficulty is it not more equitable to turn away from the vagaries of such judgments toward examining the unfairness of placing an additional burden upon a mother and a family that is regarded as falling short of a eurocentric 'ideal'. Is it not time to recognize that the women who seek reunion with their children are asked to be 'doubly mother', given their transgression from the norm in the initial separation from their child. They must meet an 'ideal' of motherhood premised in terms other than their own – that of meeting an 'essential womaness'. This appeal to universality is a white discourse, and a white discourse is a 'political discourse' *per se* shared, in the manner in which they work, by the very institutions which exclude and marginalize black experiences.

NOTES AND REFERENCES

1 E. Dodgson (ed.), *Motherlands* (1984) 17.
2 Currently Commons 251 (1990).
3 For purposes of s.26(1)(c) of the Immigration Act 1971.
4 op. cit., n. 2.
5 E. V. Spelman, *Inessential Woman* (1990) 56.
6 op. cit., n. 2, para. 53.
7 Commission for Racial Equality, *Immigration Control Procedures* (1985) 5.5.1.
8 id., 5.6.5.
9 S. Cohen, *A Hard Act to Follow* (1988).
10 WING, *Worlds Apart* (1985) 111.
11 R. Littlewood and M. Lipsedge, *Aliens and Alienists* (1989) 149.
12 H. V. Carby, 'White Woman Listen! Black Feminism and the Boundaries of Sisterhood' in *The Empire Strikes Back* (1982) CCCS.
13 Black Health Workers and Patients Group, 'Psychiatry and the Corporate State' (1983) 25:2 *Race and Class* 49.
14 M. Kline, 'Race, Racism, and Feminist Legal Theory' (1989) 12 *Harvard Women's Law J.* 115.
15 id., p. 131.
16 See P. Fryer, *Staying Power* (1989); H. Beckles, *Afro-Caribbean Women and Resistance to Slavery in Barbados* (1988) and *Natural Rebels* (1989); A. Davies, 'Reflections on the Black Woman's Role in the Community of Slaves' (1971) *The Black Scholar* 3.
17 Fryer, op. cit., n. 16, ch. 7.
18 M. Craton et al., *Slavery, Abolition, and Emancipation* (1976) 95.

19 Beckles, op. cit., n. 16 Appendix 5.
20 [1972] Imm.A.R. 63.
21 id., p. 65.
22 id., p. 65
23 id., pp. 65–66.
24 id., pp. 66–67.
25 id., p. 68.
26 id., p. 68.
27 [1972] Imm.A.R. 69.
28 id., p. 71.
29 id., p. 70.
30 id., p. 71.
31 [1973] Imm.A.R. 54.
32 id., p. 57.
33 [1989] Imm.A.R. 148.
34 [1972] Imm.A.R. 240.
35 [1978] Imm.A.R. 100.
36 *Ramos*, op. cit., n. 33, p. 154.
37 *Pusey*, op. cit., n. 34, pp. 241–42.
38 id., p. 242.
39 id., pp. 244–45.
40 id., pp. 102–103.
41 [1988] Imm.A.R. 121.
42 id., per Roch J. at 125.
43 id., p. 126.
44 *Ramos*, op. cit., n. 33, p. 152.
45 CRE, op. cit., n. 7, 5.6.1.
46 id., 5.6.4.
47 WING, op. cit., n. 10, p. 100.
48 See S. Westwood and P. Bhachu, 'Images and Realities' (1988) *New Society* 20; A. Phoenix, 'The Afro-Caribbean Myth' (1988) *New Society* 10; E. Lawrence, 'Just Plain Common Sense: the 'roots' of racism' in CCCS, op. cit., n. 12.
49 See D. Spender, *Men's Studies Modified* (1981).
50 See S. Harding, *Feminism and Methodology* (1987) 9.
51 L. Stanley and S. Wise, *Breaking Out* (1983) 181.

Finding a Strategy in Litigation: Sexually Exploited Patients in Therapy

INTRODUCTION

It has long been recognized in the context of medicine that sexual contact between a doctor and her/his patient raises serious medical and ethical problems. A question arises as to whether the therapist/patient relationship with its intense emotionality, often necessarily involving a sexual element (see below), raises particular problems in this respect, over and above those present in the context of medicine. Until recent years the issue of sexual abuse of patients in therapy was largely invisible in Britain. Only now is it beginning to be recognized as an unresolved problem which can result in devastating damage to patients, especially where they have previously suffered sexual abuse. Increasing numbers of people in the United Kingdom are now using the services of therapists, both privately and through National Health Service referrals, and are thereby exposed to the potential risk of sexual abuse.[1] There is growing awareness of the problem which was previously addressed only by a minority of professionals. At a recent conference of the British Psychology Society at Scarborough in 1992 Dr Sue Llewelyn, pointing to American studies suggesting that up to one in ten therapists have sexually abused their clients, concluded that there was similar cause for concern in Britain.[2] Moreover, although abuse obviously can and does occur where the therapist is female,[3] American research has shown that the typical abusing therapist is a man in his early forties, while the client is typically female, single, and in her twenties, suggesting that there may be particular or additional problems which can occur in the male therapist/female patient dyad.

Any research in this area will necessarily rely heavily on experience gained in North America where media attention to the problem of therapists' exploitation of their patients has resulted in its recognition as a serious social and legal issue. Formerly, North American women claiming to have been sexually exploited by their psychotherapists were treated cynically and sceptically. However, the research of Dr Alan Stone[4] led him to the conclusion that *such claims were rarely fabricated*:

Kent Law School, The University of Kent at Canterbury, Canterbury, Kent CT2 2NY, England

39

> If once on the basis of my professional training I presumed that such complaints were false, I now presume that they are true.[5]

In the light of the increased use of therapy in the United Kingdom and proposed changes in professional structure (see below), patient exploitation is an emerging social and ethical issue and one which particularly affects women. As such, it demands a feminist analysis of the problem, including a consideration of the potential scope of legal redress available to patients who have suffered in this way.

THE NATURE OF THE THERAPIST/PATIENT RELATIONSHIP

There is at present no overall professional control of the practice of psychotherapy in Britain.[6] Entry into the 'profession' of psychotherapy is therefore not regulated or restricted. The absence of a national code of practice means that professional standards are regulated by the individual organization to which the psychotherapist may belong. For example, the British Association of Psychotherapists claims its members will always act in the best interests of the patient, but does not refer specifically to sexual misconduct. On the other hand, the British Association for Counselling *does* have a clause addressing the issue:

> Counsellors must not exploit their clients financially, sexually, emotionally, or in any other way. Engaging in sexual activity with the client is unethical.[7]

An overall organization of the profession is now being attempted by the United Kingdom Standing Conference on Psychotherapy (UKSCP) which aims to regulate standards, prevent unskilled practitioners from working as psychotherapists, and devise a national professional ethical code of practice.

In this context there may be strong arguments for an ethical prohibition on sexual relationships between therapists and their clients. It might be said that a sexual relationship between therapist and patient is always potentially exploitative because all patients in therapy are necessarily dependent and vulnerable. Appelbaum and Jorgenson suggest four justifications for such an ethical prohibition. First, the patient's capacity to decide whether to engage in sexual contact with her therapist is significantly impaired both by her underlying distress and the closeness of her relationship with the therapist. Secondly, there is potential for abuse of confidential information about the patient's particular vulnerabilities. Thirdly, it is generally agreed that sexual involvement reduces the effectiveness of the treatment; and finally, the therapist has a responsibility to act in the patient's best interests.[8]

Indeed, it may be argued that, because of the conflict in roles between being a lover and a therapist, it is dishonest for a therapist to claim that sexual involvement will not affect the effectiveness of the treatment:

> To encourage patients to believe they can gratify sexual desires with their therapists and continue to receive the treatment they need is to deceive them.[9]

The term 'transference' is used in psychotherapy to describe the powerful feelings which patients develop toward their therapists. This phenomenon often involves undergoing past emotional experiences in order to create the potential for more healthy emotional responses in the future. It has been described as:

> ... a specific illusion which develops in regard to the other person, one which, unbeknown to the subject, represents, in some important features, a repetition of a relationship towards an important figure in the person's past.[10]

The response of the therapist to these feelings should represent a healing of the old wounds. Yet the transference phenomenon confers an immense power which the therapist is well aware of:

> Psychoanalysts have long recognized that the nature of their work exposes them to emotional stimulation of every variety and intensity – from the patient's irritation to his fury, from trepidation to terror, from liking to sexual passion, from moodiness to profound despair. . . . Accordingly, it is not always easy for the analyst to maintain sufficient neutrality to be consistently able to help the patient understand what he is experiencing, why he is experiencing it and what its consequences are. . . . It is his responsibility, however, to retain that sufficient degree of neutrality. . . . It is his work ideal to do so.[11]

When people go to a psychotherapist for help they are particularly vulnerable. Their feelings of distress can result in an overvaluation of others and in the dependency which is an integral part of the therapeutic relationship:

> The therapist will often encourage dependency in the early stages of therapy so as to build up a strong therapeutic relationship which will make it easier for him later to encourage the client to make more and more of his own decisions. The therapist will utilize his own prestige to reinforce the power of his suggestions.[12]

Because of their responsibility for their patients' well-being, analysts must accept the development of strong and genuine feelings on the part of patients, but, at the same time, never engage with them.[13] It is the therapist's responsibility to 'harness the force of the transference' without 'the charge of suggestion – of inserting foreign material into the patient's mind . . . while making use of the forces that make such an intrusion possible in the form of a genuine emotional tie'.[14] It would therefore *always* be an intrusion by the therapist to respond in kind to the patient's erotic feelings, which have, after all, been deliberately created by the development of the transference for very different (psychotherapeutic) reasons. Patients seeking help are vulnerable even before they enter therapy but become more so as they are coerced by the transference which often results in erotic idealization of the therapist. Indeed, for this reason, a recent Canadian report, investigating the problem of sexual abuse of patients, recommended a two-year time lapse before sexual relationships between former doctors and patients are appropriate *but a complete lifetime prohibition where the treatment is psychotherapeutic.*[15] Psychotherapists are therefore acknowledged as being in a particular position of power and trust, even above that of other doctors. The fact that almost all professional bodies and mental health organizations condemn sexual contact between psychotherapists and their patients signifies recognition that the patient's dependence, which flows from the inherent inequality of the relationship, should be used only for the good of the patient herself.

However, there are some in the profession who believe that the 'professionalization' of psychotherapy (involving longer and more intensive training and higher academic standards of entry) would only further the interests of the 'profession' and not necessarily produce better results for clients. Onyett and Davey comment that:

> ... people experiencing the enduring effects of social inequality (by dint, for example, of their race, gender, sexual orientation, and socio-economic status) are particularly vulnerable to distress, and are more likely to experience unhelpful, or even abusive responses from services. The latter includes practitioners abusing their power within the (so-called) therapeutic relationships. . . . Better outcomes may be achieved through employing people in psychotherapeutic roles who share the same social and cultural background as people who use their service or who have been ex-users of services themselves. . . . By establishing psychotherapy as a graduate profession, as is proposed, the UKSCP risks impeding access to psychotherapeutic roles for people already experiencing the effects of social inequality.[16]

There may therefore be strategic drawbacks to professionalization from the patients' point of view, as stricter standards of entry and more intensive professional training will increase the power imbalance between patient and therapist. There is also little evidence that the mere existence, without more sanctions, of a national professional ethical code would have any effect on the problem of patient exploitation.

However, ethical codes of practice may *not* be irrelevant particularly in the context of possible litigation. Indeed, formal recognition by the profession that this type of behaviour is harmful could help lawyers engaged in litigation to establish the existence of a legal duty of care owed by therapists to their clients in this context. Moreover the *symbolic* value of such legal recognition may be significant. As Catharine MacKinnon has pointed out, sexual wrongs must often be transformed into *legal* wrongs before they are condemned by society.[17]

SEXUAL EXPLOITATION IN THERAPY: A FEMINIST ISSUE?

> Despite the fact that men have moral, legal, and ethical responsibilities not to allow themselves to become sexually involved with their female patients . . . there is a largely concealed epidemic . . . of exploitative sexual contact in violation of this forbidden boundary.[18]

It has already been observed that patient sexual abuse is a problem particularly affecting women. Indeed, evidence to the Canadian task force on patient sexual abuse appears to confirm this. The task force received 303 reports of abuse, only sixteen of which involved sexual abuse of male patients.[19] Moreover, in the United States of America, an estimated eighty-eight per cent of reported incidents of sexual misconduct involve male therapists and female patients.[20] This suggests the need for a specifically feminist approach to the problem of patient sexual abuse.

One difficulty in analysing and discussing a hidden problematic element in social behaviour lies in finding the appropriate vocabulary for it. This difficulty has been highlighted by feminists in the context of sexual harassment, which, before it became an everyday phrase in the 1970s (largely as a result of feminist efforts to articulate it), was a 'literally unspeakable' phenomenon.[21] Similarly, therapist-patient sex abuse has been described as 'psychiatry's problem with no name'.[22] Terms such as 'sexual impropriety' and 'inappropriate sexual behaviour' seem to trivialize the potentially devastating effects of patient abuse. Thus, one of the challenges for feminists and others must be to find ways to articulate what has hitherto remained socially and legally invisible.

In this context, women are not assisted by the prevailing language employed to characterize sexual relationships. In particular, the narrow conception of 'consent' creates significant problems for feminists seeking to identify the wrong inherent in patient sexual abuse. Traditionally, the state, reflecting prevailing social perceptions, deems sexual relations as consensual, private matters, providing that no violence or obvious element of exploitation (for example, sex with minors) occurs. The issue of the apparent 'consent' given by women who enter a sexual relationship with men in power is thus problematic. For example, a woman succumbing to sexual pressure from her boss may have great difficulty in claiming she was coerced, even though that might well be her experience. Similarly, a failure to recognize the potentially coercive nature of the therapist/patient relationship will result in any sexual contact being perceived as consensual, provoking no social or legal condemnation.

Yet, as with other types of sexual exploitation in relationships of trust, such as sexual harassment and incest, abuse of patients is evidence of the way in which women's relationships with men are rarely free from sexual demand. Socially and culturally, a woman becomes accustomed to sexual pressure and often uses diplomacy or humour to deal with it. This does not mean it is not damaging. Even if she resists, she is injured because the vital element of trust in the relationship will have been lost. If she compromises or responds, then the purpose of the important relationship is undermined and devalued. Whether or not a sexual relationship with her therapist represents 'unwelcome' attention to the patient, the fact that it occurs within a relationship of power and trust means that it will inevitably harm her, influencing the decisions of both parties as regards her health and well-being.[23]

That the relationship is inevitably tainted with a power imbalance, problematizing its 'consensual' characterization, is well established. In his analysis of the nature of professional power, Terence Johnson explains how the skill and education associated with professionalism combine with other sources of social power to reduce the common area of shared experience between client and professional:

> The power relationship existing between practitioner and client may be such . . . as to enable the practitioner to increase the social distance and his own autonomy and control over practice by engaging in a process of 'mystification'.[24]

The 'mystification' leading from the imbalance in knowledge often results in the client's passive submission to the judgement of the professional and a greater exposure to possible exploitation.

Sexual abuse of patients therefore represents an abuse of the privileges (including status and autonomy) that society grants to professionals. Furthermore, the structures of society often legitimize not only the power itself but also the *abuse* of this power. For example, the traditional professional tendency not to believe women's allegations of sexual abuse (above) reflects a perpetuation of Freudian theories of fantasy.[25] Inevitably, the attitudes of Freud's followers were shaped by similar prejudice:

> We learn – often even without deeper analytic investigation – that rape fantasies are variants of the seduction fantasies so familiar to us in the lying accounts of hysterical women patients. Both rape and seduction fantasies are deliberately passed on to other persons as true, and they have the typical pseudologic character we found in the more romantic and fantastic lies of puberty.[26]

This denial of women's accounts and experiences is clearly evidenced in the context of therapist/patient sexual abuse:

> Twenty years ago female patients who claimed that they had been sexually exploited by their psychotherapists were apt to be written off as having psychotic transferences. The presumption, derived from psychodynamic theories, that these reports represented hysterical wish-fulfilling fantasies, was applied even to victims of rape and incest.[27]

The social legitimation of professional abuses of sexual power is also apparent in the autonomy which society and law accord to professionals and the general failure to recognize a gender dimension in the power inherent in 'professionalism'. Traditionally, society has allocated a role of passivity and compliance to women and an active boundary-challenging role to men. Moreover, these roles are socially eroticized and so become desirable to both sexes. As MacKinnon observes, a woman thus comes to want what is not in her own interests and, being socialized to passivity, frequently sees no alternative to acquiescence. Thus, it is often difficult to distinguish consenting sex from coercive sex:

> Some women eroticize dominance and submission; it beats feeling forced. Sexual intercourse may be deeply unwanted, the woman would never have initiated it, yet no force may be present. . . . Force may be used, yet the woman may prefer the sex – to avoid more force or because she, too, eroticized dominance.[28]

The existence of a 'professional' relationship, defining the connection between male therapist and female client, with its accompanying power imbalance, reinforce such elements of dominance and submission which MacKinnon sees as inherent in currently constituted heterosexual relations.

Thus, any social or legal approach employing consent as a way of defining and delineating legitimate sexual liaisons may be an inadequate response to sexual exploitation involving abuse of this learned feminine passivity.[29] In response to this perception, it has been suggested that sexual relations in the therapeutic relationship should be analogized to the perpetration of child abuse. The law denies that children under sixteen years of age are capable of consenting to sex with adults because of the inherently coercive nature of a relationship, based on such an imbalance of judgement and power. Similarly, although both parties may be adult, psychotherapists are in positions of such trust and authority that they often assume the psychological role of a parent to such an extent that any violation of this relationship can be equated psychologically with an act of incest.[30] However, such an approach is, from a feminist perspective, highly problematic through (in effect) equating women with children for purposes of social and legal responsibility. Thus, to legally prohibit sexual relations between therapist and patient on the grounds that the patient is *de jure* incapable of giving her consent to such relations may be to employ a double-edged sword and one which has traditionally worked to women's disadvantage.[31] At the same time, an accurate understanding of the transference phenomenon points strongly towards a recognition that 'consent' as generally understood is not applicable in the context of the patient/therapist relationship.

One way of responding to this dilemma might be to shift the focus away from the patient and onto the behaviour of the therapist. Thus in Wisconsin, for example, it is a crime for a therapist to engage in sexual activity with a patient (see below). In this context, presence or absence of consent becomes irrelevant to the legal characterization of the wrong. Yet while such an approach has much to recommend it in its focus on the wrongfulness of the therapist's action (in risking the patient's best interests in pursuit of his own desires), there may well be other drawbacks to the criminalization of such behaviour (see below).

A final important element in the sexual exploitation of patients is the silence of professional colleagues, which can amount almost to approval of the misconduct. Professional loyalty and fear of scandal are only part of the explanation. Rutter identifies another contributory element – the envy aroused when men hear about their colleagues' sexual exploits.[32] He explains that even men who have never engaged in sexual contact with their patients participate in it vicariously in their fantasy lives. They may therefore be unwilling to expose the sexual misdeeds of their colleagues:

> This psychological picture, which acknowledges that even ethical professional men wish to leave open the possibility that one day they will have a sexual encounter with a woman under their care, helps to account for the deeply rooted male tendency toward silence, inaction, and suppression of information when it comes to revealing other men's sexual-boundary violations.[33]

Women victims in particular often collaborate in this silence because of a tendency to blame themselves. In common with survivors of acquaintance-rape and incest, their guilt and shame can prevent them from reporting the violation. When they do act, they often come up against humiliating disbelief from authorities, which discourages them from taking any further action.

It is therefore apparent that many factors – for example, consent, sexual and professional power, male and female sexuality – highlighted by feminists in the context of analyses of other forms of sexual abuse including rape, incest, and domestic violence, are equally present in relation to patient sexual abuse, suggesting that a feminist understanding of the nature of the problem is crucial both to its recognition and resolution.

THE GROWTH OF LEGAL INTERVENTION

In the mid–1970s, some psychotherapists in the United States of America advocated the use of criminal measures in relation to the sexual exploitation of patients.[34] However, traditional sex crimes such as rape, dependent as they are on evidence of physical force, did not easily extend to the sort of psychological coercion likely to characterize therapist/patient sexual abuse. Accordingly, seven states (California, Colorado, Florida, Maine, Minnesota, North Dakota, and Wisconsin) passed statutes making psychotherapist-patient sexual contact a separate crime. Moreover, in California and Florida sexual contact with *former* patients is also a criminal offence if the therapist terminates the therapeutic relationship in order to begin a sexual relationship with the patient. Four states (California, Illinois, Minnesota, and Wisconsin) have also provided by statute a civil cause of action for patients sexually exploited by their psychotherapists. The widest is that of Wisconsin which covers any person suffering harm as a result of sexual contact with a therapist who is administering or has administered psychotherapy to that person.[35]

However, despite statutory intervention, most cases of therapist/patient sexual abuse take the form of malpractice suits in negligence. The most significant of these is *Roy* v *Hartogs* (1975) where the court, holding that the relationship of a psychotherapist to a patient was similar to that of guardian to ward, found that a duty of care not to engage in sexual contact arose even where the patient had consented to such contact:

> There is a public policy to protect a patient from the deliberate and malicious abuse of power and breach of trust by a psychiatrist when that patient entrusts to him her body and mind. . . . Consent obtained under such circumstances is no consent and should stand for naught.[36]

More recently the Canadian task force emphasized the need for legal regulation in this area to protect vulnerable patients from exploitation.[37] They argued that Canadian law already recognized that many social relationships involved an imbalance of power justifying legal intervention whether in the form of the doctrines of duress, undue influence, and unconscionability in contract law, or by way of statutory provisions to prevent the exploitation of weaker parties in certain institutional relationships, for example, consumers, tenants, employees, and children. The task force concluded that the greatest potential for challenging exploitation in the doctor/patient relationship lay in the law of fiduciary relationships which had already been expanded in Canada to recognize the protection of non-economic as well as economic interests:

> To deny relief because of the nature of the interest involved, to afford protection to material interests but not to human and personal interest would, it seems to me, be arbitrary in the extreme.[38]

46

The task force argued that a fiduciary duty should be recognized in some aspects of the doctor-patient relationship where the patient was particularly vulnerable to an abuse of power, including in relation to sexual contact. Their position received some support from the trial court decision in *Norberg* v *Wynrib* (1990) where a patient, alleging sexual abuse, sued her doctor for assault, negligence, and breach of fiduciary duty:

> Regardless of the nature of their relationship, it is clear that a physician has a duty to act in utmost good faith towards a patient. It is trite to say that a physician must never allow his personal interests to conflict with his professional duty. In this case, Dr Wynrib clearly did this. . . . He showed a total disregard for the best interests of his patient.[39]

On first appeal, the majority did not agree that the doctor's breach of duty should be characterized as fiduciary but on further appeal to the Supreme Court of Canada ((1992) 92 D.L.R. 449), the original finding of the trial court was upheld, thus suggesting the possibility of new legal ways to conceptualize the wrong of patient sexual exploitation.

POTENTIAL LEGAL STRATEGIES IN THE UNITED KINGDOM

It is a matter of debate whether law is the best way to deal with professional misconduct in psychotherapy or whether it is sufficient to establish a system of licensing or registration coupled with the threat of revocation (along the lines of the General Medical Council in the medical profession). Reliance on an autonomous system of self-regulation by the profession would, however, provide a very thin shield of protection for vulnerable patients. For this reason a legal approach may be necessary to encourage awareness of responsibility and to provide a clear statement that this type of exploitation is not only unprofessional and inappropriate but also unacceptable to society as a whole because of its damaging results. For the moment, the strategy to be followed by lawyers confronted with claims of this sort needs to be formulated in accordance with the range of potential rights and remedies currently available.

1. Contract Law

Where a contract exists between therapist and patient, there may be a potential cause of action for psychiatric damage. Although, traditionally, contract law has not awarded damages for emotional as opposed to economic harm, there have been instances where limited recovery has been allowed. Thus, in *Cox* v *Philips Industries* (1976), the plaintiff received £500 damages for 'vexation, frustration and distress'[40] arising out of the breach of an employment contract. *Cox* was subsequently overruled in *Bliss* v *South East Thames Regional Health Authority* (1985) but the latter case nevertheless still leaves open the possibility of recovering damages for emotional harm arising out of breach of contract:

> Where damages fall to be assessed for breach of contract rather than in tort it is not

permissible to award general damages for frustration, mental distress, injured feelings or annoyance occasioned by the breach . . . except . . . where the contract which has been broken is itself a contract to provide peace of mind or freedom from distress.[41]

An agreement between therapist and patient might well fall into the category of contracts 'to provide peace of mind or freedom from distress', and so an action in contract could constitute a possible means of redress. However, it is only likely to be of value in the private health sector where the relationship between therapist and patient can properly be characterized as contractual. Recipients of public healthcare may well have to rely solely on tort law (see below).

2. Criminal law

Experience in the United States of America indicates some inclination towards dealing with the problem of therapist/patient sexual abuse through the mechanism of criminal law (see above). However, while of considerable symbolic value in demonstrating society's intolerance of such activity, in practical terms it is fraught with problems. These include the traditional criminal focus on violence in the context of sex crimes (see above), the fact that in a criminal case the victim becomes a mere witness and is not entitled to independent representation, and the requirement of a heavier burden of proof than in civil cases.[42] Moreover, there are serious political and ideological problems raised by the criminalization of sexual behaviour. As with pornography (see Lacey's article in this collection), the legal prohibition of sexual behaviour between therapist and patient may well become a tool in the hands of moral fundamentalists seeking to proscribe a much wider range of sexual activities.

3. Tort Law

Again, drawing upon American experience, the strategy with the greatest legal potential for challenging therapist/patient sexual abuse, undoubtedly lies in tort law.

(a) Battery

Because battery is a form of trespass and therefore actionable *per se* it may have a (small) potential in some cases of sexual exploitation by therapists, as the essence of the wrong involved in battery lies solely in the fact that the contact is unwelcome – it need not result in actual harm. However, if the plaintiff consents to physical contact there is no cause of action. An argument that the consent of a patient in therapy is never truly freely given would be certain to fail, because the law in this area traditionally takes no account of the social or psychological pressures which may be present in a relationship.[43]

(b) Negligence

Negligence may provide a more flexible route for the seeker of redress in this

48

context. Traditionally, four elements are recognized as necessary to bring an action for negligence. These are, first, establishing that a legal duty of care exists between the parties; secondly, proving there has been a breach of that duty; thirdly, proving that there has been actual loss or injury which is causally linked to the breach; and finally proving that the type of harm was foreseeable, that is, that the damage was not too remote.[44]

(i) Duty of Care

The close relationship which is necessarily built up by therapists with their patients and the recognized responsibility they bear for their patients' well-being constitutes a strong argument for establishing a duty of care in this area. Moreover, it has long been recognized that doctors owes a duty of care in relation to their patients' physical well-being. The stumbling-block is the *psychological* nature of the harm suffered by victims of therapist/patient sexual abuse. Traditionally, the courts have declined to recognize a duty of care in relation to the negligent infliction of 'purely emotional harm' except in a narrow range of cases concerning recovery for 'nervous shock'.[45] However, these cases have, with one exception,[46] been concerned with accidents caused by the defendant resulting in physical injury to others, witnessed by the plaintiff causing consequent severe emotional harm. Indeed, the English courts were slow to recognize a duty of care even in these situations.[47] Moreover, the recent case of *Alcock* v *Chief Constable of South Yorkshire*, arising from the Hillsborough football ground disaster, suggests that the courts may be taking an increasingly narrow view of the scope of nervous shock recovery.[48] Thus, the legal climate may not be propitious for arguments seeking to extend the scope of nervous shock recovery to circumstances where physical injury is neither alleged nor present in either the victim or a third party.[49] Nevertheless, in order for a negligence action to succeed, it would be necessary to persuade the courts to recognize a duty of care in these circumstances.

(ii) Breach

In cases involving allegations of professional negligence, the courts have adopted a fairly cautious approach to the articulation of a standard of care, merely requiring that professionals should possess a minimum degree of competence and should exercise reasonable care in the discharge of their duties. Moreover, this standard of care is, more often than not, determined by reference to the profession itself, that is, the standard which members of the profession normally achieve (as per *Bolam* v *Friern Hospital Management Committee*[50]) rather than that which in the opinion of the court they *ought* to achieve.[51]

If the law *is* to take its standards directly from the profession, on the Bolam principle, it becomes very important strategically to ensure that professional organizations do formally recognize their power and responsibility towards patients in the form of a clear declaration of professional ethical standards. Such an approach might assist lawyers in establishing not just the standard of care to be adopted but also the existence of a legal duty of care in the first place (see above).

(iii)   Causation
There could well be considerable technical problems in establishing factually that a sexual relationship was the cause of the patient's distress, and the onus of proving this causal link rests on the plaintiff. The standard of proof is satisfied only if the plaintiff proves that the defendant's breach made a material contribution to her injury:

> Mere proof that the defendant's breach increased the risk of injury is not of itself sufficient to discharge that onus; in particular, where a pathology may in the instant case have been caused by any one or more of a number of factors, it is necessary for the plaintiff to prove affirmatively that at least one factor for which the defendant is in law responsible, caused or made a material contribution to that pathology.[52]

There is no doubt that sexual exploitation can cause great suffering. The Canadian task force discovered that the psychological damage includes intense anxiety, fear, panic, depression, self-mutilation, and suicidal behaviour.[53] Victims also described how the experience had adversely affected their education, personal relationships, and performance as parents and employees. Under the principle laid down in *Wilsher* v *Essex Area Health Authority* the court would, however, require proof through medical evidence not only that the damage had actually occurred but also that it was more likely to have been caused by the defendant's breach than by any other factors which the defence might introduce.

There are inherent difficulties in presenting evidence through expert witnesses, especially in cases of professional liability. Because any 'scandal' rebounds on the whole profession, it may be difficult to find a suitable expert to attest to the causal link between the act and the damage. Professionals in general are very reluctant to criticize one another. Moreover, in this instance, the person most familiar with the psychological state of the plaintiff and therefore in the best position to give information about her condition is the defendant, and this poses further evidential problems. Ultimately, of course, the biggest stumbling block which a plaintiff in these circumstances has to confront is the difficulty of disentangling aspects of her previous psychological condition, for which she sought therapeutic help in the first place, from those manifestations of harm which derive directly from the defendant's acts and about which she is complaining. The rigidity of the *Wilsher* decision, combined with a common law tradition which approaches psychological as opposed to physical injury with scepticism and suspicion, makes establishing causation a particularly difficult task in these circumstances.

(iv)   Remoteness of Damage
In a negligence action the type of harm incurred must have been foreseeable. It therefore needs to be proved that, given the special nature of the therapeutic relationship, the introduction of a sexual element will have predictably damaging psychological consequences, not only because the patient will be

emotionally harmed by the violation of trust but also because she will be denied the healing which she was seeking by consulting a therapist in the first place.

Contemporary understanding of the therapist/patient relationship, particularly in relation to the psychotherapist's management and cognizance of the phenomenon of transference (above), makes the damage resulting from therapist/patient sexual contact foreseeable almost to the point of inevitability. Thus, so long as such an understanding finds its way into courtroom arguments (and here the issue of raising public awareness of the problem assumes significance), there should be little difficulty in establishing that the psychological damage which results from the therapist's actions is within the legal bounds of remoteness.

(v) Limitation Period
A final problem to be faced by a victim of therapist/patient sexual abuse who attempts to bring a negligence action is the limitation period.

Where a plaintiff claims damages for negligence in respect of personal injuries, the limitation period is three years (Limitation Act 1980 s.11(1)), beginning from the date when the cause of action accrued or 'the date of knowledge', that is, when the plaintiff becomes aware of the negligence. However, this 'date of knowledge' will be experienced simultaneously with the trauma caused by sexual exploitation, and victims will often feel unable to face the added stress involved in bringing a legal action against their former therapist.

The Canadian task force addressed this problem in their report arguing that:

> ... based on the information now available about post traumatic stress disorders, there must be specific attention paid to the reality that sexual abuse survivors do not always report quickly.[54]

Thus, the task force recommended that there should be no limitation period whatsoever on sexual assaults occurring in relationships of trust or dependency, particularly with any health care professional. It would be desirable if negligence claims for personal injury involving psychological harm could also acknowledge the plaintiff's need for a period of recovery before bringing an action.

CONCLUSION

Sexual exploitation in therapy occurs as a result of a number of factors including professional, social, and legal denial of the problem, leading to under-reporting by women due to ignorance, guilt, and shame.[55] Internal professional problems could be alleviated by the improved training methods now being called for by many professionals,[56] with specific emphasis on how to deal with the combination of power and the eroticized transference which is a recognized part of the therapeutic process.[57]

51

Socially, the situation will only be improved with the provision of more information for the general public. Patients are often very ignorant of the standard and methods of treatment they should expect, and this ignorance encourages implicit trust of the therapist even when patients are being exploited. Moreover, there is a need for a change in attitudes towards abuse victims particularly with regard to the frequent tendency to blame victims for allowing the abuse, based on misconceptions about the victim's apparent 'consent'.

From a legal perspective, this paper supports the imposition of a strict duty of care between therapists and patients. Our society is becoming more and more dependent upon the services of therapists and counsellors and we must therefore ensure that those to whom these vulnerable people are turning for help are made accountable to the law through the recognition of a duty of care. This argument would be strengthened by the profession's own acknowledgement of this duty. But, in any case, it is important for lawyers to recognize that a strictly legal approach, uninformed by a wider understanding of the nature of this particular problem, is unlikely to achieve much in the way of results. Strategically, the way forward must embrace not just litigation but a much broader campaign of public education aimed at securing professional responsibility, a societal change of attitude and, where appropriate, legislative reform.

NOTES AND REFERENCES

1 The British Association of Psychotherapists estimates that the number of enquiries received has risen in the last ten years from six or seven per week to sixty or seventy per week. Membership of the British Association for Counselling has risen from under 2,000 in 1982 to 9,600 in 1992 and it now receives over 100 enquiries per week.

2 Celia Hall, *The Independent*, 11 April 1992. A recent survey of 300 clinical psychologists working for the NHS, carried out by Warwick University, revealed that a startling one in five patients may be sexually involved with their therapists (Public Eye BBCTV, 13 November 92).

3 See Hall, op. cit., n. 2.

4 A. Stone, *Law, Psychiatry and Morality* (1984).

5 id., p. 192.

6 The need for regulation was recognized as long ago as 1971 in the Foster Report, 'Inquiry into the Practice and Effects of Scientology' (1971; Cmnd. para. 158). In 1978 a professional joint working party proposed the establishment of a statutory body called the Council for Psychotherapy, which would have the task of regulating entry, controlling standards, and drawing up a code of ethics. To date none of the working party's recommendations have been implemented. By contrast, consider the disciplinary provisions of the medical profession which are the responsibility of the General Medical Council (GMC), a body created by the Medical Act 1858. The GMC annually compiles a list of registered doctors (the Medical Register), and inclusion on the list is a condition of practice. The GMC is distinguishable from the British Medical Association (BMA) which is an unofficial, voluntary, professional body. The BMA has a code of ethics and an internal disciplinary system but the ultimate sanction available is expulsion from the BMA (not striking off the Medical Register, which only the GMC can do). A doctor expelled by the BMA would still be free to practise unless the GMC also decided to take action.

7 'Code of Ethics and Practice for Counsellors' AGM/9/90 at para. B.2.2.6.

8 P. Appelbaum and L. Jorgenson, 'Psychotherapist-Patient Sexual Contact After Termination of Treatment' (1991) 148: 11 *American J. Psychiatry* 1466 at p. 1469. Considerations such as these have begun to be highlighted by organizations in the United Kingdom, attempting to bring the problem to the public notice. For example, the Prevention of Professional Abuse Network (POPAN) was established in 1990 with the aim of addressing the issue of sexual abuse in psychotherapy. The co-ordinators' research indicates that it is a widespread problem, similar in nature to child abuse and/or incest twenty years ago in that it has not yet been properly addressed by society. The work of such organizations is an important step towards social recognition of this issue, a precondition to any broader solution.

9 id., p. 1469.

10 J. Sandler *et al.*, 'Notes on Some Theoretical and Clinical Aspects of Transference' (1969) 50 *Int. J. Psychoanalysis* 633.

11 R. Schafer, 'On the Nature of the Therapeutic Relationship' in *The Family and the Law*, eds. Goldstein and Katz (1963) 171.

12 W. U. Snyder, *Dependency and Psychotherapy* (1963) 5.

13 J. Forrester, 'Rape, Seduction and Psychoanalysis' in *Rape*, eds. Tomaselli and Porter (1986) 78.

14 id., p. 79.

15 Independent Task Force on Sexual Abuse of Patients (hereinafter referred to as 'task force'), *The Final Report* (1991) 41. The task force was commissioned by the College of Physicians and Surgeons of Ontario.

16 S. Onyett and T. Davey, 'UK Standing Conference on Psychotherapy: Room for an Alternative View?' (1992) 42 *Clinical Psychology Forum* 23.

17 C. MacKinnon, *Feminism Unmodified* (1987) 104.

18 P. Rutter, *Sex in the Forbidden Zone* (199) 19.

19 Task Force, op. cit., n. 15, p. 83.

20 Gartrell *et al.*, 'Prevalence of Psychiatrist-Patient Sexual Contact' in *Sexual Exploitation in Professional Relationships*, ed. G. Gabbard (1989).

21 C. MacKinnon, *Sexual Harassment and Working Women* (1979) 27.

22 V. Davidson, 'Psychiatry's Problem with No Name' (1977) 37 *Am. J. Psychoanalysis* 43.

23 Appelbaum and Jorgenson, op. cit., n. 8, p. 1469.

24 T. Johnson, *Professions and Power* (1972) 43–44.

25 MacKinnon observes: 'The theory of the unconscious was devised to explain how women invent experiences of childhood sexual abuse, because Freud did not believe, finally, that they could have happened.' (op. cit., n. 17, p. 51).

26 H. Deutsch, *The Psychology of Women* (1945) Vol. 1, p. 256.

27 Stone, op. cit., n. 4, p. 191.

28 C. MacKinnon, *Towards a Feminist Theory of the State* (1989) 177.

29 In the United States of America sexual harassment law goes some way to recognizing this inadequacy in the development of the so-called 'consequences approach'. This assumes 'that it is easier to measure the effect' [such as depression and anxiety] 'that unwanted sexual propositions have on female victims than it is to determine whether a female victim's lack of overt resistance to them is a sign of her tacit consent to them': see R. Tong, *Women, Sex and the Law* (1984) 76. Such an approach may be of potential value in the context of therapist/patient sexual abuse.

30 Rutter, op. cit., n. 18, p. 88.

31 Until well into the nineteenth century, married women were deemed incapable of consenting for purposes of making a contract or holding property, thus facilitating their sexual, social, and economic control by men (see S. Atkins and B. Hoggett, *Women and the Law* (1984) 105–109).

32 Rutter, op. cit., n. 18, p. 62.

33 id., p. 63.

34 Masters and Johnson, 'Principles of the New Sex Therapy' (1976) 133 *Am. J. Psychiatry* 548.

35 Stone, op. cit., n. 4, pp. 195–200.
36 *Roy* v *Hartogs* (1975) 366 NYS 2d 297, pp. 300–301. See also *Zipkin* v *Freeman* 463 SW 2d 753 (Mo. 1968). Actions for negligent inflictions of emotional distress (*Rowe* v *Bennett* 514 A 2d 802 (Me. 1986)), intentional inflictions of emotional distress (*Destefano* v *Gravrian* 763 P 2d 275 (Colo. 1988)) and breach of contract (*Anclote Manor Foundation* v *Wilkinson* 263 So 2d 256 (Fla. Dist. Ct. App. 1972) have also been successful.
37 Task Force, op. cit., n. 15, Legal Appendix p. 2.
38 *Frame* v *Smith* (1987) 42 DLR (4th) 81, per Wilson J. at p. 104. A fiduciary duty is the obligation of a person holding a position of trust or confidence with respect to another person to act solely for that person's benefit.
39 *Norberg* v *Wynrib* (1990) 44 BCLR (2d) 47 (BCCA).
40 [1976] 3 All E.R. 161.
41 [1985] I.R.L.R. 308 at p. 316.
42 Criminal law traditionally requires proof 'beyond a reasonable doubt' whereas in civil law, the wrong must be established 'on the balance of probablities'. The problem is compounded by the inevitable absence, given the circumstances of the therapeutic relationship, of witnesses to the crimes alleged. On the question of victim representation, there is a growing tendency in certain jurisdictions to confer representation rights to victims, particularly in the context of sex crimes (for example, France and the United States of America).
43 *Latter* v *Braddell* [1881] LJOB 448. For further discussion of the consent issue in this context, see J. Conaghan and W. Mansell, *The Wrongs of Tort* (1993) ch. 7.
44 M. Brazier (ed.), *Street on Torts* (1988) ch. 11–17.
45 The 'legal' term 'nervous shock' means a recognized psychiatric illness such as clinical depression rather than 'ordinary' grief, sorrow, or distress, *Attia* v *British Gas* [1987] 3 All E.R. 455 at 462. In the United States of America a tort of '*intentional* infliction of emotional harm', deriving from the old English case of *Wilkinson* v *Downton* [1897] 2 Q.B. 57, has been invoked in the context of therapist/patient sexual abuse (see above, n. 33). No such tort as yet exists in English law although there are those who argue for its development, both generally (see, for example, F. Trinidade, 'The Intentional Infliction of Purely Mental Distress' 6 *Oxford J. of Legal Studies* 219), and in the specific context of sexual harassment (J. Conaghan and W. Mansell, op. cit., n. 43). In any case, the likely scope of such a tort in the present context is limited first by the requirement that the harm be inflicted *intentionally* (or recklessly), and secondly because, to ground a cause of action, the therapist's behaviour must be demonstrably 'outrageous' and the patient's consequent emotional distress 'severe', American Law Institute Restatement 2d of Torts (1966) s.46 and Comment.
46 In *Owens* v *Liverpool Corporation* [1938] 4 All E.R. 727, a tramcar negligently collided with a hearse during a funeral procession, overturning the coffin. A nervous shock claim by the relatives of the deceased, who witnessed the impact, was successful; the court held that recovery for 'mental shock' was not limited to cases in which apprehension as to human safety was involved, but extended to every case where injury by reason of mental shock resulted from the negligent act of the defendant.
47 There was initially no cause of action for nervous shock unless accompanied by physical injury to the plaintiff. However, in *Dulieu* v *White & Sons* [1091] 2 K.B. 669 the plaintiff successfully claimed damages for nervous shock after the defendant's carriage crashed into the building where she was working, although she was not physically harmed by the accident. Subsequent case law developed the scope of recovery to its present (uncertain) limits as laid down in *McLoughlin* v *O'Brien* [1982] 2 All E.R. 298, and, more recently, in *Alcock* v *Chief Constable of South Yorkshire* [1991] 4 All E.R. 907 (below). In the context of this paper, the nervous shock cases pose a problem because of the strict limitations which the courts choose to impose upon the recovery of damages in negligence for 'purely emotional harm', not resulting from physical injury.
48 [1991] 4 All E.R. 907. Sixteen relatives of spectators who had been crushed to death at the stadium claimed damages for nervous shock which they alleged was caused by seeing or hearing news of the disaster. None of the appellants were successful, however, because either they were not at the football match and had only learnt of the disaster through television or

radio reports, or else their relationship was not considered sufficiently close to the primary victim. The decision is generally viewed as a retreat from the more liberal approach to recovery implict in *McLoughlin* v *O'Brien* (above, n. 47). See also *Ravenscroft* v *Rederiaktiebolaget Transatlantic* [1992] 2 All E.R. 470.

49 Some American jurisdictions are more flexible. Consider, for example, the Californian case of *Molien* v *Kaiser Foundation Hospitals* 27 Cal. 3d 916 (1980), which permitted recovery of damages for the negligent infliction of emotional harm in circumstances where a defendant doctor's misdiagnosis (of venereal disease) had resulted in the break-up of the patient's marriage causing consequent emotional distress to her husband, the plaintiff.

50 [1957] 1 W.L.R. 582 at p. 586.

51 The Bolan test was approved by the House of Lords in the context of medical cases in *Maynard* v *West Midlands Regional Health Authority* [1985] 1 All E.R. 635, where it was also recognized that mere differences of opinion and practice cannot be used as a basis for a conclusion of negligence. A more objective approach to professional liability had been suggested in *Midland Bank* v *Hett, Stubbs & Kemp* [1979] Ch. 384, where Oliver J. observed that 'the extent of the legal duty in any given situation must, I think, be a question of law for the court' (at 402).

52 M. Powers and N. Harris, *Medical Negligence*(1990) 293. See also *Wilsher* v *Essex Area Health Authority* [1988] A.C. 1074.

53 Task Force, op. cit., n. 15, pp. 84–85.

54 Task Force, op. cit., n. 15, p. 195.

55 T. Garrett and B. Thomas-Peter, 'Sexual Harassment', *The Psychologist*, July 1992, p. 321.

56 Garrett and Thomas-Peter, op. cit., n. 55; Hall, op. cit., n. 2; J. Russell, 'Breaking Boundaries: A Research Note' *Counselling*, May 1990; Rutter, op. cit., n. 18, p. 193.

57 Garrett and Thomas-Peter, op. cit., n. 55.

Self and Subjectivities: Languages of Claim in Property Law

ANNE BOTTOMLEY *

It must be stressed that her work is not a *true* description of women or femininity, a position that is superior to false, patriarchal conceptions (truth, after all, is engaged in precisely the relation of doubles, or mirror reflections that is the hallmark of phallo-centrism). Her aim is quite different: it is to devise a strategic and combative understanding, one whose function is to make explicit what has been excluded or left out of phallocentric images. Unlike truth, whose value is eternal, strategy remains provisional; its relevance and value depend on what it is able to achieve, on its utility in organizing means towards ends.[1]

FATAL ATTRACTION

I will call her Janet because she has had four surnames already. She was married for the first time at the age of 18; but that marriage only lasted a year. Next at the age of 19 she met a man, Stuart Eves. He was a married man. They could not marry. So they started living together. She took his name and had two children by him. After [four and a half] years that relationship broke down. Now both have got divorces from their former spouses and have remarried. The question arises as to the house where they lived.[2]

And so begins a well-known story; a story of promise and betrayal; of an innocent young girl and an older man; of a house and of the hard work put into making a home for the family:

The house was very dirty and dilapidated. They went in and made their home there. She did a great deal of work to the house and garden. She did much more than many wives would do. She stripped the wallpaper in the hall. She painted woodwork in the lounge and kitchen. She painted the kitchen cabinets. She painted the brickwork in the front of the house. She broke up the concrete in the front garden. She carried the pieces to the skip. She, with him, demolished a shed and put up a new shed. She prepared the front garden for turfing. To add to it all, they had their second child.[3]

Not only a story of a dishonest and cheating man, but another woman: ' . . . *he met another woman called Gloria. He met her when he got a job as a mini-cab driver.*'[4] She became more than an ally to the man:

*Lecturer in Law, Rutherford College, University of Kent, Canterbury CT2 7NX, England

With special thanks to the following who have all contributed, in diverse ways, to the writing of this paper: Elizabeth Cowie, Andrew Dart, Christine Dickin, Elona Major, Belinda Meteyard, Katherine O'Donovan, Nick Jackson, and Christopher Stanley.

> *. . . Gloria made an upset. She raised her voice and said that Janet would not get a penny out of Stuart Eves. She threatened Janet with violence. Janet was very upset and afraid of what might happen if she stayed in the house. So she left and Stuart and Gloria moved in with an Alsatian dog.*[5]

But as in all good folk stories, there is a happy ending made possible by a good fairy:

> *. . . a few years ago even equity would not have helped her. But things have altered now. Equity is not past the age of child bearing. One of her latest progeny is a constructive trust of a new model. Lord Diplock brought it into the world and we have nourished it.*[6]

The story is indeed a familiar one. This case is known by all law students who have studied equity or property law.[7] However, consideration is rarely given to the narratives deployed in the judgment, other than an attempt to extrapolate a 'purely' legal one in order to uncover the *ratio(nes)*. Read as a story narrated by the judge, our attention is immediately focused on the wronged woman. Denning's choice of detail, as well as his sentence construction, underline the obvious injustice of her treatment, particularly after all her good work. His reference to this as '. . . *more than many wives would do . . .* .' serves to highlight not only her role as wife/mother but her very lack of formal status, which would at least have received recognition in law with some consequent benefits.[8] Clearly implied is the point that women with that formal status would receive better treatment in law than she, even if their cases were less deserving on the facts. She is as a wife without the 'protection' of wife status. She is mother (and Denning makes a point of Stuart's lack of paternal responsibility in not paying maintenance to the children);[9] she is innocent youth (Janet) against glamour (Gloria) and an irresponsible, dishonest man. It is clear from the very first sentence of the judgment that Denning will find some way of recompensing her; it becomes then a question of how he achieves it. Before we turn to his construction of the legal argument, we need to listen to the resonances of his construction of Janet as subject.

PRESUMED INNOCENT

The vortex of wife/mother/innocent is compelling. Denning plays with each motif but it is when they are brought into relation that they become particularly powerful. The counterpoint provided by Gloria underlines the distinction between the damsel in distress and the dangerous glamour of a figure which I can only construe as a combination of harridan and courtesan; certainly a dangerous woman (to the point indeed where one might even construct the man as weak rather than wicked). Janet is transformed into the victim who needs the protection of law. The need to construct quite such a powerful image of her is due partly to the weakness of the relevant evidence in this case,[10] and partly to the fact that Denning is, in terms of the substantive law he seeks to employ, undoubtedly trying to expand legal doctrine in a new and controversial direction.

Whilst we may recoil from the patronizing tone with which Denning constructs Janet, we must not loss sight of the consequences, both for herself and for other women, of such a construction. Overdrawn it may be, but the paradox is that whilst we have no real sense of 'Janet', we are given one glimpse of her which makes it clear that she would, to some extent, have recognized herself in Denning's judgment:

> So far as I was concerned, we were husband and wife, and I did trust him. I never ever thought anything was going to happen while we were building the home up: as far as I knew we were going to stay there.[11]

She was indeed, in one sense, the wife/mother/innocent. The creation of this subjectivity does, however, leave us with some unfortunate consequences. Not only does it reinforce traditional models of femininity as a ground for intervention but it specifically operates to provide a trope against which the claims of other women might be judged. Indeed, in later judgments Denning did deploy the tryptic against women who could not stand madonna-like within the figure.[12] However, for some women this representation of them does, importantly, represent a sense of self which is both real to them and the source of their sense of betrayal. That it reproduces themes from which we would want to distance ourselves, and that it can be used against women who fail to conform, does not mean that we should lose sight of this. Not only would this be an injustice to the individual woman but, in a broader context, the loss of the figure of wife/mother/innocent as at all relevant to the legal arguments has been significant, as is evidenced in major cases since Denning's retirement.[13]

UNBEARABLE LIGHTNESS OF BEING

It has been a major theme of feminist work in this area of law to try and find legal strategies (or more statically 'legal forms') which will mitigate the structural inequalities from which women suffer without reproducing models of dependency. This is particularly problematic when a legal system privileges the free market model of equal individuals freely entering into legal relations. It has been a difficult task for feminists to argue that what might seem a more progressive philosophy of treating women as equals is too often blind to actual inequality, and therefore reproduces or exacerbates it. This problem is stark enough when examined in terms of marriage and divorce law, but is even more problematic when examined outside a status structure. What are the elements which we would want recognized in claims to property ownership outside a marital relationship? Are there any arguments for making gender-specific points, and if so at what cost?

In English law, the formulation of claims has been almost entirely through the law of trusts. There is another line of cases which bears upon a claim to occupation rights alone and which has been formulated in part through contract law, but, to date, the focus in this country has been on trusts and the related concept of proprietary estoppel. This has opened up space for a great deal of judicial creativity. To date, no statutory intervention has been made in this area and we are reliant on case decisions and interpretation.

It may seem strange that in dealing with claims to real property (land) we should find ourselves in such fluid territory. Our maps are relatively few. On the one hand, we have primary source material, reported cases which have reached the higher courts; on the other, we have academics, whose traditional role is generally understood to be not simply to offer us a reading of the cases but to render them intelligible by placing them, as far as is possible, into a coherent relation. The promise of most academic work (and the fantasy of most students) is that we will be able to excavate the hidden map, place all locations within this map and then simply guide others around it. We may argue about who has the better map but we rarely (at least in public) argue about the very act of mapping itself. The act of mapping is, of course, an act of control, in which fundamental decisions and choices will be made and then rendered invisible. More significantly, however, what becomes lost is an understanding that a map is, and can be, no more than a representation.[14] In this area in particular, because the case material is so confused and its history so controversial, paradoxically, the act of mapping becomes an even greater challenge to the orthodox academic and an even greater need for the student who craves certainty in an uncertain world. None of this is an argument against maps *per se*, but it expresses a concern that we do not become caught within maps of our own making with no sense of either our responsibility for them, or the proper use to which they should be put. For me, maps offer possible directions and moments of grounding. I need both. But I also know that I cannot be finally contained within; I need to be constantly vigilant of fracture, paradox, and externalities which may render my maps confused. Without acknowledging that confusion as being my experience of my reading, I would be involved in a fundamental breach of faith. This sense of disorder, and an ability to live with it rather than to try and control it by forcing a map upon it, is fundamental to my understanding of law, particularly in this area, and particularly as both woman and feminist. It is, in its many manifestations, the excess which lies at the very core of the attempt to dominate with internal coherence and rationality. Whilst it continues to try and externalize this excess by figures of other (whether, as in this area, as equity or woman or simply a judgment we can ignore because it does not fit easily into our map) our task must be 'to bring it home'.[15]

This does not mean then that we can be at all cavalier in our use of legal materials. Indeed it calls for greater vigilance in our use of them and hence an insistence on close case reading. It also frees us to look more closely at the narratives and figures employed by judges as they construct their strategies of decision-making. As we open ourselves to a more fluid – and, at the same time, much deeper reading, we listen to the deployment of language and watch the representation of the characters which appear before us. We then have to double back on ourselves and reconsider our own initial reading of, and response to, the case material.

The factors which made Denning's judgment in *Eves* controversial were, primarily, his blurring (one might argue avoidance) of three elements within a more orthodox approach to trusts. The first is the need to focus on the acquisition of the property rather than a more general consideration of the way in which the couple ran their lives. The second is the traditional concern to find evidence of an agreement about the ownership of the property. The third element is the preference for monetary contributions, or contributions in kind, to the acquisition or (substantial) improvement of the property. Clearly, then, an orthodox approach would suggest that many of the factors Denning took into account in his judgment were extraneous.[16] Our problem then could be couched in these terms. Should we support or defend the development of an area of law which allows the play of a figure of woman/victim and privileges women who can be ascribed within the wife/mother role?

SEX, LIES, AND VIDEOTAPES
OR
SILENCE OF THE LAMBS

We first need to consider the disadvantages women face when they have become cohabitees and do not formally share the ownership of the property with their partners. Certainly birth and childcare are major factors contributing to women's economic 'vulnerability', and it is not surprising that so many of the reported cases concern women who have become dependent due to these factors. Their very withdrawal from the labour market means that few of them can make any significant financial contribution to the acquiring of a home. Indeed, if and when they do earn (small) amounts of money, they too often use that money to support the family rather than pay a mortgage. This situation is well illustrated in *Burns* v *Burns*.[17] Denning's approach in *Eves* made it clear that he was well aware of this problem; to constrain a claim to within a financial nexus would severely disadvantage the very women he thought most in need of the protection of law. Although Denning's figure is wife/mother we should not ignore the recent evidence which again confirms that domestic labour is still the preserve, in most homes in this country, of women rather than of men and that there is very little real evidence of any fundamental change in this pattern.[18] Whilst I would not want to use this evidence, at this point anyway, for any argument that it itself should be rewarded, I would want to suggest that a woman without children may also, although not as radically, be economically disadvantaged in terms of access to paid labour (in particular, for example, in relation to overtime work or the extra work required to make one a candidate for promotion). Given all these factors, and against the general background of women's overall position in the labour market, it is not surprising that few women are in a position to be able to base a claim entirely within a formal cash-contribution nexus.[19]

However, our problems go beyond simply those of entry to the labour market. The entry of women into a domestic-sexual relationship may well signal the beginning of a narrative of differing expectations which lies at the

60

base of potential conflict between men and women. By looking at the fragments of evidence we have in the cases of the woman's account of the beginning of their relationship and of the process of living together, rather than focusing on the breakdown of the relationship, we can begin to excavate the possibility of patterns of gendered behaviour. Obviously such evidence needs to be handled with care; it is constructed within the court setting in order, as far as possible, to build a case. But I find it significant that the same themes came up over and over again. Perhaps we should begin to see them as 'normal' and therefore to be addressed, and recognize that at the core of many on-going relationships there lie problematic issues which might well pre-figure the patterns of conflict and separation. My focus here is on (our) expectations, and on our construction of our experiences of our domestic lives, and to question to what extent gender difference is visible – different enough and visible enough to the point where we cannot afford to be blind to it. Having made this point, I must emphasize that I am talking in terms of motifs and narratives rather than arguing that this is the case for all couples on all occasions. I do not hold to a simplistic structural argument that power relations are simply about men holding power to the detriment of women; in my opinion we have to face both the depth of division between men and women as well as the specificity of power relations within differing familial settings.[20]

The evidence suggested by so many of the cases is that whilst there may be mutual (?) dreaming about what the couple will do together, there is rarely concrete discussion about the practicalities of economic relations, especially should the couple separate. A further problem seems to be that in this genre of material almost invariably the couple are not free to marry; the narrative of expectations therefore becomes more confused as the woman is promised marriage at some point in the future, and often the sorting out of property relations becomes linked in any discussion to that event. By implication, then, we are dealing with women who feel doubly betrayed; marriage has not come about and they find themselves without any certain claim to the property they have jointly lived in as a home. It is at this point that what is rendered visible is the very real possibility that they have committed themselves to the relationship, more so than their male partners, and hence have given more on trust than an individual still possessing a distinct sense of separate identity is likely to have done. Leaving aside those cases where there is a distinct trick, it often seems that we are dealing here with a basic failure in communication and a fundamental difference in expectations.

We need to look at the use of language, to move from a focus on financial contributions to a focus on intentions. From my reading of the cases the first issue is simply silence. But equally important are the different ways in which the genders seem to construe what is spoken. Evidence given in one recent case arising under the equitable jurisdiction is not, in my opinion, unusual and illustrates this point:

> As soon as we heard he was likely to get the money, we looked round, looked for a suitable home for us and children. I always understood we were going to share whatever we had, big or

little. We always discussed it as being ours. The only discussion was in very general terms. We needed a house; we would go out and look for one we could own as a couple for a family. When we found [the house], he said he was glad he would be able to provide a proper home, a place where we could be secure. I understood it would be jointly ours. He'd always indicated it would be a joint venture. Everything we did in the past had been jointly done. If you live with someone, you don't 'dissect'. It was the accepted thing.[21]

This was accepted in the court of first instance and the Court of Appeal as evidence of an agreement to share on the basis of which Mrs Rosset acted to her detriment and therefore acquired an interest in the property. I would argue that other factors in the case inclined the courts towards a preference to accept Mrs Rosset's evidence rather than that of her husband (it was accepted that he had explicitly lied on at least one occasion). However, in the House of Lords a more orthodox judge was able to utilize the tools of specificity and explicitness to find against Mrs Rosset. He wanted explicit evidence that there was an agreement about ownership.

I pause to observe that neither a common intention by spouses that a house is to be renovated as a 'joint venture' nor a common intention that the house is to be shared by parents and children as the family home throws any light on their intentions with respect to the beneficial ownership of the property.[22]

Lord Bridge did recognize that such a requirement of evidence of an agreement specifically on the point of ownership could pose a problem:

Spouses living in amity will not normally think it necessary to formulate or define their respective interests in property in any precise way. The expectations of parties to every happy marriage is that they will share the practical benefits of occupying the matrimonial home whoever owns it. But this is something quite distinct from sharing the beneficial interest. . . . These considerations give rise to special difficulties for judges who are called on to resolve a dispute between spouses who have parted and are at arm's length as to what was their common intention or understanding . . . when they were still living as a united family and acquiring a matrimonial home in the expectation of living in it together indefinitely.[23]

Here the problem is presented as primarily one of time; but I would suggest that we need also to consider the problem of specificity. It seems to me that this is not only a requirement of a certain jurisprudential approach but also a mode of reasoning and language use which is more conducive to men than women. This may in part be due to material factors and differences in socio-economic strengths and roles, but evidence drawn from psychoanalytical material would suggest that this division derives from the construction of gender identity. In other words, it is far more deeply embedded than a simple analysis of economic difference and consequent relative power relations would reveal.

I have suggested two particular uses of language which need to be thought about – the use of silence and how it might be interpreted, and the use of specificity, a clear focus of the discussions. There is some evidence from the case material to suggest that women too often read silence as positive assent and lack of specificity as covering a number of issues with equal firmness rather than evading the particular issue.

There is also evidence of the great difficulty some women experience in raising issues about property as well as their difficulty in persuading their

62

partners to confront the issue through discussions. Take, for example, the case of *Coombes* v *Smith*.[24] This is a case of first instance (and therefore at the most can only be persuasive precedent) but is much referred to in the textbooks as evidence of a narrower definition of law (not to the benefit of the party making the claim) than had previously seemed to be the case in the higher courts. The judge accepted that *'the plaintiff was manifestly a completely honest witness'*. Unfortunately, throughout the case there is clear evidence of a disparity between what was being said and what was being heard:

> . . . sometime during 1980 or 1981, the plaintiff asked the defendant what security she or [her daughter] would have if something happened to him. The defendant replied, 'Don't worry, I have told you I'll always look after you' or words to that effect. The plaintiff said in evidence, 'I didn't ask that sort of question in the early days. I thought things would be O.K. I let things drift along, then as time went on I started to ask him.[25]

Later:

> . . . the plaintiff once again raised the question of putting the property in joint names, but the defendant refused saying, 'Don't dictate to me.'[26]

It is quite clear from the case that the woman did, over the course of the relationship, begin to try and discuss her position in relation to the property but 'silence' operated in a number of ways: first, by their initial mutual silence on the issue, secondly by the man's later refusal to deal with it (except in the most general terms), thirdly by his literal silencing of the issue when raised, and finally by her retreat in the hope that the situation would eventually be resolved. Each aspect worked crucially against her once the case came to law. She was hopelessly optimistic to the point that she heard statements with an interpretation which was based on an attempt to find the reassurance she came to need after the 'honeymoon' period was over. The man never actually moved in with her, despite repeated assurances that he would leave his wife to do so. Then, in 1984 he:

> . . . confessed to the plaintiff that he had left his wife and moved in with another woman some seven months previously. But he still professed an intention to move in with the plaintiff. He told her he couldn't let her waste ten years of her life, saying, 'leave me a couple of days to sort it out and you will have a lodger,' referring as the plaintiff understood it, to himself. However, consistently with what had happened before, the defendant did not move in.[27]

One could easily be forgiven for thinking that by this time the woman should have known better and withdrawn from a hopeless situation. Unfortunately, economic as well as emotional dependency now came into play: she had a child and only a part-time low-paid job. She had no assets of her own. She continued to rely on his assurances and to seek what evidence she could to confirm that his promises would eventually be performed. But as the man's lawyer argued:

> . . . where a man and a woman live together, they always expect or hope that the relationship will be a permanent one . . . what they say at this point cannot be relied upon when the relationship breaks down.[28]

Again we return to specificity:

> ... a belief that the defendant would always provide her with a roof over her head is, to my mind, something quite different from a belief that she has a right to remain there against his wishes. Moreover, all the statements relied upon by the plaintiff were made by the defendant while the relationship with the plaintiff was continuing. There is no evidence before me of any discussion at all between the plaintiff and the defendant as to what would happen in the event of the relationship breaking down and of the defendant choosing to live with another woman.[29]

All these points, in relation to both cases, are concerned with the need to find an agreement or an assurance upon which the plaintiff acted. Both cases exemplify the problems for women in having to move into a frame of language-use which seems more conducive to men than to women. This is essentially different from, although clearly closely related to, expectations based on the socio-economic construction of gender roles. We need to continually distinguish these aspects as well as to play them through in relation to each other.

THE COOK, THE THIEF, HIS WIFE, AND HER LOVER

In the House of Lords in *Rosset*, Lord Bridge stated that there were two ways to establish a beneficial interest:

> [first] ... *The finding of an agreement or arrangement to share ... based on evidence of express discussions between the partners, however imperfectly remembered. ... Once a finding to this effect is made it will only be necessary for the partner asserting the claim to a beneficial interest ... to show that he or she has acted to his or her detriment ... [secondly, when] ... the court must rely entirely on the conduct of the parties both as the basis from which to infer a common intention to share the property beneficially and as the conduct to be relied on to give rise to a constructive trust.*[30]

The second head is concerned with conduct which contributes towards the purchase of the property or towards a substantial improvement which increases its value. In one of the most controversial aspects of the judgment, Lord Bridge defined the concept of contributions extremely narrowly:

> ... *direct contributions to the purchase price by the partner who is not the legal owner, whether initially or by payment of mortgage instalments will readily justify the inference necessary to the creation of a constructive trust. But, as I read the authorities, it is extremely doubtful whether anything less will do.*[31]

Mrs Rosset was typical of a housewife with children; she had no paid job and no capital and was therefore unable to make financial contributions even if she had wished to. Instead she contributed time and labour to finding the house, helping with aspects of the purchase, and then being involved in the restoration and decoration work, including undertaking some of the labour herself. In the words of Nicholls J. in the Court of Appeal she was *'busying herself about the property day after day'*.[32] Not only did Lord Bridge in the House of Lords regard such efforts as *'so trifling as almost to be de minimis'*[33] in terms of the overall value of the house but, more significantly, he drew a line distinguishing between activity undertaken in her role *qua* wife and activity undertaken which might have been used as evidence that she would have only undertaken such activity if she had believed herself to be an owner:

> ... it would seem the most natural thing in the world for any wife, in the absence of her husband ... to spend all the time she could spare and to employ any skills she might have ... to accelerate the progress of the work quite irrespective of any expectation she might have of enjoying a beneficial interest in the property.[34]

What is required is not only labour which can be valued, but labour which can be dissociated from any wifely role and in which it can be proven that the woman specifically directed the activity towards ownership rather than simply use of the property. We are drawn back to forms of specific thinking which seem at variance not only with women's socio-economic activities but with the very way in which they think them. As Nourse LJ said in the earlier case of *Grant* v *Edwards*:

> There remains this difficult question: what is the quality of conduct required ... [from which to infer the common intention that the parties should share ownership]? It would be possible to take the view that the mere moving into the house by the woman amounted to an acting upon common intention ... [but] ... the law is not so cynical as to infer that a woman will only go to live with a man to whom she is not married if she understands that she is to have an interest in their home. So what sort of conduct is required? In my judgement it must be conduct on which the woman could not have been expected to embark unless she was to have an interest in the house. If she was not to have such an interest, she could reasonably be expected to go and live with her lover, but not for example, to wield a 14lb sledge-hammer.[35]

Which brings us back to Janet Eves.

POSTCARDS FROM THE EDGE

Janet's entry into a narrative of expectation was via the figure of a wife, a promise of 'wife-to-be', a status never achieved and therefore the very reason for her appearance in the courts having to found a claim external to marital status. That Denning uses this to argue for her claim as analogous to a wife-claim is certainly one of the threads of the rationale for his judgment. Yet, at the very same time, he constructs her as 'more than wife', a woman who goes beyond (it is beyond rather than counter to) a wife-role. Looking back at this distinction through the frame of later cases, the 'more than wife' characterization becomes significant. To begin with, it seems simply a bizarrely old-fashioned view of women-wives; as if Denning cannot really believe that contemporary women have skills (or can learn) skills outside the nursery and the kitchen.[36] If we play through this distinction based on expectations of gendered activity, it becomes obvious that Denning is differentiating (an orthodox definition of) domestic labour from other forms of labour, to her advantage. Compare this with the approach taken by Lord Bridge. Here it is not the form of labour but the context in which it is performed that becomes significant. It is what women-wives are willing to undertake within, and because of, a relationship. Suddenly there are no boundaries. The modern woman-wife will undertake any form of labour, labour which can then never be used to formulate a claim to ownership. At least in the judgement of Nourse LJ in *Edwards*, we still have a moment in which we can locate a definition which takes into account the form the labour takes, an echo of Denning's 'external' approach.

Further, evidence about general expectations within the relationship, behaviour and betrayal, now become irrelevant. Whilst we might welcome a narrowing of focus which removes the patronizing account giving by Denning (which sometimes leaves us with an uneasy sense of voyeurism), the loss of these narratives has left the women with only a very narrow range of play. The attempt to focus only on agreements and activity geared towards ownership tears one element from a much more complex framework of inter-related detail. Unless we are allowed to see the broader frame of a sexual-domestic relationship, in which trust and expectation are necessarily in play, how can we begin to demonstrate the paucity of claims which assume an ability to extrapolate and specify agreements and actions aimed at only one focus (ownership of house rather than home)?

We could simply leave the story on notes of closure and gloom; of loss and, paradoxically, of a recognition that the failure of the woman-wife narratives in recent judgments has left such women exposed and with few defences which reflect their sense of subjectivity. We could celebrate the exposure of the fragility of wife models and use the material as warnings against both actual economic (and emotional) dependency and the constructions of similar models in and through law. There could be a simple virtue in offering to women a frame which requires explicit negotiations and specific goals, for instance as in arguing for the use of a contractual model or calling for the use of express trusts. This would all be fine but of extremely limited use.

One of the major values of thinking in strategic forms rather than substantive ones is that we move from debates imbued with absolutism to a clear recognition of contingency. For some women, on some occasions, we need to be able to argue – the simplicity of this is beautiful. It no longer compels us towards judgmental stances in which we have to try and find the 'best model'. Further, it actually impels us towards careful listening: listening to the specificity of women's experience; to their/our fractured subjectivities, never finally contained in any one language of claim and yet, at the very same time, recognizing that aspects of their/our own senses of self meet legal discourse in certain narratives which we need to keep open.

We need to actually listen to the evidence of women's lives that these cases present us with, and consider our own. Too often feminist material has been prescriptive – giving blue-prints for living rather than accepting the muddles and confusions which mark most people's emotional lives, including our own. Once we are willing to truly acknowledge the complexity, contradictions, and cross-currents of our emotional lives, we can move towards not only an attempt to begin to make some sense of them for ourselves but also a reading of case material which reflects these ambiguities within the evidential material:

> It must be stressed that her work is not a true description of women or femininity, a
> position that is superior to false, patriarchal conceptions . . . . Her aim is quite different: it is
> to devise a strategic and combative understanding, one whose function is to make explicit
> what has been excluded or left out of phallocentric images.[37]

We have to acknowledge the gender specificity which marks the material. If we
accept that there is evidence not just of differing expectations but also
differences in the deployment of language then we must meet this, concretely.
To continue to examine legal forms which rely on a finding of *consensus ad
idem* (in particular the contractual model) ignores the tension between the
differing patterns of thinking; women may well find such an approach
alienating rather than enabling. Finding a way to recognize ambiguity,
paradox, and contingency may be far more valuable. However, we must
continue to emphasize that we are not looking for *one* answer. We are looking
for different possibilities in different situations, investigating different juridical
models and considering patterns of bargaining and mediation. All must be on
our agenda: ' . . . strategy remains provisional; its relevance and value depend
on what it is able to achieve, on its utility in organizing means towards ends.'[38]

In this spirit we should look back, constructively, on the juridical models
available to us and, in particular, to the remedial forms of relief available
through equity. There is never finally a closure. Even *Rosset* has recently been
given a more liberal, flexible interpretation,[39] an important reminder of the
difficulty of effecting closure in any area of law, but perhaps particularly here.
At the very centre of the attempt to control through the imposition of models
of doctrine, the excess is there to be found and to be worked with. It is simply a
question of the willingness to approach the material with an eye to the
possibilities and with an agenda of needs. This is the politics of engagement.

It is also the politics of contingency – of working with what we have now,
whilst recognizing that the power-play may shift and along with that shift we
will have to find new moments of engagement.[40]

Importantly now we need to be able to let go of our own prejudices, so that
we can truly turn the mirror back on those prejudices which surround us. We
have become caught in three nets. The first is that in the flight away from
marriage and dependency we became too entangled in the need to portray all
associated ideas and needs in negative terms. We constructed it as a closed
model and simply advised women to stay away. Secondly, we concentrated on
finding our own voices, our sense of self identity, and argued that all that
opposed this was an imposition upon us, another closed model, one
consequence of which was to privilege women's experience over that of men.
Finally, we allowed ourselves to become involved in a fiction called the 'new
man', men who would take on what we taught them and somehow, with us,
would transform the world. This led us to accept superficial change as
structurally deep and, at the same time, allowed us to ignore the violence in
which we were complicit in attempting to force our own construction on men.

Our starting points must now be more radical. Braidotti quotes de Lauretis:

> What is emerging in feminist writing is . . . the concept of a multiple, shifting, and often
> self-contradictory identity, a subject that is not divided in, but rather at odds with

language; an identity made up of heterogeneous and heteronomous representations of gender, race, and class . . . an identity that one decided to reclaim from a history of multiple assimilations, and that one insists on as a strategy.[41]

She then goes on to say:

> . . . the starting point for this redefinition of the female feminist subject is the notion of the asymmetry between the sexes, which results in the political and epistemological project of asserting difference in a non-hierarchical manner, refusing to disembody and therefore to desexualize the vision of the subject. The question then becomes: how to reconcile the recognition of the problematic nature of the construction of subjectivity with the political necessity of asserting women as the subjects of another story?[42]

NOTES AND REFERENCES

1 E. Grosz, *Sexual Subversions* (1989); for comments on the work of L. Irigaray see p. 110.
2 Per Lord Denning MR in *Eves* v *Eves* [1975] 1 W.L.R. 1338 at p. 1339.
3 id., p. 1339.
4 id., p. 1339.
5 op. cit., n. 2, p. 1340.
6 op. cit., n. 2, p. 1340. This is not the place to explore more fully the use of female imagery in relation to equity. Here it takes the form of childbirth; in other places it might take, for example, the form of a reference to women's clothing (*Tinsley* v *Milligan* [1992] 2 All E.R. 391 at 416 per Lloyd LJ: 'We are not obliged to draw up our skirts . . .'). The gendering of equity as female (the other, the excess) in opposition to the non-gender of (common) law (the word is man) continues the heritage of figuring justice (as opposed to law) as woman in representations of justice. The complex of configurations behind the use of Woman (from gentle mercy-mother through unruly woman to strong and vengeful woman) are explored in Bottomley, *Figuring Dike* (forthcoming).
7 The basic position in English law is that, whilst a presumption is made that the holder of legal title is 'the owner' of the property (in terms of having rights to the proceeds of sale, decisions about administration and sale), that in fact this might be shared with (an)other(s) by reason of either an express agreement (a written trust) or as a result of the parties' actions (an unwritten trust). The basis of a claim for the existence of an unwritten trust is found in the Law of Property Act 1925 s.53(2), which provides that the requirement of writing does not affect 'the creation or operation of resulting, implied, or constructive trusts'. See further, K. Gray, *Elements of Land Law* (1987) ch. 10.
8 Primarily the right to apply for financial provision on divorce under the Matrimonial Causes Act 1973 (as amended). The 1973 Act gave the courts the power to transfer property between spouses for the first time, a provision of which Denning was only too aware, having himself given his own notorious judgment in *Wachtel* v *Wachtel* [1973] 1 All E.R. 829, the first case to go to appeal under the Act. In *Eves* he makes much of the fact that this jurisdiction is not open to the plaintiff, and his judgment can certainly be read as an attempt to provide (as far as he can) an analogous form of relief. Under the Family Law Reform Act 1987 applications can now be made for the transfer of property to provide for children (whether their parents are married or not). This device can be used to provide for a form of transfer between parties but (see note 7 above) the property would be held on trust to the benefit of the child. For a recorded example of this being used alongside an application for declaration of a trust see *Hammond* v *Mitchell* [1992] 2 All E.R. 109. (Note: for any reader specifically interested in issues of litigation in this area, this case makes particularly fascinating reading.)
9 At p. 1339.
10 Following the House of Lords judgments in *Pettitt* v *Pettitt* [1970] A.C. 790 and *Gissing* v *Gissing* [1971] A.C. 894. Denning would have been looking for evidence of an intention to share the beneficial interest plus (or as evidenced by) contributions to the purchase of the

property or substantial improvement to the property. The actual evidence of her physical labour was minimal; despite his attempt to highlight it, it comes over as 'very thin'. He partly covers this by gendering the labour, emphasizing that it was more than women would normally undertake; contrast to the labour of the husband in *Pettitt*.

11 Janet Eves giving evidence as quoted by Denning in *Eves*, op. cit., n. 2, p. 1339.

12 See, for example, *Horrocks* v *Foray* [1976] 1 W.L.R. 230.

13 See *Burns* v *Burns* [1984] Ch. 317; *Lloyds Bank* v *Rosset* [1990] 1 All E.R. 1111. Whilst the former was the first major case to make the post-Denning era, the latter is the major judgment in that it is a decision of the House of Lords.

14 On mapping see, for example, D. Harvey, *The Condition of Post-Modernity* (1989).

15 I am of course using psychoanalytical sources here. particularly the Lacanian models of 'excess' and 'other'. I would not wish, however, to locate my references there but would rather refer the reader to R. Braidotti, *Patterns of Dissonance* (1991) for the way in which she engages with this material, which is, importantly in my opinion, not over-reverential to yet another map.

16 If the case were heard today it would have been the trick which would have become the focus of the argument. The reasoning would then have taken on the characteristics of a decision based on proprietary estoppel.

17 [1984] Ch. 317.

18 See *Social Attitudes Survey* (1992).

19 Women who are truly financially independent are not often going to appear in these cases – they are more likely to have insisted on a formal agreement at least, or, even more likely, on shared legal title. Indeed, the need for their contribution to mortgage repayments may well have necessitated a formal sharing of the property, even if it had not been simply the decision of the couple. On the consequences for one woman of taking a solicitor's advice not to hold the property in joint names, see *Equity and Law Home Loans Ltd* v *Prestidge* [1992] 1 All E.R. 909. On another man's trick which enabled him to put the property in his name alone, see *Hammond* v *Mitchell* [1992] 2 All E.R. 109.

20 I have been particularly influenced by Christiane Olivier, *Jocasta's Children* (1989) in which she considers the origins of the different use of language between men and women. I prefer a reading of this material which is not determinist or absolutist and which, while recognizing dominant narratives and structures in interpersonal relations, does not finally hold out possibilities solely within these frames. A major step in not being caught within these structural limitations is simply to recognize them. This does not seem to me to be a new form of determinism, but rather a new possibility of overcoming by facing the extent to which our lives are fractured by gender difference. See also Braidotti (op. cit., n. 15).

21 Mrs Rosset's evidence, quoted in the Court of Appeal in *Lloyds Bank* v *Rosset* [1988] All E.R. 915 at 928. (In fact the couple in this case were married.)

22 [1990] 1 All E.R. 1111 at 1117 per Lord Bridge.

23 id., at 1115.

24 [1986] 1 W.L.R. 808.

25 id., p. 811.

26 id., p. 812.

27 id., p. 812.

28 id., p. 817.

29 id., p. 818.

30 op. cit., n. 22, p. 1118.

31 id., at 1119.

32 op. cit., n. 21, p. 931.

33 op. cit., n. 22, p. 1118

34 id., p. 1118.

35 [1989] 2 All E.R. 426 at 433.

36 See Denning's equally quaint view of what men are (in)capable of in *Wachtel*, op. cit., n. 8.

37 Grosz, op. cit., n. 1.

38 id., p. 110.

39 in *Hammond* v *Mitchell* [1992], op. cit., n. 19.

40 Hence in the 1980s it was important for us, as feminists. to raise issues about the development of mediation; see, for example, Bottomley, 'Resolving Family Disputes: A Critical View' in *State, Law, and the Family*, ed. M. D. A. Freeman (1984). Many of the issues of power which we raised then have since been accepted into a 'general concern' in developing mediation; see for example, G. Davis, *Partisans and Mediators* (1988). This has now freed us to turn and consider the positive benefits we might seek from mediation practices. However, our critics still often expect from us the same position we held in the 1980s, as if we are fixed in a historical vacuum.

41 T. de Lauretis in *Feminist Studies/Critical Studies*, ed. Lauretis (1986) 9, quoted by Braidotti, op. cit., n. 15, p. 281.

42 id., p. 281.

Pregnancy and the Workplace: A Question of Strategy?

JOANNE CONAGHAN *

INTRODUCTION

Women in Britain currently constitute over forty-five per cent of the workforce. This represents a considerable increase in the economic activity of women in the post-war period, particularly married women.[1] It becomes increasingly misleading to view paid work as predominantly the province of men although this perception still characterizes most textbook presentations of labour law.[2] Despite the reality of women's substantial presence in the labour force, the implications of that presence have not been fully recognized. In particular, British employers, judges, and policy-makers have failed to properly confront the issue of pregnancy in the workplace, either conceptually or practically; for example, there is uncertainty about when pregnancy discrimination contravenes the Sex Discrimination Act 1975 (hereinafter cited as 'the SDA').[3] Moreover, employers vary greatly in their response to pregnant workers. For some (usually small employers in the private sector), pregnancy is still in itself a reason for dismissal, whereas for others (typically large employers in the public sector), it is the subject of an elaborate scheme of rights, negotiated by trade unions and incorporated into individual contracts of employment.[4] Statutory maternity rights in Britain are notoriously meagre.[5] Originally introduced in the 1970s, these rights have since been substantially restricted[6] and currently constitute the meanest set of provisions in the European Community ('the EC').[7]

Yet, despite this confusion of law, policy, and practice, empirical evidence reveals that pregnant women are increasingly resuming economically active roles after the birth of their babies. The number of women returning to work within nine months of birth has almost doubled since 1979, rising from twenty-four to forty-five per cent of women working during pregnancy.[8] Women today are three times more likely to return to full-time work than in 1979.[9] Significantly however, there has been no real increase in employer arrangements to help returning mothers.[10] While most women exercise whatever rights are available, the reality is that the limited income replacement and right to return to work which British law provides, combined with the enormous gap between supply and demand in terms of the availability of

*Lecturer in Law, Eliot College, University of Kent, Canterbury CT2 7NS, England

71

decent and affordable childcare,[11] leave women with children in a significantly disadvantaged position in relation to the terms upon which they return to the workplace. The 'working mother' is still vulnerable to job loss during the period of her pregnancy and thereafter. She is still more likely to work part-time, and part-time work continues to be economically disadvantaged.[12] She is also more likely to experience downward vertical mobility leading to lower pay and poorer working conditions.[13] The constraints imposed by mother-hood in an essentially unsympathetic working environment become another resource for employers to use in their increasing quest for flexibility. A woman's lack of bargaining power, directly consequent upon the absence of significant legal protection of her economic position during pregnancy and thereafter, makes her economic vulnerability easy to exploit.

Despite the expansion of the female workforce in the last thirty years and the increasing tendency of pregnant workers to return to work, the reality of paid work for many women in the 1990s continues to be dogged by all the hallmarks of disadvantage, discrimination, and exploitation which have characterized their experience hitherto. This suggests that legislative efforts to combat such disadvantage, through the Sex Discrimination Act 1975 and the Equal Pay Act 1970, have been of little or no success. The virtues and shortcomings of this legislation have been subject to considerable discussion elsewhere and it is not my intention to rehearse them here.[14] I wish to address a broader question, namely, what do feminists want for women workers and how can they best achieve it? Are they striving for an end to discrimination and the realization of equal opportunity, or are they pursuing some broader goal which sees the securement of justice for women workers as part of a struggle to secure justice for workers generally? How should these goals be pursued? Should feminists work towards achieving greater statutory *rights* for women workers? To what extent should they rely on the traditional tactics of the trade union movement? Might the market be harnessed to serve the interests of women workers? Or, is it necessary in order to liberate women workers, to work towards the end of capitalism itself?

This essay seeks to explore such questions by focusing upon their particular significance in the context of pregnancy in the workplace. By narrowing the focus of study, I hope to consider the question of goals and strategies without losing sight of context, namely the daily lives of working women. At the same time, I hope to avoid assuming a homogeneity in women's working experience by focusing on an issue eliciting a broad variation of responses from employers, workers, and the state, reflecting an underlying diversity in approach to, and experience of, the issue in question.[15]

GOALS AND STRATEGIES

What objectives underlie calls for better maternity arrangements? Certainly they are not always motivated by a 'feminist' concern to secure justice for women. While it tends to be assumed that the primary goal of British maternity law in the 1970s was to improve women's status in the labour market, it is clear that health and safety considerations[16] and demographic changes in the labour market (particularly in relation to its gender-composition)[17] were also of significance. At the same time, while acknowledging the mixed motives behind the maternity provisions, feminists should consider to what extent women can nevertheless benefit from them. If, as the evidence shows, women workers are currently disadvantaged both by their biological role as child-bearers and their social role as primary child-carers, justice for women clearly demands that, at the very least, such disadvantages should not continue. In the context of the current paucity of British maternity law, it becomes important to consider what strategy might best secure this end or its approximation.[18] Drawing upon experience to date, one can identify at least three strategies which feminists have employed (or been complicit in) in order to improve the position of pregnant workers. The first strategy, most closely associated with the United States of America, but also visible in United Kingdom debates about the scope of the Sex Discrimination Act 1975, relies upon the concept of sex equality (the 'equality' strategy). The second strategy, which has to a considerable extent informed campaigns to secure maternity rights in Britain, locates pregnancy in the context of security of earnings and thus as an aspect of workers' rights (the 'workers' rights' strategy). The third strategy, most evident in the context of the European Draft Directive on the Protection of Pregnant Workers (hereinafter cited as 'the Pregnancy Directive'), which, for the last few years, has been proceeding through the EC legislative process, invokes health and safety reasons for protecting pregnant workers (the 'health and safety' strategy). Each strategy has its strengths and limitations. The crucial question is – which strategy currently offers the best opportunity to improve the position of pregnant workers?

THE EQUALITY STRATEGY

Equality is a concept whose precise meaning has long beset and beleaguered political theory and practice. The history of the women's movement suggests that there has rarely been unanimity among feminists as to equality's meaning. While one can trace a certain conceptual progression from the notion of 'formal equality', informing nineteenth- and early twentieth-century campaigns for female suffrage, to the goal of 'equal opportunity' embedded in the British equality legislation, this progression has frequently been accompanied by disagreement about equality's implications in a given situation.[19]

Such disagreement is nowhere more evident than in the debate about pregnancy which dominated feminist jurisprudence in the United States of America in the 1980s.[20] A controversy arose as to whether or not pregnancy should be accorded 'special' consideration in the workplace or whether it should be treated like other short-term 'disabilities'. This led to further consideration of the meaning of equality with its concomitant reliance on notions of sameness and difference. Did equality require that women and men be treated in the *same* way or did it permit distinctions based on sexual difference? What was 'sexual difference' for these purposes?

The legal background to the controversy is important in understanding how and why it arose. The United States of America has been curiously unique among Western industrialized countries in failing to provide any significant legal protection to pregnant workers. While states vary in the provisions offered, and while improvements in basic legal provisions have recently occurred,[21] it still remains the case that most American women depend on their employers rather than the law for their maternity arrangements.

Until the 1970s, pregnant workers in the United States of America were routinely subjected to discriminatory treatment, both in law and practice. Employers hired and fired on account of pregnancy and implemented mandatory leave policies (often state-initiated) requiring pregnant workers to leave work with no guarantee of reinstatement and no compensation for lost wages or benefits. Legal challenges to these discriminatory practices were not initially successful. For example, in two notorious challenges to employer disability schemes which expressly excluded pregnancy,[22] the Supreme Court ruled that pregnancy was *not* a gender-based classification and therefore violated neither the Equal Protection Clause of the Fourteenth Amendment to the American Constitution nor Title VII of the Civil Rights Act 1964 (hereafter cited as the 'CRA'). The outcry inspired in particular by the *Gilbert* decision resulted in the passing of the Pregnancy Discrimination Act 1978 (hereafter cited as the 'PDA') which amended Title VII by providing that pregnancy discrimination *could* constitute sex discrimination where pregnant women were treated differently from 'other persons . . . similar in their ability or inability to work'.[23]

However, such an approach fell far short of guaranteeing pregnant workers legal protection. Where an employer implemented no disability scheme, or treated all 'disabled' employees equally badly, women could not complain. Moreover, only a handful of states compelled employers to initiate disability schemes.[24] An even smaller number had, or enacted within their fair employment provisions, specific maternity leave requirements. Yet it was precisely such provisions, entitling pregnant workers to a protected period of maternity leave, which provoked such fierce controversy among feminists. The controversy first surfaced in relation to a Montana statutory provision; it reached its high point in a federal court challenge to a California statute, the California Fair Employment and Housing Act (hereafter cited as the 'FEHA') which required employers of fifteen or more employees to grant up to four months unpaid maternity leave with a right to reinstatement.[25]

California Savings and Loan Association argued that the FEHA was inconsistent with, and therefore pre-empted by, federal legislation (Title VII to the CRA 1964 as amended by the PDA 1978), because it treated certain employees (pregnant workers) *preferentially* on the basis of sex. Feminist groups divided on the issue: the Coalition for Reproductive Equality in the Workplace (hereafter cited as the 'CREW') filed an *amicus curiae* brief in

74

support of the statute, while both the National Organisation of Women (NOW) and the American Civil Liberties Union (ACLU) argued that the Californian law should be struck down in favour of a provision requiring employers to provide leave for all temporarily disabled employees, whatever the source of their disability. Ultimately, the Supreme Court decided by a majority to uphold the FEHA, despite a minority dissent criticising the decision as contrary to the plain meaning of the PDA.[26]

Why should feminists have divided so bitterly over this issue? One explanation lies in the way in which the debate was framed, namely, in terms of equality. This must in turn be understood against a legal and political background of developing anti-discrimination laws, but limited welfare and employment provisions. Feminist lawyers approached the issue in accordance with the legal tradition in which they found themselves, a tradition in which anti-discrimination was an emerging theme. In this context pregnancy, as a biologically constituted difference between men and women, had historically been used to justify discrimination *against* women. Feminists, espousing an 'equal treatment' position, were understandably wary about calling attention to this difference in order to gain particular benefits, pointing to where arguments about women's 'difference' had got them in the past.[27] They also argued that emphasizing the special or unique nature of pregnancy risked reinforcing stereotypical notions of women's 'natural' role as mothers.[28] Thus, pregnancy should be viewed as a short-term disability and feminists should campaign for better disability provisions for *all* workers.[29]

Advocates of 'special' treatment, by contrast, insisted that pregnancy was neither a disability nor an illness and that it did not benefit women to characterize it as such, serving only to reinforce the damaging association of pregnancy with illness and vulnerability. Moreover, to subject pregnancy to the same conditions as disabilities generally was to fail to recognize that pregnancy *was* a unique and *enabling* condition requiring specially tailored policies. Furthermore, it failed to acknowledge the social *value* of pregnancy and child-bearing.[30] Finally, it was contended that differential treatment was not inconsistent with equality; to assert 'difference' was not to assert 'inequality' as such. To require pregnant workers to conform to standards laid down without taking account of pregnancy was to require women to conform to a male norm, to assimilate to established male working patterns rather than to forge new ones.[31]

In the event, neither argument won the day. Indeed, feminist scholars have increasingly concluded that equality is an almost wholly indeterminate concept.[32] At the same time, the feminist legal preoccupation with equality, viewed in terms of sameness and difference, has become subject to considerable and diverse criticism. Thus, for example, feminists in the United States of America have been accused of pursuing equality at the expense of working women's real needs, for example, for childcare and maternity/parental leave arrangements.[33] Moreover, socialist feminists have charged those engaging in the equality debate with making an 'idealist error', by speculating about women's needs in the realm of abstract ideals while ignoring the reality of their material lives, particularly as shaped and constructed by class and race.[34] From a different theoretical perspective, Maria O'Brien Hylton criticizes feminists for ignoring economic factors and prioritizing the interests of middle-class women. She alleges that feminists are wrong to pursue 'isolated policies' such as parental leave because, unless accompanied with counterbalancing employment policies to increase the demand for relatively unskilled labour, they will benefit middle-class women at working-class women's expense, as employers meet the costs imposed by cutting unskilled jobs.[35] The underlying thrust of such arguments is to highlight the abstract, uncontextualized nature of the equality debate with its consequent failure to substantially address practical politics.

The most devastatingly effective critique comes from Catharine MacKinnon. She argues that both the equal and special treatment positions suffer from the same fatal flaw – they both posit and rely upon a male norm or ordering:

> There is a politics to this. Concealed is the substantive way in which man has become the measure of all things. Under the sameness standard, women are reserved according to our correspondence with men, our equality judged by our proximity to his measure. Gender-neutrality is thus simply the male standard, and the special protection rule is simply the female standard, but do not be deceived masculinity or maleness is the reference for both.[36]

MacKinnon argues for an approach to sexual equality which focuses primarily on power and dominance and only derivatively on questions of sameness and difference. More important than identifying difference or justifying different treatment, is the need to ask why it is *women* who are perceived to be different and who, on account of their difference, are accorded unequal treatment. Why is it women who at one and the same time must assert their sameness to men (and thereby their entitlement to equal treatment) and their difference from men (and thus their need for special treatment), inevitably inviting the accusation that they want to have it both ways.[37] Ultimately, this is a question of hierarchical ordering, a question of who gets to define the standard by which difference is measured.

Close analysis reveals that the concept of equality is perfectly consistent with either the equal/special treatment position, depending on how difference is defined. If equality requires that like cases be treated alike, the position of feminists who espouse equal treatment is to assert that men and women are, for all relevant purposes, alike and therefore entitled to equal treatment. Hence the tendency to equate pregnancy with other 'similar' disabilities. Those arguing for special treatment, on the other hand, assert that pregnancy constitutes a significant difference between men and women. Equality does not require similar treatment because men and women are in fact differently situated.

Either position is supportable. If pregnancy is perceived in terms of its immediate financial and administrative consequences in the workplace, then it is arguably 'similar' to other disabilities.[38] On the other hand, characterized as a normal, natural, often voluntary condition, pregnancy is distinguishable from disability resulting from disease or injury.[39] Thus, whether or not pregnancy is perceived as the same as or different from other disabilities depends on the measure of comparison. What is crucial is the power to decide what counts as difference, and how the difference counts.[40] This suggests that the important issues in the equality debate are those of power, not philosophy.

The feminist deconstruction of difference discourse has clearly been theoretically enriching. It is less clear whether or not it has significantly benefited working women. The aftermath of *Cal-fed* has stimulated the introduction of pregnancy and/or parental leave policies (above) but it is important to recognize the limits of the decision, which, while ruling that states have the power to mandate maternity leave policies, are not required to do so. Meanwhile, moves to introduce a federal parental leave scheme (see above, note 21) have continually been obstructed by interests more concerned about the perceived economic costs of parental leave than with securing sexual equality (below). Yet, from the perspective of the equality debate, the concept of parental as opposed to maternity leave is particularly attractive: it no longer demands that men and women be accorded different treatment and constitutes a legislative recognition of the value of child-bearing and parenting to society in general.[41] The difficulties which the policy has nevertheless encountered suggest that the feminist focus on equality in the United States of America in the context of pregnancy is somewhat misplaced and that the real obstacles to developing maternity and parental leave policies, obstacles which have more to do with economics that philosophy, have not really been addressed.

Meanwhile, it is worth observing that nor has the concept of equality served British women well. While the majority of pregnant workers' rights derive from social security or employment protection laws (see above, note 5), pregnancy has emerged as a sex discrimination issue also. Under the EPCA 1978, it is automatically unfair to dismiss a woman on grounds of pregnancy. However, this right is subject to a qualifying period, originally six months employment with the same employer (1975), but raised in 1985 by the Conservative Government to two years. Thus, pregnant women who have worked for less than two years for the same employer have no protection from dismissal under the EPCA. Consequently, some have argued that dismissal in such circumstances constitutes unlawful sex discrimination under the SDA 1975.

In an early case, *Turley* v *Allder Department Stores Ltd.* ([1980] I.R.L.R. 4) the Employment Appeal Tribunal upheld an industrial tribunal's decision that dismissal on grounds of pregnancy was *not* sex discrimination because, since a man could not become pregnant, it was not possible to compare a woman with a man, as the SDA required, in order to establish *less favourable* treatment. The tribunal thus adopted an approach similar to the majority in *Geduldig* and *Gilbert* in holding that pregnancy discrimination was not sex-based. This position was rejected by the EAT in *Hayes* v *Malleable Working Mens Club and Institute* ([1985] I.R.L.R. 367) which, in taking an approach similar to the American PDA, recognized that pregnancy discrimination *could* constitute sex discrimination if a man, in circumstances 'not materially different' (for example, sick or disabled) – would not have been treated in the same way.[42]

While an improvement on *Turley*, the Hayes approach troubled some feminists in its characterization of pregnancy in terms of illness and/or physical vulnerability.[43] Moreover, it has become increasingly apparent that the 'comparability' approach is substantially limited in the protection it affords pregnant women because an employer need only show that he would have treated all comparable employees equally shabbily in order to avoid liability under the SDA for pregnancy dismissal.

In 1990 the British comparability test was severely undermined by the European Court of Justice's (ECJ) decision in *Dekker* v *Stichtung Vormingscentrum voor Jonge Volwassen (VJV Centrum) Plus* (see above, note 3). Although the case involved a hiring rather than a firing, the court held that, for purposes of the EC Equal Treatment Directive (No. 76/207), there was no need for a male comparator in cases where a woman's treatment arose out of her pregnancy. Pregnancy discrimination constituted sex discrimination in itself because, as pregnancy was a condition unique to one sex, decisions based on pregnancy were, unavoidably, sex-based decisions. Subsequently, the British Court of Appeal in *Webb* v *EMO Cargo* (see above, note 3) sought to distinguish *Dekker* and reinstate the comparability test, arguing, among other things, that any interpretation of *Dekker* holding that pregnancy dismissal was necessarily sex-based discrimination required an untenable distortion of the plain meaning of the SDA.[44] While opinions differ as to whether or not the SDA can be reconciled with *Dekker*[45] and, while the extent of the obligation on British courts to interpret domestic legislation consistently with EC directives is still being worked out,[46] United Kingdom courts clearly consider the concept of discrimination embodied in the SDA as inconsistent with the broader protection of pregnancy in the workplace offered by *Dekker*. Thus, while pregnant women continue to lose their jobs often in circumstances where the employer has given only the most cursory consideration to the impact of the pregnancy on workplace arrangements, feminist lawyers can offer women little in the way of assistance, while employers invoke equality to justify treatment which too often flies in the face of justice, fairness, and basic common sense.

THE 'WORKERS' RIGHTS' STRATEGY

Can women use their status as workers to combat the economic disadvantages which pregnancy generally entails? From this perspective, the issue is less likely to be viewed in terms of equality and more in terms of practical needs, for example, for job security and better childcare provision. In part, this is an expression of the traditional liberal aspiration to maximize freedom of choice – women wish to be able to choose to have children without compromising their economic independence – but more realistically, it reflects a desire, common to all workers, to combat the relative powerlessness which the employment relationship inevitably entails. Typically, this concern has expressed itself in the collective organization of workers in trades unions for purposes of collective bargaining. But since the 1960s there has been an increasing tendency to seek some measure of protection for workers through law by the introduction of statutory rights.

Within this framework, the concerns of pregnant workers emerged as an issue to be addressed. Thus, the Employment Protection Act 1975 introduced a number of rights for pregnant workers, including the right not to be unfairly dismissed on grounds of pregnancy, and limited rights to maternity pay and leave (see above, note 5). These rights formed part of a larger package of rights (including unfair dismissal and redundancy pay) aimed at guaranteeing workers' security of earnings, and were an integral part of the 'social contract' struck between the government and trades unions during the period of the 1974–1979 Labour administration. As such, the provisions were characterized by a strong emphasis on the primacy of voluntary collective bargaining as the best means of securing protection for workers. Thus, the rights introduced were regarded as statutory minima, a 'floor of rights', upon which collective bargaining could build.

In addition to the introduction of employment protection provisions, pregnant women were also entitled to certain social security payments, including a limited income replacement entitlement in the form of maternity allowance.[47] Thus, by the end of the 1970s, pregnant workers in Britain possessed an (albeit limited) set of maternity rights deriving from their status as workers. Such a regime continues to operate in a modified if more restricted form today.[48]

While the British approach to pregnancy in the workplace is superior to that in the United States of America, certainly in terms of the economic protection it affords pregnant workers, limitations in the scope of the United Kingdom provisions testify to fundamental underlying problems. It has already been observed that Britain compares unfavourably with its European partners in terms of maternity rights. Moreover, empirical research reveals that a substantial number of pregnant workers are not covered even by the limited rights which British law does offer.[49]

The question arises as to why the workers' rights strategy has failed to secure more for pregnant workers. One answer lies in the form of the relevant legal provisions. Based on a concept of 'work' and 'worker' which is stereotypically male, that is, full-time, long-term, unionized, and free from domestic responsibilities, the legal provisions fail to capture the varied biographies of women's working lives.[50]

The qualifications for full entitlement to maternity rights exemplify this well. As with employment protection legislation generally, to qualify for her rights to maternity pay, leave, and reinstatement, a woman must be an 'employee', that is engaged on a contract of service rather than a contract for services.[51] She must be continuously employed for two years by the same employer for sixteen or more hours per week (or between eight and sixteen hours for a period of five years).[52] Inevitably, these provisions ensure the exclusion of self-employed women,[53] women working 'casually', for example as child-minders or homeworkers,[54] women on temporary contracts or with interrupted work patterns,[55] and some part-time women workers. Clearly then, the conception of work upon which the maternity provisions are based does not accommodate the wide and varied working patterns of women.

The provisions are also conceptually 'male' in their dependence on collective bargaining. The idea that employment protection provisions should act as a stepping-stone to the securement of greater rights through collective bargaining presupposes that the workers affected are in a position to bargain effectively. In the case of women workers, this assumption is highly problematic: women have traditionally worked in sectors of the labour market where union recruitment has been difficult and collective bargaining power weak.[56] Moreover, the failure to significantly improve upon the legislative minimum is well evidenced. A survey in 1980 revealed that only eighteen per cent of employers made more generous maternity arrangements than the law provides. More contemporary research evidences no significant change in this position in 1990 (see above, note 10). The strategy to facilitate improved employment protection through collective bargaining has, in the context of maternity rights, clearly failed.

The employment protection route is also flawed in its exclusive focus on the world of paid work in isolation from other aspects of workers' lives, particularly their families. This reflects a conventional labour law conception of the workplace as autonomous and self-regulating, a conception which has traditionally informed analyses of the collective bargaining process. The separate consideration of home and work fits closely with the biography of the full-time, male breadwinner, upon whom the exigencies of domestic life rarely impact, but it is thoroughly misleading in the context of women's working experience. Not only are women's employment opportunities significantly limited by the prevailing gender division of labour in the home, but even where no such constraints are present, women's experience at work, what they do, and how it is valued, is unquestionably shaped by social assumptions about their proper role and function in the family. The gender division of labour at home and at work do not operate independently but constantly inform and reinforce each other.[57] This is nowhere more apparent than in the context of pregnancy in the workplace. The traditional approach, which viewed pregnancy and maternity as matters which had nothing do to with the workplace, has given way in recent years to an approach which, confronted with the inevitability of women's substantial presence in the workforce, enables pregnant workers (in a limited fashion) to depart from and re-enter the labour market without significant disruption of workplace practices. It is only employees who have proved their worth by remaining with an employer for two years who are entitled to be 'rewarded' with the measure of job security implicit in the current provisions governing leave and reinstatement.[58] Otherwise, employers are not required to adapt their working practices to the exigencies of pregnancy.[59] Thus, to the extent that British law recognizes an interaction between pregnancy and the workplace, it is an interaction taking its shape and definition from employer perceptions of workplace needs. Current maternity provisions in no way challenge the existing 'order' of the workplace and hold out little hope of bringing about the substantial reorganization necessary to free women from the disadvantages of existing arrangements.

In part, the limitations inherent in the provisions reflect their genesis as a response to labour market changes rather than working women's needs. But, in so far as the provisions also evidence a legislative attempt to secure some measure of equality for women, the failure of reformists to step outside the parameters which inform conventional perceptions of the workplace significantly weakens the effectiveness of their strategy as a whole. Because the maternity provisions reinforce an existing tendency to conceive of home and work as separate and independent entities, because they do not challenge the prevailing view that childcare is the responsibility of mothers rather than fathers,[60] the province of the family not the workplace, they reinforce the very ideologies they purport to challenge.

In this context, parental leave again seems an obvious solution. By extending to fathers the right to substantial leave, the law would go some way towards encouraging the idea if not the actuality of shared parenting. The significant demands on workplace organization which such a policy would make, if properly implemented, would inevitably compel the recognition of parenting activity as a legitimate determinant of workplace practice and organization. A draft directive on parental leave produced by the European Commission in 1983 and providing (among other things) each parent with a minimum of three months leave within two years of the birth/adoption of a child, still awaits the approval of the Council of Ministers, not least because of the determined opposition of the British Government.[61] This opposition reflects the Government's broader commitment to 'deregulating' the labour market and freeing employers from the 'burdens' which employment protection legislation allegedly imposes.[62] This renders existing maternity provisions and reform efforts vulnerable to the politics of a government not in sympathy with the general idea of workers' rights. While the political climate of the 1970s made the pursuit of maternity provisions through a strategy of 'workers rights' both viable and effective, the ideological shift towards market regulation in the 1980s significantly undercut gains already achieved while holding out little prospect for further progress (see above, note 6).

This suggests that 'rights' conferred by law are not nearly so secure as rights rhetoric implies. The existence of a 'right', carrying with it the notion of a fixed and natural entitlement, can often be counterproductive in creating a false sense of security among its beneficiaries while at the same time providing its opponents with good grounds for resisting its further extension or even justifying its restriction.[63] Thus, it may be that the 'workers rights' strategy, while bringing limited benefits in the 1970s, is of little use in the changed political and economic climate of the 1990s.[64]

The most fruitful strategy currently employed to improve British maternity provisions invokes health and safety reasons for expanding the legal protection of pregnant workers. Indeed, the only additional maternity 'right' to emerge from thirteen years of Conservative government, the right to reasonable time off for antenatal care (see above, note 59), was introduced in response to concerns about the increased peri-natal mortality rate in the United Kingdom.[65] In the context of European law, agreement has finally been reached in relation to the Pregnancy Directive which, among other things, confers additional employment protection rights on pregnant workers. The directive, proceeding on the basis of Article 118A EEC, is an individual directive within the meaning of Article 16 of the 'Framework' Health and Safety Directive of 1989 (Directive 89/391/EEC), a collection of 'measures to encourage improvements in the safety and health at work of pregnant workers and workers who have recently given birth or are breastfeeding' (Preamble). These measures include first, proposals to ensure the protection of pregnant and breastfeeding women against exposure to harmful agents and processes including, where necessary, the reorganization of the working conditions and hours of pregnant/nursing mothers;[66] secondly, the right to a substantial period of paid maternity leave;[67] and finally, the prohibition of dismissal on pregnancy-related grounds.[68]

'Health and safety' may seem oddly misplaced grounds for asserting rights to maternity pay and leave but, in the context of European law and politics, it may make more sense to rely on such arguments rather than to make the case in terms of equal opportunities or workers' rights. The commission's choice of base (Art. 118A EEC) enabled the directive to proceed by a qualified majority procedure, avoiding a requirement of unanimity among the Council of Ministers.[69] The scope of Art. 118A includes 'improvements, especially in the working environment, as regards the health and safety of workers' (para. 1), interpreted by the commission to include measures such as maternity pay, leave, and protection from dismissal 'in order to guarantee workers . . . the exercise of their health and safety protection rights' (the Pregnancy Directive, Art. 11).

The commission's characterization of such provisions has not gone uncontested. Indeed, one of the British Government's main objections to the directive has been that it misrepresents 'employment rights' as matters of health and safety. Furthermore, from a feminist perspective, there are reasons for feeling uncomfortable with a health and safety approach. First, it reinforces a social and legal tendency to associate pregnancy with ill-health, an inaccurate depiction of a perfectly healthy and natural condition. Secondly, a traditional concern for women's health and child-bearing functions, evident in such measures as protective labour legislation (see above, note 19) has, more often than not, produced and legitimated social and legal practices which exclude and disempower women (see above, note 27). The conception of women as 'the weaker sex' which has served to legitimate their oppression throughout history is closely related to the idea that pregnancy confers upon women a particular vulnerability.[70] Thirdly, a concern for health and safety during pregnancy encompasses the health of the foetus as well as the mother. Katherine De Gama argues that the emerging legal construction of the foetus as 'a locus of rights' seriously threatens women's physical autonomy;[71] in the field of paid work, concern for the foetus has often justified the imposition of restrictions on women in the form of foetal protection policies.[72] Indeed, the Pregnancy Directive contains provisions which are strangely resonant of such policies. Under Articles 5 and 6, an employer must protect a pregnant worker from exposure to any agent, process, or working conditions deemed by the directive to be injurious to the health and safety of the mother and/or child (Annexes I and II). This includes, where necessary, the removal of the worker from the workplace during the period of risk (Art.5(3)). It was originally envisaged that, where such circumstances arose, a woman would be fully compensated, suffering no loss of pay or employment rights (OJ C 281/3, Art. 4(3)). However, the agreed draft contains no such guarantee: affected workers will be granted leave 'in accordance with national legislation and/or national practice' (Art. 5(3)). A worker may find herself financially disadvantaged by a health and safety provision which requires her employer to take all necessary measures to ensure her physical protection with no obligation to maintain her employment rights beyond that imposed by national legislation and/or practice (Art. 11(1)).

The commission's strategic choice of a health and safety approach to issues of pregnancy in the workplace has subordinated any equal treatment aspiration. The focus on maternal health, for example, makes the case for paternity leave more difficult to argue. Moreover, the emphasis on pregnancy rather than on parenting means that little consideration is given to cases of adoption where parents are equally in need of time off to adjust and provide for the arrival of a new child. At the same time, the health and safety focus, *without* an accompanying commitment to equal treatment, has resulted in the enactment of measures such as Article 5 which are of questionable benefit to women.

The original draft of the directive (September 1990, OJ C 281/3) contained provisions which had much more far-reaching equal treatment implications. Maternity leave was to be subject to a requirement of *full* pay without the imposition of qualifying conditions beyond the need to be employed or registered as unemployed at the time the pregnancy commenced (OJ C 281/3, Art 5(4)). The general thrust of the draft was to provide the necessary measures to ensure health and safety without compromising women's employment rights. Moreover, the commission viewed the proposals as no more than 'minimum provision', considering that a more onerous imposition of obligations on member states might have an adverse effect on women's employment.[73]

However, opposition to the directive, coming from Britain in particular, inevitably produced a much more attenuated set of rights. Contesting the appropriateness of Art. 118A EEC as a base for maternity leave provisions, the United Kingdom Government argued that such leave was a social security matter not to be foisted on an unwilling member state by a qualified majority procedure. While finally abstaining from the Council of Ministers' vote to adopt the compromise agreed draft in December 1991, Britain ensured that the provisions adopted were much less radical than those originally put forward.[74]

On 5 November 1992, the United Kingdom Government published the Trade Union and Employment Rights Bill containing, among other things, legislative proposals for the implementation of the new directive. Clause 20 of the Bill amends the EPCA 1978 provisions currently governing maternity leave (see above, note 5). An employee will now be entitled to fourteen weeks maternity leave without loss of contractual benefits and regardless of her length of service. Clause 21 proposes to amend section 60 of the EPCA 1978 to make the right to protection against unfair dismissal for pregnancy-related reasons similarly independent of a service qualification. It appears that the existing longer period of maternity leave, ending at twenty-nine weeks after the date of confinement, will continue to apply to workers with two or more years service (Schedule 2 of the proposed Bill). It also appears that, for the moment, the current arrangements for Statutory Maternity Pay (see above, notes 5 and 49) will continue. According to Clause 22, a new Schedule 3 will enable a pregnant employee to be suspended from work for health and safety reasons (subject to a right to be offered suitable alternative work) with an accompanying entitlement to remuneration (a week's pay in respect of each week of the period of suspension).

If and when implemented, these provisions will undoubtedly confer significant additional benefits on pregnant workers. Yet, the verdict on the new directive and its implementation must remain mixed. While it undoubtedly extends maternity leave and the right to reinstatement to a number of British workers hitherto denied such a benefit, and while the protection from dismissal on pregnancy-related grounds can only be welcomed, it does not bring women in Britain much closer to the benefits (particularly financial) enjoyed by their European counterparts and at the same time carries a legacy of ideas and practices which, in viewing pregnancy primarily in terms of ill-health, weakness, and female vulnerability, may do more to disadvantage women than to assist them.

CONCLUSION

An examination of the strategies which feminists and others have deployed in the context of pregnancy in the workplace spawns a number of conclusions. Chief among these is the recognition that consideration of *context* – political, legal, and economic – is crucial to any strategic evaluation of the likely effects of a particular legal engagement. An approach which relies on 'workers' rights' may be of value in the context of the British political climate in the 1970s but is less likely to produce results in the post-Thatcherist 1990s.

Likewise, an approach which relies on liberal 'entitlements' such as the 'right' to equality, may be more in keeping with the legal tradition in the United States of America than the social welfarist approach implicit in British maternity law. Interestingly, many of those favouring the 'equal treatment' position in the equality debate in the United States of America adopted an approach which, in demanding improved disability provision for all workers, was not dissimilar in style or substance from the British reliance on 'workers' rights' (see above, note 29). But such a strategy in the American context is highly problematic: the promotion of workers' rights is presented as an *imperative* of equality, as defensible in lowering standards as raising them, so long as the same standards apply across the board.[75] A second and related problem with the equal treatment espousal of workers' rights is that in an environment where few employment rights exist and the opposition to the very idea of them is considerable (see below), it may make more strategic sense to go for a little (improved maternity/parental leave provisions) than a lot (universal disability provisions).

The experience in the United States of America teaches us another salutary strategic lesson – the importance of avoiding entrapment in theoretical and ideological straitjackets. The equality approach should be regarded as valuable in so far as it produces results, *not* because it conforms to scholarly standards of logic and/or coherence. Equality is better viewed *as a means* than an end. To treat it as an end, as is the case with much of the American literature, is to vest it with particular content and meaning, accessible through rational discussion and analysis. Yet, the long and tortuous analyses which characterize the American debate suggest that equality has little fixed meaning except that which those with the power to define choose to allot it. This is not to say that equality is valueless in the struggle to achieve a just society (both for men and women) but rather to suggest that its value is tactical rather than inherent, pragmatic rather than principled. In the context of pregnancy, experience to date suggests that the strategic value of equality, certainly in its traditional Aristotelian form, has yet to be proved.[74]

The avoidance of ideological entrapment similarly requires the retention of an open mind in relation to health and safety characterizations of the pregnancy issue. While many feminists may be justifiably wary of a health and safety approach, there may be good reasons for remaining flexible about its application in particular contexts, as recent European legal developments clearly illustrate. In this context, it is worth distinguishing between health and safety measures which are predominantly worker-focused (as with the European directive) and those which are exclusively foetus-centred. The latter are much more likely to result in legal provisions which do not benefit women.

Another important insight to emerge here is the presence of an ideological and political continuity in the range of opposition to maternity/parental leave arrangements. Whatever strategy is pursued, the invariable mode of resistance invokes the language of profit and costs, against an ideological backdrop of contractual and market freedom. Thus, in the United States of America the main opposition to the federal parental leave proposals came from business and financial organizations, including the United States Chamber of Commerce, the National Association of Manufacturers, numerous small business groups, and a large coalition of assorted business groups.[77] In Britain, the Conservative Government has systematically reduced the scope of maternity provisions in the interests of 'efficiency', promoting small businesses, and 'freeing' employers from the 'burdens' of an 'over-regulated' market.[78] In the same vein, they have opposed both the European Parental Leave and Pregnancy Directives, alleging that increased costs, decreased competitiveness, and rising unemployment would be the likely consequences of their implementation.[79]

These practical political concerns raise a host of broader questions about the regulation of the workplace too rarely addressed by feminists, engaged in the struggle to secure improved maternity/parental leave policies. Chief among these is who pays for such policies: parents, employers, or the state? Who should assume the primary financial responsibility for child-bearing - the individual or society? What principles should determine an allocation of responsibility here? To what extent should the state assume responsibility for the welfare of its citizens generally? Is it not an infringement on individual freedom to restrict the power of employers and employees to strike their own deals in relation to maternity/parental leave arrangements? What are the likely consequences for employers and employees of legally regulating the employment relationship?

Those who oppose or resist the introduction of maternity and parental leave arrangements have very definite answers to these questions. Invoking the rhetoric of individual freedom and market efficiency, they pose a powerful challenge which feminists are slow to take up. There is a certain wariness among feminist theorists, no doubt well-founded, of engaging in discourses which are predominantly economic in tone. The feminist theoretical encounter with Marxism in the 1970s is popularly regarded as a salutary reminder of the dangers of engaging with 'male' agendas, not just because they are inclined to eclipse or marginalize women's issues but also because they tend to close rather than to open space for debate.

Engaging with the market economics of neo-liberalism inevitably brings feminists back to addressing questions about the nature of capitalism and class, questions which have been off the theoretical agenda for some time. But, it is incontrovertibly the case that such issues are at the bottom of much of the opposition to pregnancy policies, and also that those who espouse them are generally in positions of considerable political and economic power. Feminists must address them, both on their own terms and more broadly. The argument that maternity policies furnish employers with a disincentive to employ women, for example, must be taken seriously, carefully weighed, and considered in any feminist strategic evaluation. Likewise, the current prevalence of neo-liberal ideology in the context of labour market regulation must be understood not so much as a departure from labour market policies of the 1970s but as their expression in different economic conditions. Just as demographic changes in the 1970s made the introduction of maternity provisions both acceptable and desirable to many employers, so also did they shape and inform policy formation in the 1980s and 1990s.

Nor should feminists regard the questions raised by opponents of maternity and parental leave policies as exclusively economic. Lurking not far from the surface of neo-liberal economics are some highly problematic assumptions about the social role of the family and the gender division of labour.[80] Zillah Eisenstein, in particular, has unravelled the complex gendered vision which informs such ideas.[81] The point is not simply, or even, that feminists should address economics in devising legal strategies but rather that issues which pose as 'economic' (just as with political, philosophical, or religious issues) should be fully interrogated and their gendered nature and implications understood. This points to a wide and multi-faceted concept of 'lawyering', redefining not just the boundaries separating law from other disciplines and institutions (politics, the market, religion) but also those which traditionally designate the perceived separation of theory and practice.

NOTES AND REFERENCES

1 Equal Opportunities Commission, *Women and Men in Britain 1992*; V. Beechey, 'Women's Employment in Contemporary Britain' in *Women in Britain Today*, eds. V. Beechey and E. Whitelegg 77 at p. 80.
2 See J. Conaghan, 'The Invisibility of Women in Labour Law: Gender-Neutrality in Model Building' (1986) 14 *Int. J Sociology of Law* 377; R. Hunter, 'Representing Gender in Legal Analysis: A Casebook Study in Labour Law' (1991) 18 *Melbourne Univ. Law Rev.* 305.
3 Compare *Dekker* v *Stichting Vormingscentrum voor Jonge Volwassen (VJW-Centrum) Plus* [1992] I.C.R. 325 with *Webb* v *EMO Cargo* [1992] 2 All E.R. 43 discussed below. See also I. Hare (1991) 20 *Ind. Law J.* 124.
4 Recent research by the Policy Studies Institute reveals a significant divergence between public and private sector maternity arrangements; S. McRae, *Maternity Rights: the Experience of Women and Employers* (1991) pp. 50, 77.
5 The current provisions are embodied in the Employment Protection (Consolidation) Act 1978 (hereafter cited as 'the EPCA') sections 33–48, 56, 56A, 60; Social Security Act 1986 sections 46–50; Statutory Maternity Pay (General) Regulations 1986 (S.I. 1986 No. 1960).
6 J. Conaghan and L. Chudleigh, 'Women in Confinement: Can Labour Law Deliver the Goods?' (1987) 14 *J. Law and Society* 133, pp. 140–143.
7 For details, see Equal Opportunities Commission, *Pregnant Women at Work: A Response to the EC's Proposed Directive* (1990), Appendix 1.
8 McRae, op. cit., n. 4, p. 197.
9 id., p. 197.
10 id., pp. 50–54.
11 See, in particular, European Commission's Childcare Network, *Childcare in the European Community 1986–1990* (1991).
12 The economic disadvantages of part-time work are not universally agreed upon; see C. Hakim, 'Employment Rights: A Comparison of Part-time and Full-time Employees' (1989) 18 *Ind. Law J.* 69; R. Disney and E. Szyszczak, 'Part-time Work: Reply to Catherine Hakim' (1989) 18 *Ind. Law J.* 223. On the correlation between part-time work and motherhood, see A. Morris and S. Nott, *Working Women and the Law* (1991) 60.
13 id., p. 62.
14 See, for example, N. Lacey, 'Legislation against Sex Discrimination: Questions from a

Feminist Perspective' (1987) 14 *J. Law and Society* 411; A. Morris and S. Nott, op. cit., n. 12; K. O'Donovan and E. Szyszczak, *Equality and Sex Discrimination Law* (1988).

15 It has been suggested that pregnancy in the workplace should not be characterized as a 'woman's' issue because reproduction is better viewed as of general social value. While clearly a more preferable characterization of the issue, pregnancy in the workplace is unavoidably a *feminist* issue because, given the current gender division of labour, it so often results in real and repeated acts of injustice against women workers.

16 See E. Ellis, 'Parents and Employment: An Opportunity for Progress' (1986) *Ind. Law J.* 97, p. 101.

17 R. Lewis and B. Simpson, *Striking a Balance? Employment Law after the 1980 Act* (1981) 12.

18 'Justice' is an elusive aspiration. Moreover, identified here with the need to end *disadvantage*, it is closely associated with, if not absorbed by, the ideal of equality. This creates problems, given the difficulty of attributing to equality any agreed or fixed content (see below). Moreover, the feminist pursuit of 'justice for women' is further problematized by an emerging scepticism about alleged claims to universality implicit in the category 'woman'; C. Smart, 'The Woman of Legal Discourse' (1992) 1 *Social and Legal Studies* 29. Feminists are presented with an unavoidable political dilemma because traditional understandings of feminism as a 'movement to end women's oppression' are inevitably challenged. This paper hopes to show that an emphasis of *strategy* combined with an effort to *particularize* situations of 'injustice' will avoid many of the pitfalls into which feminist theory might otherwise fall.

19 See, for example, feminist disagreement in the late nineteenth/early twentieth century over the benefits of gender-specific protective labour legislation; O. Banks, *Faces of Feminism: A Study of Feminism as a Social Movement* (1981) ch. 7 and ch. 9. More generally, see A. Phillips (ed.), *Feminism and Equality* (1987).

20 See, for example, L. J. Krieger and P. N. Cooney, 'The Miller-Wohl Controversy: Equal Treatment, Positive Action, and the Meaning of Women's Equality' (1983) 13 *Golden Gate Univ. Law Rev.* 513; W. Williams, 'Equality's Riddle: Pregnancy and the Equal Treatment/ Special Treatment Debate' (1984) 13 *New York Univ. Rev. Law and Social Change* 325; L. Finley, 'Transcending Equality Theory: A Way Out of the Maternity and Workplace Debate' (1986) 86 *Columbia Law Rev.* 1118; C. Littleton, 'Reconstructing Sexual Equality' (1987) 75 *California Law Rev.* 1279; C. Bacchi, 'Pregnancy, the Law, and the Meaning of Equality' in *Equality, Politics, and Gender*, eds. E. Meehan and S. Sevenhuijsen 71; L. Vogel, 'Debating Difference: Feminism, Pregnancy, and the Workplace' (1990) 16 *Feminist Studies* 9.

21 Some twenty-six states have introduced pregnancy disability and/or parenting legislation in the wake of the decision in *California Savings and Loan Association* v *Guerra* (1987) 107 S. Ct. 683 (the *'Cal-Fed'* case), discussed below (Vogel, op. cit., n. 20, p. 30). A further reform stimulus has come from recent efforts to secure statutory parental leave *at federal* level. The Parental and Disability Leave Act first made its appearance in the House of Representatives in 1985. Versions of the Bill (consisting of progressively weaker provisions) were regularly placed before Congress until the Family and Medical Leave Act was finally adopted in 1990. The Act, which provides some employees with a period of unpaid parental or family leave, was subsequently vetoed by President Bush although the recent election of Bill Clinton is likely to break the prevailing deadlock between the legislature and executive. The Act has encouraged a number of states to enact their own parental or family leave legislation. For a fuller account of the federal legislation and its genesis, see M. O'Brien Hylton, 'Parental Leaves and Poor Women: Paying the Price for Time Off' (1991) 52 *Univ. Pittsburgh Law Rev.* 476, pp. 478–484.

22 *Geduldig* v *Aiello* (1974) 417 U.S. 484; *General Electric Co.* v *Gilbert* (1976) 429 U.S. 125.

23 CRA 1964 s.701(k).

24 See S. Kamerman, A. Kahn, and P. Kington, *Maternity Policies and Working Women* (1983) 97.

25 Cal. Govt. Code, s.12945(b)(2) (West 1980 & Supp. 1987).

26 Per White J.; Marshal J. gave the majority opinion holding first, that preferential treatment of pregnant workers was not inconsistent with the PDA when considered in terms of its

underlying purpose and objective, that is, the promotion of equal opportunities for women and the prohibition of pregnancy discrimination. Secondly, even if the court's interpretation of the PDA was incorrect, the California statute did not *require* preferential treatment of pregnant workers because employers could avoid it simply by granting disability leave entitlements to all their employees.

27 See, in particular, *Bradwell* v *Illinois* (1873) 83 U.S. (16 Wall.) 130 (justifying the exclusion of women from practice at the bar on the grounds of their 'natural' differences) and *Muller* v *Oregon* (1908) 208 U.S. 412 (upholding restrictions on women's working hours on grounds of their inherent physical weakness and maternal functions).

28 Williams, op. cit., n. 20, p. 358.

29 Williams, op. cit., n. 20, p. 326; Vogel, op. cit., n. 20, pp. 20–22, 25–27.

30 Finley, op. cit., n. 20, pp. 1138–39, 1174–77.

31 A. Scales, 'Towards a New Feminist Jurisprudence' (1981) 56 *Indian Law J*. 375, pp. 435–436; Littleton, op. cit., n. 20, pp. 206, 218–19, 233–236.

32 Finley, op. cit., n. 20, pp. 1149–52. Indeterminacy may be strategically advantageous to feminists; see D. Majury, 'Strategizing in Equality' in *At the Boundaries of Law: Feminism and Legal Theory*, eds. M. Fineman and N. Thomasden (1991) 320, pp. 324–327.

33 id., p. 333.

34 S. G. McCloud, 'Feminism's Idealist Error' (1986) 14 *New York Univ. Rev. Law and Social Change* 278.

35 Hylton, op. cit., n. 21. 'Economic' critiques of equality surface in both left-wing and right-wing politics. McCloud's approach reflects the politics of the left in its utilization of the Marxist contrast between idealism and materialism (McCloud, op. cit., n. 34, p. 280, notes 8, 9), while Hylton's approach is more reminiscent of the politics of the right which often marshalls economic arguments against feminist policies by highlighting their allegedly negative effects on women's employment (see below). Underlying the left-wing critique is a rejection of the liberal world-view, including its veneration of 'the market', both normatively and prescriptively. Underlying the right-wing critique is a reaffirmation of the market as the best regulator of economic affairs. Thus, a surface similarity of left and right approaches masks fundamentally opposing starting positions.

36 C. MacKinnon, *Feminism Unmodified* (1987) 34.

37 W. Williams, 'The Equality Crisis: Some Reflections on Culture, Courts, and Feminism' (1982) 7 *Women's Rights Law Reporter* 175, p. 196.

38 See the approach taken by Brennan J. in his influential dissents in the *Geduldig* and *Gilbert* decisions (see above, n. 22).

39 See Stewart J.'s majority opinions in *Geduldig* and *Gilbert* (above, n. 22). However, in thus distinguishing pregnancy, he is able to deny that it is sexually discriminatory to treat pregnant workers less favourably than other workers.

40 The majority and minority opinions in *Geduldig* and *Gilbert* diverged precisely because they selected different measures of comparison.

41 N. Taub, 'From Parental Leaves to Nurturing Leaves' (1984–85) 13 *New York Univ. Rev. Law and Social Change* 381.

42 SDA 1975 s.5(3).

43 N. Lacey, (1986) 15 *Ind. Law J*. 43.

44 Per Glidewell LJ, pp. 56–57.

45 See Hare, op. cit., n. 3.

46 See the ECJ decisions in *Von Colsen & Kamann* v *Land Nordrhein-Westfalen* Case 14/83 [1984] E.C.R. 1891 (holding that national courts are obliged to interpret national law in accordance with directives the law was passed to implement) and *Marleasing SA* v *La Comercial International de Alimentacion* Case C–106/89 [1990] E.C.R. I–4135 (holding that national courts are obliged to interpret domestic legislation as far as possible in light of the wording and purpose of any relevant directive, whether or not the legislation preceded or succeeded the directive in question). Together these cases suggest that British courts *are* obliged to intererpet the SDA consistently with *Dekker*. This is one of the issues before the House of Lords on appeal in *Webb* (above, n. 3). The House of Lords have referred the case to the E.C.J.

47 For details, see Conaghan and Chudleigh, op. cit., n. 6, p. 135.

48 For details and analysis of the current provisions see Conaghan and Chudleigh, op. cit., n. 6; A. Morris and S. Nott, 'The Legal Response to Pregnancy' (1992) 12 *Legal Studies* 54. The most significant change to the provisions introduced by the Conservative Government in the 1980s was to merge maternity pay under the EPCA 1978 with maternity allowance, creating a new 'Statutory Maternity Pay' Scheme administered by employers (above, n. 5); J. Conaghan, 'Statutory Maternity Pay under the Social Security Act 1986' (1987) *Ind. Law J.* 125. However, as a result of the adoption by EC countries of the Pregnancy Directive, further change is now imminent: see the Trades Union and Employment Rights Bill, currently proceeding through Parliament, discussed below.

49 McRae's study reveals that sixty per cent of women in work during pregnancy qualify for maternity leave and the right to reinstatement, still leaving a significant forty per cent without any statutory entitlement to leave or reinstatement (op. cit., n. 4, p. 146). Eighty per cent of women receive some form of maternity pay, either Statutory Maternity Pay (payable by an employer) or maternity allowance (paid by the DSS) (id., p. 91). However, maternity pay is not generous. The higher rate of SMP, six weeks at nine-tenths of a week's salary followed by twelve weeks at a lower fixed rate (currently £46.50 per week) is conditional upon a two-year continuous service qualification. The lower rate (eighteen weeks at £46.50 per week) requires six months continuous employment while even maternity allowance (currently eighteen weeks at £42.25 per week) is subject to a minimum national insurance contribution requirement.

50 Conaghan and Chudleigh, op. cit., n. 6; Conaghan, op. cit., n. 2; Hunter, op. cit., n. 2. It might be argued that, in the 1980s, patterns of work changed so significantly for workers generally (for example, with the growth of self-employment, part-time and temporary work, the decline of trades unions, and the dramatic increase in unemployment), that the model of work which employment protection legislation reflects no longer typifies anything at all. Certainly at the time of its introduction in the mid–1970s it corresponded most closely with the working patterns of workers with the most say in shaping its contents, that is, male unionized employees.

51 EPCA 1978 s.153.

52 EPCA 1978 s.33(3)(b) and Schedule 13. See also note 49 above.

53 Self-employment increased by 1.1million (fifty-two per cent) between 1981 and 1991 to a total of 3.3million. Of this growth, men accounted for 0.8million and women 0.4million (*Employment Gazette*, June 1992, p. 269).

54 Homeworkers are typically although not necessarily regarded as self-employed; see *Nethermere (St Neots) Ltd* v *Taverna* [1983] I.R.L.R. 103.

55 Temporary workers make up about 5.6 per cent of the workforce as a whole and about 7.3 per cent of the female workforce (*Employment Gazette*, April 1991, p. 181). The biography of women's working lives is often characterized by interruption during the child-bearing years; Beechey, op. cit., n. 1, pp. 80–83.

56 Conaghan, op. cit., n. 2, pp. 383–385.

57 The theoretical literature on the gender division of labour and the relationship between work in the home and in the labour market is extensive. See in particular S. Walby, *Patriarchy at Work* (1988); M. Barrett, *Women's Oppression Today* (revised ed., 1988); V. Beechey, *Unequal Work* (1987).

58 Department of Social Security Report, *Reform of Social Security, Volume Two* (1985; Cmnd. 9518) para. 5.22.

59 Subject to any obligation to pay Statutory Maternity Pay (see above, notes 5 and 49). Moreover, under the EPCA 1978 s.31A, employers are required to permit pregnant employees reasonable time off work for ante-natal care. The *Dekker* decision significantly challenges the limited approach to employer responsibility which current British law reflects; see Morris and Nott, op. cit., n. 48, pp. 67–68; see also the implications of the Pregnancy Directive and its anticipated implementation in the United Kingdom, discussed below.

60 There is still no legal entitlement to paternity leave in Britain. On the progress of the European Draft Directive on Parental Leave, see note 61.

61 Draft Directive on Parental Leave and Leave for Family Reasons, OJ C 315/84. The original proposals were significantly diluted to take account of member's objections including those of Britain. The requirement of unanimity among the Council of Ministers suggests that the proposal has little hope of being enacted, at least during the lifetime of the present Conservative Government.

62 Department of Employment, *Lifting the Burden* (Cmnd. 9571); *Building Businesses not Barriers* (1986; Cmnd. 9794). For further elaboration of the Government's deregulationist philosophy, see Conaghan and Chudleigh, op. cit., n. 6, and below.

63 The current Government, for example, often highlights the long period of maternity leave (forty weeks) which British law provides while at the same time omitting to draw attention to the stringent qualifying conditions or the fact that most of it is unpaid. See, for example, 'Party Policies on Equal Opportunities' (1992) 42 *Equal Opportunities Rev.* 12, p. 21. On rights in feminist theory, see C. Smart, *Feminism and the Power of Law* (1989) ch. 7.

64 In the late 1980s, the European Social Charter expressed the hopes of many who sought to develop workers' rights through European rather than British legal mechanisms. However, the concessions secured by Britain in the Maastricht Treaty (allowing them to 'opt-out' of a Protocol aimed at extending the scope of the qualified majority voting procedure to facilitate the implementation of the charter's provisions), followed by the re-election of the Conservative Government in 1992, have all but buried the issue in the United Kingdom. For a full analysis of the charter's provisions, see L. Wedderburn, 'The Social Charter, European Company and Employment Rights' (1990; Institute of Employment Rights).

65 Lewis and Simpson, op. cit., n. 17, p. 47.

66 Arts. 3–7 and Annexes I and II.

67 Members states must ensure that pregnant women enjoy at least fourteen weeks paid maternity leave at a rate corresponding to no less than the national minimum sick pay rate (£45.30 per week in the United Kingdom), including a two-week period of compulsory leave in and around the time of confinement (Art. 8). Member states may impose eligibility requirements but these must 'under no circumstances provide for periods of employment in excess of 12 months immediately prior to the presumed date of confinement' (Art. 11(4)). Significantly, Art. 1(3) provides that the directive must not have the effect of reducing the legal rights that pregnant workers already enjoy under national legislation.

68 Art. 10.

69 See D. Muffat-Jeandet, 'The Proposed Pregnancy and Maternity Directive' (1991) 20 *Ind. Law J.* 76, pp. 77–78.

70 An earlier draft of the pregnancy directive (OJ C 281/3) contained within its preamble allusions discomfitingly resonant of such a perception, referring for example to the particular 'vulnerability', 'sensitivity', and 'delicate condition' of pregnant workers. The agreed draft of the directive has, significantly, removed most of these references.

71 K. De Gama, 'A Brave New World? Rights Discourse and the Politics of Reproductive Autonomy' in this collection.

72 S. Kenney, 'Reproductive Hazards in the Workplace: the Law and Sexual Difference' (1986) 14 *Int. J. Sociology of Law* 393.

73 'Draft Directive on Protection of Pregnant Workers' (1990) 203 *European Industrial Relations Reports* 16, p. 17.

74 After agreement by the Council of Ministers in December 1991, the new proposals (above, notes 72–74) went before the European Parliament, which voted, among other things, for a maternity pay level at eighty per cent of full earnings. On returning the matter to the Council of Ministers, the acceptance of the directive was further delayed, first by Britain's insistence that maternity pay remain at the sick pay level, and secondly by Italy's refusal to support the directive because the level of pay was too low. Agreement was reached to proceed with the directive *with* the sick pay linkage on 19 October 1992.

75 For an appropriate British parallel, see debate surrounding the 1986 repeal of gender-specific protective labour legislation; J. Jarman, 'Equality or Marginalization: The Repeal of Protective Legislation' in Meehan and Sevenshuijsen, op. cit., n. 20, p. 142.

76 The notion of equality is intuitively very powerful and its value does not, in my view, diminish

because 'rational' analysis cannot produce any 'true' or 'correct' version of it. While I remain open to the possibility of a philosophical articulation of equality which avoids many of the pitfalls of the debate in the United States of America, I am not sure, in this case, that the penny is worth the candle. The journey from idea to actualization is long and hazardous and invariably ignorant of the forces ranged against it. Moreover, as Diana Majury points out, the pursuit of a formulaic approach to equality is more likely to trap and constrain rather than to liberate discussion (op. cit., n. 32, pp. 327–331).

77 K. Kovach, 'Creeping Socialism or Good Public Policy: The Proposed Parental and Medical Leave Act' (1987) *Labour Law J.* 427, p. 429.
78 Conaghan and Chudleigh, op. cit., n. 6.
79 Ellis, op. cit., n. 16, pp. 107–108; Department of Employment Supplementary Memorandum, 'The Costs of the Social Action Programme to the UK', para. 13, HC 7 (1990–91); Select Committee on European Legislation, HC 1990–91, 29–ii, para. 5, 21 November 1990.
80 See, for example, G. Gilder, *Wealth and Poverty* (1981).
81 Z. Eisenstein, *Feminism and Sexual Equality: Crisis in Liberal America* (1984).

Theory into Practice?
Pornography and the Public/Private Dichotomy

NICOLA LACEY *

'The feminist total critique of the liberal opposition of private and public still awaits its philosopher'.[1] So concluded Carole Pateman in an important article written a decade ago. During the intervening years, there has been an explosion of feminist literature reflecting upon issues raised by public/private dichotomies in social and political thought, much of it concerned with legal analysis or questions of legal policy and reform. Yet, notwithstanding this theoretical development, questions around public/private dichotomies have lost little of their power to bewilder, as each confidently asserted critique raises further questions of theory and strategy. Indeed, it sometimes seems that the more we criticize the public/private dichotomy, the more we get trapped within its conceptual framework.

In this paper, I want to return to this well-worked terrain with two purposes in mind. First, I want to distinguish several different concerns which have informed feminist preoccupation with the public/private dichotomy. Drawing on feminist political and social theory, I shall explore how each of the different concerns I identify feeds into questions of legal policy. Secondly, I shall turn my attention to one concrete area, namely pornography, in which feminist activism – including that directed to law reform – has been informed by the public/private critique. Pornography is an issue which, perhaps above all others, has been controversial *within* feminist thought, and in which issues of theory and strategy connect particularly closely. I hope to shed some light on why the pornography debate has been such a problematic one for contemporary feminism by looking at it again in the light of a more differentiated appreciation of the public/private critique. In particular, I shall try to identify the negative consequences which unjustified inferences from the public/private critique have had on feminist politics around pornography.

DISENTANGLING PUBLIC/PRIVATE DICHOTOMIES

The idea that 'the personal is political' has been a central tenet of the

*Fellow in Law, New College, Oxford OX1 3BN, England

I would like to thank Susanne Baer, Joanne Conaghan, and Katherine O'Donovan for giving me useful comments on an earlier draft of this paper.

contemporary women's movement, though its precise meaning is less than clear. At its broadest, the idea has issued in a thorough-going reassessment of the traditional conception of what is properly within the realm of public debate and critique, by unearthing and making visible issues of gender which have been ignored in political theory and practice. One particular theoretical ploy has been to focus on a supposed liberal division of the world into public and private spheres: a strictly limited public sphere is appropriate for the enforcement of justice, whilst the state leaves relations and distributions in the private sphere untouched.[2] But though the idea of privacy as an essential constituent of individual autonomy has been central to the liberal tradition, public/private divisions are not confined to liberal or libertarian thought. The delineation of a 'private' sphere beyond the scope of politics is a feature of Marxist thought too: the sphere of reproduction within the family does not form the object of revolutionary critique or practice except in specifically feminist versions of Marxist theory.[3] Feminists have pointed out that, since women's lives have in many societies been lived to a greater extent than men's within the so-called private sphere, the implication of the public/private division has meant that fundamental sources of women's oppression politically invisible and hence ignored. But both the arguments on which the feminist critique focuses and the critique itself have been obscured by the difficulty of identifying precisely what is meant by the public/private divide. In what follows, therefore, I shall try to distinguish between a number of different issues which are relevant to the debate.

1. Public and Private Spheres: Normative and Descriptive Arguments

The claim most commonly associated with public/private ideology, that the world divides into public and private *spheres*, presents two immediate questions. First, what are these spheres – what do public and private denote in this context? Secondly, is this a descriptive or a normative claim? I shall look at each in turn.

As far as the identification of public and private spheres is concerned, two basic accounts have been influential. In the first, the division is between the state and civil society. Particularly in nineteenth-century *laissez-faire* versions of liberalism, a central idea was that the role of the state should be strictly limited, with the market governing relations other than family relations in civil society. The continuing influence of such ideas is reflected in the ideology of recent governments in the United Kingdom and the United States of America. In the second account, the division is between the state and/or the market on the one hand and the family on the other. The family is constructed as the quintessentially private sphere in which human relations must be allowed to develop away from the scrutiny let alone intervention of state or market institutions. In each case, the ideas of 'public' and 'private' roughly correspond to 'regulated' and 'unregulated', and the claim is offered variously as descriptive and as normative. On one level, the idea of a division between state and civil society or between the market or state and the family is offered

94

as a characterization of the world. At another, it is connected with substantive political arguments about the appropriateness of regulation in the relevant areas.[4] Clearly, this means that we need to assess the various kinds of public/private sphere claims in terms of different criteria.

First, let us examine the descriptive version of the public/private dichotomy. To what extent is it sensible to see our social world as divided into spheres corresponding to state/civil society, market/family? Obviously, these categories have a certain degree of institutional validity. But, at the level of political and sociological analysis, taking these categories as a starting-point would be very crude. 'The' state consists of many interlocking institutions and practices, as does 'the' market; 'families' can be defined in different ways and come in a variety of forms. Nor does this three-tier institutional characterization seem an adequate starting-point for social theory. For modern capitalist societies also develop a 'public sphere' or set of 'publics' which constitute not only the state or state institutions but also non-state fora for public, political debate – social movements, trades unions, pressure groups and so on.[5] Here, too, politics, in the broad sense of 'the critical activity of raising issues and deciding how institutional and social relations should be organized',[6] goes on.

What of the specific attempt to understand social institutions as public or private in the sense of their being (at least predominantly) regulated or unregulated by state power? Historically, it could fairly be said that in, for example, mid-nineteenth century Britain the operation of the market and contractual relations were relatively unregulated by the state, or that in mid-twentieth-century Britain legal regulation was not applied to some significant aspects of family life and relations. But we are talking here of *relativities* rather than clear divisions. Indeed, the very institution of contract law always, in some sense, regulates market transactions, even though the degree to which the state controls the terms on which parties may contract with each other has steadily increased. Similarly, in spite of a great deal of rhetoric about privacy in the family sphere, a moment's thought reveals that many aspects of family life are hedged around with legal regulation – marriage, divorce, child custody, social welfare rules, to name but the most obviously relevant areas of law. Moreover, it would be wrong to see direct *legal* regulation as the touchstone for state involvement. In all sorts of indirect ways – economic, administrative, and political – state institutions have a crucial and often deliberate impact on the conduct of family life.[7] Indeed, it might be argued that in late twentieth-century Britain we have seen an increasing willingness to regulate the family, whilst *laissez-faire* attitudes to the market (not always realized in political practice as opposed to rhetoric) have experienced a revival. As for the non-state 'publics' referred to above, the question of regulation or non-regulation seems inappropriate, yet their importance to the conduct of social life further blurs any supposed division between public and private spheres. We may be able to make relative judgements, and draw crude distinctions between family, market, and state at an institutional level. But the search for the public/private division in terms of the presence or absence of state-directed or state-sponsored regulation is as hopeless as the analysis of society merely in terms of state, market, and family is inadequate.

This conclusion becomes even clearer when we take into account the difficulty in attaching any general significance to a distinction between regulation and non-regulation, or between intervention and abstention. In any given case it can be unclear analytically whether to characterize the state's position as one of regulation or non-regulation.[8] For example, the exemption of married men from charges of rape of their wives which persists in many jurisdictions is generally seen in terms of non-regulation. Yet it discloses a certain view of the marriage relationship which is positively inscribed in law. In such cases, abstention amounts to a form of regulation. And even where a regulation/non-regulation distinction can be drawn analytically, its significance is called into question by the fact that decisions *not* to regulate made by state or other institutions with the power to do so are every bit as much *political* decisions as are decisions to regulate. Clearly, both within and beyond liberal theory, the shape of arguments for regulation and non-regulation cannot be taken to be identical. But the strong liberal presumption in favour of non-regulation which proceeds from the commitment of some of the most influential versions of modern liberalism to a *negative* conception of freedom – freedom as the absence of constraint – has obscured the way in which state decisions not to regulate are themselves political and call for justification.[9]

Another problematic feature of the characterization of family or civil society as private in the sense of unregulated has to do with what such a characterization presupposes about the regulator. This is generally conceived in simple terms as 'the state'. But, as I have already observed, the state is not monolithic; it is rather a set of diverse institutions. This gives rise to further complexities in identifying regulation or non-regulation. What are we to say of issues such as wife-battering – always 'regulated' in the sense of being within the purview of criminal law, but frequently 'unregulated' because of the decisions of law enforcement agencies? The picture is fragmented, even leaving aside the operation of powerful regulation which cannot be identified with 'the state'. Once we incorporate non-state power, and acknowledge the difficulty of distinguishing between state and non-state bodies in a world where 'public' and 'private' power are inextricably linked with each other, the picture threatens to disintegrate.[10] The very idea of power as something which is deliberately exercised by identifiable agents, as opposed to, or at least also, subsisting in discourses and practices spreading throughout the social body – including those other 'publics' ignored by the traditional public/private distinction – misses important aspects of how subjects' positions are constituted and maintained in the social world.[11] Finally, the descriptive association of women with 'the private sphere', particularly in the sense of the family, is itself problematic. For whilst it is both true and highly significant that women still bear a disproportionate responsibility for domestic labour, the converse suggestion that women have lived their lives exclusively or even mainly in the private sphere of the family is quite unsustainable. Working-class women in particular have worked outside the home to a far greater degree than the public/private critique has tended to acknowledge. At a descriptive level, the idea of a private, unregulated family simply collapses when subjected to scrutiny.

Now let us move from the descriptive to the normative. The idea that the state's use of coercive force to curtail citizens' behaviour calls for special justification lies at the heart of liberal political philosophy. In Mill's famous formulation, the only justification for state intervention to curtail individual freedom lies in the prevention of harm to others.[12] Individual freedom is the paramount liberal value. State power threatens that freedom in a peculiarly dangerous way, and must be strictly limited. Leaving aside for the moment Mill's unitary conception of state power, the implications of his argument depend on how freedom is conceived. To the extent that we recognize that genuine freedom depends not only on being left alone – not interfered with, regulated, or scrutinized – but also on being provided with certain positive goods and facilities, we will be alert to the freedom-enhancing as well as the freedom-threatening potential of state or state-sponsored action. This, certainly, was a position to which Mill was sympathetic, and it has come to be known as the idea of *positive freedom*. However, in modern debates about the proper limits of state action, the tendency has been to focus on *negative freedom* – freedom as being left in peace.[13] On this view, a conceptually neat and rhetorically powerful way of realizing the argument for human freedom is in terms of the delineation of a 'private sphere' – famously described in the Wolfenden Report as that which is 'in brief and crude terms, not the law's business'.[14] The central thrust of feminist critique has borne upon this normative interpretation of liberal theory. For, it has been argued, the practical consequence of non-regulation is the consolidation of the *status quo*: the *de facto* support of pre-existing power relations and distributions of goods within the 'private' sphere. In effect, if not explicitly, much of the feminist critique espouses a positive conception of freedom. It exposes the way in which the ideology of the public/private dichotomy allows government to clean its hands of any *responsibility* for the state of the 'private' world and *depoliticizes* the disadvantages which inevitably spill over the alleged divide by affecting the position of the 'privately' disadvantaged in the 'public' world.

The feminist critique, then, is a direct attack on the idea of public and private spheres, which it sees as a politically and ethically inadequate realization of liberal arguments about individual freedom and the proper role of the state. The attack consists in both a normative argument about positive freedom and an analytical argument about the interdependence of regulated and unregulated spheres. Liberal theory which depends on the public/private distinction is self-defeating in that the guarantees of justice and equality held out to citizens in the 'public' sphere are worth systematically less to those who are pre-politically disadvantaged. The limits of the scope of politics and justice asserted by liberals such as Rawls, in other words, are inconsistent with the realization of the general values which they claim to espouse.[15] Also notable from a critical point of view is a tendency to couch the normative argument in superficially descriptive terms, in a way which is at once intellectually

97

indefensible and rhetorically powerful. As we saw above, the project of delineating public and private spheres at a descriptive level is fraught with difficulty. Yet the substantively normative argument often proceeds by simply announcing a particular issue to fall 'within the private sphere' and 'hence' to be inappropriate for regulation. The statement of the Wolfenden Committee quoted above is an excellent example: the labels 'public' and 'private' are used in question-begging ways which *suppress* the normative arguments which they actually presuppose so that the debate sounds common-sensical rather than politically controversial. One of the main successes of feminist critique has been to expose the *politics* – the 'power-laden' character[16] – of 'privatization' of this kind. It ought to go without saying that this repoliticization of attributions of 'privacy' is quite different from an argument for the propriety let alone the efficacy of state regulation: to say that what has been thought of as private is within the scope of political *critique* is not to say that it must necessarily be *regulated*. Unfortunately, as we shall see, this crucial distinction has not always been observed.

2. Public and Private Values

At an explicit level, most of the debate around public/private dichotomies has centred on the idea of public and private spheres. But just below the surface has been another equally important set of ideas to do with the place of the public/private opposition within a set of dichotomies which structure Western thought. Other dualisms include objectivity and subjectivity, reason and passion, self and other, culture and nature, and, crucially for feminist thinking, male and female. Many feminist theorists have argued that the male/ female opposition maps onto these other dichotomies, identifying, for example, femaleness with emotion, passivity, subjectivity, nature; male with reason, objectivity, activity, culture.[17] They have also observed that in Western culture one half of each pair is valued above the other, and that the halves with which women and femaleness are associated are the less valued. This kind of analysis in turn maps onto the public/private dichotomy. For, it is argued, what we need to focus on is not so much empirical (and highly problematic) claims about women's lives being lived disproportionately in the private sphere but rather *cultural associations* between femaleness, the private and under-recognized values and attributes. On this view, the importance of the public/private dichotomy lies in the fact that the cultural construction of the public sphere as the sphere in which universal reason holds sway implicitly marginalizes or is inhospitable to women, because reason and hence the public, are culturally associated with the masculine, whereas the private, conversely, is associated with the feminine – with particularity, emotion, the body, *otherness*. The task of feminist critique, then, is to expose the gendered nature of the concepts in terms of which our notions of 'the public sphere' are constructed, and to offer alternative conceptions which would render the 'public' genuinely accessible not just to women as well as men, but also to all those whose 'particularity' currently marks them as 'different' and hence as excluded from the unity of the public.[18]

Another aspect of this feminist argument relates to the very nature of public/private and the other dualisms as *dichotomies*. Here feminist thought participates in a broad project of exposing and challenging ways in which our thinking is structured around pairs of ideas which are opposed in the sense that the attribution of one excludes the other: that which is public cannot be private; that which is male cannot be female, and so on. By showing how each side of each dualism depends on the other for its own meaning – subjectivity can only be understood by differentiating itself from objectivity, maleness takes its meaning from femaleness, and so on – this 'deconstruction' shows how the less valued half acts as a 'dangerous supplement' to the other. Each member of the pair refers to the other at the same time as it suppresses it. Thus, the self-sufficiency of the more powerful side of the dichotomy is fragile, being undermined in the very moment in which it is expressed. This kind of deconstruction proceeds on the assumption that we need to erode the power of hierarchically ordered dichotomies as part of a liberating political pro-gramme. For the fact that one side of the dualisms has cultural status helps to invest people related to those attributes or values with greater power. Hierarchically dichotomized thinking operates by way of suppressing the implied reference to the 'other'; by marginalizing that 'other', it forms an important part of the politics of the powerful as realized through language.

As always, it is easier to identify the problem here than to find a way of resolving it. Some deconstructionists affirm the inevitability of working *within* the dichotomies: since they are part of our cultural and linguistic heritage, they cannot be left behind by an act of political will. There must therefore be a phase – for some deconstructionists it is a phase which will never end – in which we work to unearth the 'dangerous supplement', to effect a revaluation of that which has been suppressed.[19] Since gender neutrality is unrealizable, the only possible immediate goal is to attack gender hierarchy – to expose the contingency (and hence the *politics*) of the current cultural hierarchy. This is disappointing, for to the extent that we stay within the dichotomized categories, our only political option seems to be to change the position of particular groups within those structures – merely substituting one oppressed, marginalized group for another.[20] The hope of a genuinely radical politics would be to escape oppression altogether, and this, in the view of many critical theorists, entails transcending the dichotomies rather than reversing them. But how is such a project to be effected; how is the logic of binary oppositions, in which deconstruction itself seems to participate, to be escaped? Two possibilities (they are not mutually exclusive) have been suggested. The first is exemplified by Cornell's feminist reading of Derrida. Whilst Cornell acknow-ledges the need to 'take off' from within the dichotomies, the openness of language, particularly as realized through devices such as metaphor and metonymy, opens a utopian moment within deconstruction. Different mean-ings and possibilities can be glimpsed or imagined which may gradually allow us to transcend the oppressive social relations expressed in the current dichotomies.[21] In the work of other theorists such as Young, in which deconstruction plays a less central role, the possibility of transcending the dichotomies proceeds from a decided rejection of the idea that the world must be understood in terms of their binary straitjacket. Rather, it is argued, we can move to a realization of difference as multiple and relational, hence undermining the dichotomized construction/understanding of the world and rejecting the limited political options that its either/or analysis seemed to force upon us.[22] Each of these strategies needs to be borne in mind in considering feminist critique of public/private dichotomies.

3. The Value of Privacy

One final aspect of the debate about public and private needs to be distinguished. This is the argument about what, if any, value should be ascribed to privacy. Clearly, the idea that privacy in the sense of a space around the individual or a particular association from which she or it is entitled to exclude others, connects closely with liberal notions of individual freedom, contributing to liberal arguments about the desirability of an unregulated private sphere, particularly the family. But a commitment to the idea that privacy can be of value and should sometimes be respected does not entail a commitment to a private *sphere* in any of the senses generally understood by that term. Evidently, the value of privacy is contextual – it depends on the particular area of life we are thinking of, and the circumstances which prevail. This means that an approach to protecting privacy which operates by delineating a relatively concrete *sphere* seems inappropriate. But, from a feminist point of view, it is far from clear that a critique of the public/ private dichotomy should bring with it a total rejection of the notion that privacy can be valuable and ought sometimes to be protected by the state and other powerful institutions.[23] Indeed, given the double burden inherent in current social arrangements, privacy is one of the many things which women tend to lack. This needs to be emphasized because some feminist critiques have been taken (not always without justification) to imply that privacy is a value which has nothing to recommend it to women.[24]

PROBLEMS FOR THE PUBLIC/PRIVATE CRITIQUE

Now that we have a clearer view of the different aspects of the public/private dichotomy and the critique which it has generated, we can begin to focus on some of the specific difficulties which the critique has encountered. The main problems associated with the division between public and private spheres can be summarized as follows. In its 'descriptive' guise, it inappropriately 'reifies' spheres which cannot be clearly identified by means of careful concrete sociological analysis. The construction of public and private spheres as analytical categories exaggerates the extent of actual institutional divisions, suppresses the ways in which women's as well as men's lives are lived across 'public and private spheres', and gives insufficient attention to concrete social practices and historical changes. Secondly, the analytical categories are applied to particular areas and practices as if descriptively, but with normative conclusions being drawn from the 'descriptive' denotation of publicity or privacy. The premises on which these conclusions are based are hence obscured and protected from critical scrutiny. Thirdly, the assumption that the world can be divided into separate spheres obscures the interdependence of those spheres and the spill-over from oppression in one sphere to subordination in another. Finally, the analysis is crude in its focus on 'the state' and 'state intervention' as the touchstones of 'the public' and of regulation, when in fact both the state and the means of regulation are multiple rather than unitary. Many different modes of regulation exist – overt and covert, legal and administrative, more or less coercive – operated by a variety of state institutions. Indeed, the very idea of state as opposed to non-state agencies (yet another form of public/private dichotomy) is inappropriate in a world where 'public' and 'private' power are inextricably linked. The critique of the public/private dichotomy questions the common assumption that politics has to do exclusively or at least primarily with the state. It also suggests that we should reject the idea that power can be understood exclusively in terms of sovereignty: rather than seeing power as something which is wielded by particular persons or agencies in a conscious or overt way, we must also attend to the operations of power in a diversity of state and non-state institutions, practices, and discourses.

Unfortunately, however, the critique of the division between public and private spheres which has generated these insights has itself not always escaped the problems it has identified. The difficulty lies in the fact that once one engages in a critique of the division, one gets sucked into the very categorization one is attempting to undermine. One good example is provided by the last two chapters of Katherine O'Donovan's *Sexual Divisions in Law* (1985). This book, which broke new ground in feminist legal scholarship in the United Kingdom, devoted much of its argument to a critique of the public/private dichotomy. Yet O'Donovan's models of reform essentially consist in turning the values which characterize one side of the dichotomy against practices on the other. In doing so, O'Donovan elides two aspects of the public/private divide which we have distinguished: public versus private *spheres* and the sexualization of the public/private dichotomy at the level of *values*. Evidently, the idea of 'making a man more like a woman', and the public more like the private, precisely does not transcend the dichotomy it critiques, for it speaks in the unreconstructed terms of the dichotomy itself. And, despite her vision of transcending the dichotomy via a world of reds and greens and blues, Frances Olsen's sophisticated analysis too makes little progress in this transformative direction. In 'The Family and the Market',[25] most of her argument, like O'Donovan's, consists of an analysis of the way law reform has mapped the values associated with the private onto the public, and vice versa. Because the critique of the ideological power which the public/private dichotomy has as part of a sexualized and hierarchical cultural discourse is mapped back on to a division between public and private spheres which has effectively been exploded as a myth, the argument reaches a kind of deadlock in which the promise of genuine transformation cannot be made good. In Olsen's metaphor we begin to escape the binary and the dichotomized, but the utopian vision opened up by deconstruction is glimpsed rather than developed.

Another way of looking at this problem is to think of the public/private critique as operating at several different levels. At one level, the dichotomy is criticized as being impossibly indeterminate or even analytically incoherent; as being an inaccurate description of the world; and as implying an unattractive prescription for social organization. At a different level, the critique focuses not on the dichotomy itself but on the power which that dichotomy, incoherent, inaccurate, unattractive though it may be, has actually had in constructing or consolidating certain features of women's oppression. In spite of all its glaring defects, in other words, its discursive power in our culture is acknowledged. This involves the feminist critique in a delicate balancing act, and one which can all too easily appear to lose its equilibrium. It can seem as though our theoretical critique of the public/private distinction undermines our critique of its power: if the division is so hopelessly indeterminate, to what concrete political practices is the normative liberal argument and, more importantly, the feminist critique of it, meant to relate? It is extremely difficult, in other words, to engage in critique of the public/private dichotomy or its effects without speaking as if it had an analytic and empirical validity which the critique denies. The way out of this impasse lies in seeing that the dichotomy has operated, and continues to operate, ideologically – and ideological power does not necessarily depend upon empirical validation or logical coherence. This suggests that the critique may have focused to too great an extent on the idea of public and private *spheres*. For the ideological role of the dichotomy can be – and has been – played *without* necessarily being realized in any empirically identifiable separation of institutions, activities, or areas of life, or indeed in articulated policy.

A final problem encountered by the critique has to do with the conclusions which are to be drawn from it. All too often, feminist theorists have made the assumption that a critique of the depoliticization of the private should go hand in hand with change in the form of greater legal regulation. Consider the assumption tucked away in Alison Jaggar's otherwise careful analysis: 'By defining sexual and family relations as private . . . liberal theorists provide grounds for arguing that these assaults are no business of the law *and so* for allowing them to continue'[26](my emphasis). It is perhaps unfair to attribute to Jaggar a general view on the basis of a particular example in which law is arguably a rather obviously apt response. Nonetheless, the passage makes a strong assumption both about the appropriateness of legal intervention as a remedy for the ills of privatized wrongs and about the efficacy of such legal intervention. Both of these assumptions call for much more argument, fleshed out in particular contexts.

Whilst feminist lawyers have widely debated the strategic implications of legal regulation, the normative arguments have been less fully developed. This is perhaps because of a pervasive and understandable scepticism in feminist

102

thought about the utility of normative theories which pretend to a politically dubious universalism and fail to articulate the position from which they speak. Nonetheless, feminists should address the underlying substantive political and ethical issues which have been skated over by both public/private dichotomized discourse and its critique. This must be part of a larger feminist enterprise of reconstructing concepts such as autonomy and privacy.[27] The kind of enterprise I have in mind is well illustrated by the following passage from feminist philosopher Iris Marion Young:

> Instead of defining the private as what the public excludes, I suggest, the private should be defined, as in one strain of liberal theory, as that aspect of his or her life and activity that any person has a right to exclude others from. The private in this sense is not what public institutions exclude, but what the individual chooses to withdraw from public view. With the growth of both state and non-state bureaucracies, the protection of privacy has become a burning public issue. In welfare capitalist society, the defence of personal privacy has become not merely a matter of keeping the state out of certain affairs, but of calling for positive state regulation to ensure that both its own agencies and non-state organizations, such as corporations, respect the claims of individuals to privacy.
>
> This manner of formulating the concepts of public and private, which is inspired by feminist confrontations with traditional political theory, does not deny their distinction. It does deny, however, a social division between public and private spheres, each with different kinds of institutions, activities and human attributes.[28]

This passage captures the importance of reconstructing an adequate distinction between public and private – a distinction which is neither dichotomous nor mapped onto separate spheres – and shows how this connects with central ethical considerations. It also implies that adequate notions of public and private do not automatically map on to conclusions about regulation and non-regulation. I shall now move on to consider these theoretical points in the context of the concrete issue of pornography.

PORNOGRAPHY AND THE PUBLIC/PRIVATE DICHOTOMY

Feminist concern with pornography is certainly not new, but it has taken a particular shape and gained a new intensity over the last twenty years. In a period of reflection upon the implications for women of the sexual 'liberation' of the 1960s, many women began to be concerned with the proliferation of readily available pornography, asking questions not just about the relationship between pornography and sexual violence, or about the exploitation of women involved in the production of pornography, but also about the broader cultural implications of the spread of pornography for the status and citizenship of women. In Andrea Dworkin's work, for example, pornography is seen as central to the maintenance of women's oppression: heterosexuality constructs women as the sexual objects of men, and this objectification finds its most graphic as well as one of its most powerful expressions in pornographic material.[29] On this view, sexuality is the fundamental site of women's oppression, and pornography, along with rape, wife-beating, sexual harassment, and other forms of sexually specific violence, represent the social practices which both express and cause women's subordination and power-lessness. This analysis of pornography emphasizes its implicit or explicit violence, its dehumanization of its objects – mostly women or children, disproportionately often black women – by representing them in positions of servility, as enjoying pain or humiliation, by reducing them to particular body parts. A somewhat different account has emphasized the ways in which the proliferation of pornography has affected other areas of life. Pornography, on this view, is a regime of representation through which we see the world. Once widely available as a genre, the regime of representation which pornography engenders is not restricted to the viewing of pornographic materials them-selves. It affects the way in which consumers of pornography look at other genres – advertising, novels, and so on.[30] Moreover, the question of whether or not pornography contributes to actual sexual violence is not the exclusive or even the central concern. The point is that the profusion of the pornographic regime of representation inevitably affects the social consti-tution of femininity – affects the ways in which women can be represented and can represent ourselves across all social practices – and hence directly and adversely, albeit intangibly, affects the status of women.

My concern here is not to engage in further analysis of pornography but rather to focus specifically on the contribution which the critique of the public/private dichotomy has made to feminist analyses of pornography. In the first place, pornography in liberal society has largely been constructed as a matter of private consumption, and hence as outside the ambit of political critique or action. Without any proof of the contribution of pornography to overt acts of violence, and without any overt violence or coercion in its production, pornography has been taken to be either an instance of expression or a form of sexual practice and hence within the sphere of individuals' privacy. Feminist critique has brought pornography into the sphere of the public and has insisted upon its political relevance. This is both because of the inter-dependence argument – the argument that private oppression inevitably leads to public disadvantage – and because the traditional denomination of pornography as private can itself be shown to be disingenuous. The liberal analysis which constructs pornography as a matter of private sexual preference in one breath constructs it as a matter of public rights to free expression in the next. In what might be called a 'no-lose situation' for the producers and consumers of pornography, the production of pornography is seen as a matter of public right, and hence protected, whilst its consumption is constructed as a matter of private interest, and also protected. Both public and private sides of the dichotomy are manipulated in ways which exclude anti-pornography arguments. Another twist to the conundrum comes from the ways in which the public right to pornographic expression has often been limited to the private sphere: legal regulation of pornography tends to focus on public manifestations which cause offence. This policy compromise may be functional to the meaning of pornography by in effect making pornography easily available whilst maintaining the illusion of illicitness which forms part of the power of pornography to arouse.[31]

104

In many senses, then, issues of public and private suffuse the feminist analysis and critique of the traditional construction of pornography: the private consumption of pornography inevitably impacts on the public status of women - on women's citizenship. However, in the work of several feminist lawyers, the critique of the privatization of pornography has been developed in the form of inferences from critique to practice, and to practice in a very specific legal reformist guise. I want to consider this specific attempt at reform, because I think it illustrates some of the theoretical problems I have identified, as well as some of the pitfalls of making simple inferences from theory to strategy. In response to a local grassroots movement in Minneapolis, Andrea Dworkin and Catharine MacKinnon were invited to draft an anti-pornography ordinance.[32] The political process included lengthy hearings in which many women gave painful and appalling evidence about the effect of pornography on their lives. The hearings helped to produce a political atmosphere in which pornography was widely acknowledged to be a serious social harm with a differential impact upon women. The ordinance which Dworkin and MacKinnon drafted enunciated a very broad definition of pornography as the 'graphic, sexually explicit subordination of women through pictures and/or words' which also exhibits one or more of a number of further features. These further features included the presentation of women as dehumanized sexual objects; as experiencing sexual pleasure in rape, incest, or other sexual assault; and, perhaps most controversially, in postures or positions of sexual submission, servility, or display. Pornography in these senses was conceptualized as sex discrimination – that is, as behaviour which exploits and differentially harms women. The ordinance went on to give civil causes of action for injunctions and/or damages to anyone coerced, intimidated, or fraudulently induced into performing pornography; to anyone on whom pornography is forced in a place of employment, education, home, or any public place, as against the person forcing it on them; to anyone assaulted, attacked, or injured in a way that is directly caused by specific pornography; to anyone defamed by the unauthorized use of pornography in their proper name, image, or recognizable likeness; and to any woman acting against the subordination of women or other person who alleges injury by pornography, against anyone who produces, sells, exhibits, or distributes pornography, including through private clubs.

In many respects, the ordinance represented an inspired piece of feminist legal politics. First, the conceptualization of pornography as sex discrimination placed at the heart of the legislation a feminist view of pornography. Moreover, by pitching one constitutional standard (free expression) against another (equal protection) it in effect forced the courts in the United States of America into a position where, if they were to hold the ordinance unconstitutional, they had to do so in terms which were easily interpreted as valuing an at best dubiously worthwhile form of expression over and above the removal of sex discrimination, and as valuing men's expression over the worth or even possibility of women's. Indeed, the United States Court of Appeals, which did find the ordinance to be unconstitutional, underlined these embarrassing implications of its decision by making it clear that it accepted the premises on which the ordinance was based.[33] Secondly, the reform process itself was a model of feminist political practice. The hearings gave a public voice to women whose suffering had been hidden and silenced; indeed, they constituted precisely the kind of civic forum which illustrates the inadequacy of the traditional public/private distinction and its focus on the state. Thirdly, the important choice of civil over criminal enforcement helped to some extent to defuse the accusation that the ordinance amounted to censorship. More significantly, the process of giving individual women rights of action was symbolically apt. It sought to empower women to use a legal process whose terms are generally constructed in ways which are inattentive or even hostile to the interests and needs which many women may wish to defend legally. Finally, by defining pornography *as* sex discrimination, causal links between pornography and harms to women were taken as already established. Hence the legal process was relieved from having to deal with intractable questions about the relationship between pornography and sexual violence: these would only arise legally in the specific cases where this was what the cause of action alleged.

As is well known, however, the ordinance also raised some very difficult questions for feminist politics, and generated a bitter controversy within the women's movement. At its heart, this controversy had to do with the basic shape of the feminist analysis on which the ordinance rested: in short, the claim that pornography is a *central* means of perpetuating women's oppression. Many feminists see pornography and sexual violence as epiphenomenal rather than as central: as the product of economic and other material means of subordination.[34] For the purposes of this discussion, I shall make an intermediate assumption: that is, that pornography in the forms which predominate in our culture, whilst not being a root cause of women's oppression, is a practice which does contribute to sex discrimination, not just in the sense of sexual violence but also in the sense of contributing to the low esteem in which women are held by men and, all too often, in which we hold ourselves. Pornography is by no means the only or even the most important means of degrading objectification to which women (and indeed men) are subjected in our society, but as one such form, it is of political relevance and concern. To this extent, bringing the *issue* of pornography into public debate, and the recognition of the interdependence between privately consumed pornography and the public status of women, is entirely progressive.

However, reflection on the instrumental and symbolic implications of legislation against pornography of the kind embodied in the ordinance gives serious pause for thought about how the public/private critique is to be realized in political practice. Such a legislative strategy exhibits two features which I have already suggested are among the failings of the feminist development of the critique. First, it participates in an over-concentration on the public/private *spheres* aspect of the critique at the expense of its ideological or discursive aspects. It recognizes the discursive power of pornography, but adopts a strategy which, though it has short-term attractions because of its concreteness, is likely to be discursively counter-productive in the medium term. The price of this way of constructing pornography as a public wrong is that it has to be fitted into the conceptual straitjacket of an already legally recognized harm: in the case of the ordinance, sex discrimination. But it is unlikely that all the important aspects of the feminist critique of pornography can be captured in terms of the individualized and relatively tangible harms to which both criminal and civil law have tended to address themselves and which the idea of sex discrimination evokes. Secondly and relatedly, a legislative strategy risks falling back into the assumptions made by the public/ private dichotomy itself about the importance of the state as the main source of political/regulatory power. If the power which has kept in place the negative aspects of public/private thinking inheres in a wide variety of institutions and discursive practices, the resort to state/legal reform as a means of undermining public/private divisions looks less promising than the proponents of the legislative strategy have assumed.

Of course, the relative costs and benefits of pursuing a particular legal strategy as one aspect of feminist politics may vary in different jurisdictions. The virtually absolute constitutional protection of free speech in the United States of America presented Dworkin and MacKinnon with a very constraining legal and political framework. Conversely, the greater salience of litigation strategies as part of political life in the United States of America means that the gains to be expected of such a strategy may well have been greater than in the United Kingdom. Some of the most important problems presented by a legal reform strategy against pornography, however, would arise in most jurisdictions. For example, how many women could gather the resources, financial and otherwise, to bring cases against pornography? The experience in Britain and elsewhere of individual-initiated sex discrimination litigation is not encouraging. Even in the few cases where the best legal representation is available, and even where litigants have a very firm political commitment to their cause and a great deal of emotional and material support, research suggests that they may find it a disempowering experience rather than the reverse.[35] Strategic litigation funded by pressure groups may be a more realistic possibility, but the knock-on effects of local cases such as could have been brought under the ordinance can easily be overestimated, whilst the resources which would have to be devoted to litigation strategies, as some women's groups in Canada can attest as a result of their experience under the Charter of Rights and Freedoms, are enormous.[36] Conversely, we have to consider who might use the law in question. Given the breadth of the ordinance's definition, it cannot be doubted that such a law might be exploited by right-wing litigants to attack a wide range of sexually explicit art and literature including that evoking or expressing lesbian sexuality. These, of course, are forms which radical feminists would not see as coming within the ambit of the definition because of the background equality which may be argued to be possible in principle in homosexual but not heterosexual relations. It seems unlikely that judges would confine themselves to such an interpretation. A feminist conception of pornography, already moulded to fit a legal framework, could be further distorted in the interpretive process so as to push it towards a conservative conception inimical to the direction of feminist analysis.

Nor can we assume that a reasonable proportion of cases challenging pornographic material would succeed. Problems of proof – particularly of requirements such as being 'coerced' into pornography, 'forcing' pornography on a person, an attack or injury being 'directly caused by specific pornography' – give strong reason to think that cases would be fraught with practical difficulties, and that the success rate, as in other sex discrimination cases, would be low.[37] In any event, would the remedies envisaged by the ordinance be instrumentally effective? What level of awards of damages could be realistically expected in cases where the harm involved is intangible? How often would courts be willing to award injunctions, and how effectively would or could these be policed? If injunctions were to be awarded and enforced, the argument that the law is not a form of censorship would be hard to sustain. More importantly, what would be the impact on the working conditions in the pornography production industry? The ordinance focused on victims at the production stage only in so far as they have been coerced into performing. Such a law would have no bite against the social conditions which put women into the position where they are able to be so coerced, particularly where their performance for pornography is a rational way of making a living because of the poverty of their other options.[38] It seems unlikely that a broad interpretation of coercion such as would cohere with a feminist analysis of this issue would gain a secure foothold in legal practice.

A supporter of the legislative strategy against pornography could justly object that I have been assuming that legal reform intervenes only at a concrete, material level, underplaying the discursive aspects of law and exaggerating the difference between the discursive and the material. If power inheres to an important extent in discourses, as I have argued, then influential discourses such as law *are* material in constituting social relations, and legal interventions can deploy discursive power in seeking to change the world, as well as operating at the level of the concrete. We need, then, to look also at what are sometimes called the 'symbolic' aspects of this kind of law reform. Here again, several considerations suggest that a law such as the ordinance might be counter-productive. In the first place, if the instrumental arguments just rehearsed are correct, a symbolic message follows from them: the political meaning of having an unenforceable or unenforced law on the statute books is, at best, ambiguous and, at worst, suggests that legal policy is being used as a sop to political sentiment and as a way of avoiding the need for more effective political action. An interesting analogue here is the British (criminal) law on incitement to racial hatred – an offence which is sometimes suggested as a model for anti-pornography legislation.[39] The number of successful prosecutions since this offence was first introduced has been miniscule, and the law is widely regarded as a costless (for government) sop to concern about racism which merely serves to legitimate government's relative inaction in other more potentially fruitful areas.[40] In addition, each unsuccessful prosecution implies the *legitimacy* of the racist conduct thereby condoned. A second symbolic worry about this sort of anti-pornography law lies in its openness to use by litigants motivated by other than feminist concerns, and indeed in the need (realized in the political process in Indianapolis) to build political alliances with those on the (evangelical) right in order to enact and sustain the legislation.[41] In certain quarters the pornography debate in the United States of America has increased the image of feminism as moralistic and potentially repressive. Doubtless this is to some extent inevitable: the charge of moralism is one way of trying to marginalize a view with which one disagrees. But the feminist position has been made more vulnerable because of the quick inference from the theoretical reconstruction of pornography as public to the idea that *some* instrumental regulatory strategy must be appropriate, and hence by a failure to engage in a sufficient debate about not just the efficacy but also the ethics of legal control. At a discursive level, the implications of the legislative strategy seem at best, uncertain and at worst, damaging.

FEMINIST CRITIQUE AND FEMINIST STRATEGY: A FALSE DICHOTOMY?

I have suggested that the legal reform strategy encapsulated in the Dworkin/ MacKinnon anti-pornography ordinance makes some unjustified inferences from the theory of the public/private critique to the political practice of regulation. The idea that rescuing an issue like pornography from the insulation from political critique implicit in its 'privacy' entails a regulative strategy, gets stuck within the very categories of public and private criticized earlier in this paper. For it buys into the idea of the private as the unregulated and the public as the regulated and to the idea that the relevant regulator is the state. It misses out on, or gives insufficient emphasis to, the substantive normative arguments underlying attributions of public and private which I argued earlier were a useful part of the public/private critique. It also assumes that feminist critique is in some sense deficient unless accompanied by feminist strategic action. This entails a strong dichotomy between critique and action which is questionable, not least in the light of feminist emphasis on forms of consciousness-raising as a political practice. It underestimates the importance of undermining the discursive power of attributions of public and private by reconstructing conceptions of private and public adequate to the explication and defence of feminist politics. This is a project which has to be realized through a diversity of political practices – debates, boycotts, counter-propaganda, pickets, and so on. Of course, the publicity which tends to be given to legal fora means that a court-centred strategy may have positive secondary effects for these extra-legal politics. But the risks attendant on legal strategies are acute where we try to use new legal regulation instrumentally, to realise values which command little acceptance among those who will administer the laws in question.[42]

The idea that feminist critique must always engender reformist regulatory

109

practice is, however, one which has often recommended itself to feminist lawyers. Since in my view the elision is an unfortunate one, I want to try to unsettle it by sketching the kind of feminist politics which an adequate reconceptualization of public and private would produce. To do so, I want to return to Young's conception of the public as openness to political debate and dialogue and the (legitimate) private as that area of life from which people have the right to exclude others. This conception of public and private is entirely consonant with the idea expressed earlier in the paper that human autonomy – the value *allegedly* respected by the traditional public/private divide – may require not, or not only, non-intervention, but also positive regulation, the provision of goods and facilities, education, and so on.[43] Feminist critique has exposed the ways in which sexuality, an area of life traditionally constructed as private, impacts upon women's lives in an adverse way which should not be beyond the sphere of politics. It has argued for, *and has actually engendered*, a *public*, political debate about sexuality, and about pornography in particular. Feminist arguments are perfectly consistent with the idea that sexual practices are among those from which people have the right to exclude others and the state, but point out that the range of seriously autonomy-reducing sexual practices which call for political critique and, sometimes, action go beyond those, such as rape, traditionally acknowledged to be harmful. Thus, feminist critique has put *women's* autonomy as well as men's on the political agenda.[44] By making the link between sexual subordination and citizenship status, and by pointing out the impact of oppressive sexual practices on the value of women's speech, Dworkin, MacKinnon, and others have already begun to effect a process of social re-education, consciousness-raising, and change. Their political critique has itself undermined the traditional public/private divide in that it *constitutes* a form of political action – a discursive intervention in the production of dominant meanings, albeit one which still has an uneven hold. Unless we were to believe that a legal reform strategy was likely to be very effective in furthering this discursive and educational process, a less formalized process of campaigning and consciousness-raising in regional and national political fora seems a more sensible feminist strategy.

In short, the inference from the reconstruction of pornography as a political issue to the strategy of legislating against it seems to me to be unjustified. First, it takes an unduly narrow view of the power and role of feminist critique conceived as a form of political practice. Secondly, it falls into the trap of thinking that as feminist lawyers we have to be lawyers first and feminists second – in other words, that we have to find legal solutions to all the problems identified by feminist critique. As a general assumption this is dangerous, for questions about law reform are essentially strategic and have to be assessed carefully in the context of particular reform possibilities. At least in the United Kingdom, such an assessment in the case of pornography leads, I have argued, to the conclusion that legal reform of the kind attempted in Minneapolis is likely to be a counter-productive feminist strategy. Finally, the history of the pornography debate illustrates the importance of distinguishing between different aspects of the public/private dichotomy and its deconstruction in feminist theory. The critique of public/private divisions in social, political, and legal thought cannot of itself recommend particular political strategies. What it can do, properly differentiated, is to give us a broader conception of the political and a sense of the questions we have to confront. In their work on not only pornography but also a range of other issues – abortion, sexual harassment, rape, and so on – radical feminist lawyers have made an invaluable contribution to feminist politics, irrespective of their activities around law reform. To regard legislative reform as the invariable core of feminist legal politics is to exaggerate the power of such reform and to undervalue the power of legal critique.

NOTES AND REFERENCES

1 C. Pateman, 'Feminist Critiques of the Public/Private Dichotomy', in *The Disorder of Women* (1989) 118 at 136, originally published in *Public and Private in Social Life*, eds. S. Benn and G. Gaus (1983).
2 See S. Moller Okin, *Justice, Gender, and the Family* (1989); 'Gender, the Public and the Private' in *Political Theory Today*, ed. D. Held (1985); F. Olsen, 'The Family and the Market: A Study of Ideology and Legal Reform' (1983) 96 *Harvard Law Rev.* 1497.
3 See A. M. Jaggar, *Feminist Politics and Human Nature* (1983) 207–215.
4 Jaggar suggests that the state/civil society division is an analytical feature of liberal economics whilst the market/family division is an explicitly normative feature of liberal theory (id., pp. 143–8). I do not dissent from this, but believe that the state/civil society dichotomy also has a normative dimension, whilst the market/family dichotomy is sometimes presented as descriptive.
5 J. Habermas, *The Theory of Communicative Action* (1981) Vols. 1 and 2 (transl. T. McCarthy) (1984 and 1987). For a feminist commentary on Habermas's social theory, see N. Fraser, 'What's Critical about Critical Theory? The Case of Habermas and Gender' in her *Unruly Practices: Power, Discourse, and Gender in Contemporary Social Theory* (1989) 113. On the idea of 'civic publics', see I. M. Young. *Throwing Like a Girl and Other Essays in Feminist Philosophy and Social Theory* (1990) ch. 7; *Justice and the Politics of Difference* (1990) ch. 3, 4, and 6.
6 I. M. Young, *Justice and the Politics of Difference* (1990) 240; see also Fraser, op. cit., n. 5, pp. 166–171. The importance of this kind of public sphere to social theory is shown by the way in which writers like Arendt and Habermas have been preoccupied, in various ways, with a reduction in the vigour and richness of debate in non-state fora, and with the importance of 'communicatively achieved action contexts'. The idea of the 'decline of the political' as a symptom of a worrying dilution of democracy identified by civic republican theory, is in stark contrast to the emphasis on the state which characterizes dichotomized public/private analysis.
7 J. Donzelot, *Policing the Family: Welfare Versus the State* (1979); N. Naffine, *Law and the Sexes* (1990) 69–71; C. Smart, *The Ties that Bind: Law, Marriage, and the Reproduction of Patriarchal Relations* (1984).
8 See F. Olsen, 'The Myth of State Intervention in the Family' (1985) 18 *Mich. J. Law Reform* 835.
9 On the distinction between negative and positive freedom, see below; see Berlin's influential *Four Essays on Liberty* (1989). The preference for negative as opposed to positive ideas of freedom does not characterize all forms of liberal thought: see, for example, J. S. Mill, *On Liberty* (1859); V. Haksar, *Liberty, Equality, and Perfectionism* (1979); J. Raz, *The Morality of Freedom* (1986). But the idea of freedom as non-intervention has continued to dominate liberal political theory.

10 See P. McAuslan and J. McEldowney (eds.), *Law, Legitimacy, and the Constitution* (1986).

11 The disciplinary theory of power derives from the work of Foucault; see in particular *Power/ Knowledge: selected writings and interviews* (1980); *The History of Sexuality: Volume 1* (1976) 90ff. For discussion of the implications of this theory for debates around the public/private dichotomy, see N. Rose, 'Beyond the Public/Private Division: Law, Power, and the Family' (1987) 14 *J. Law and Society* 61.

12 Mill, op. cit., n. 9.

13 H. L. A. Hart, *Law, Liberty, and Morality* (1961).

14 Wolfenden, *Report of the Committee on Homosexual Offences and Prostitution* (1957).

15 For a particularly clear statement of this position, see Okin, op. cit., n. 2, ch. 1, 2, 5, 8. Much of her immanent critique in these chapters is directed to Rawls's *A Theory of Justice* (1971).

16 Fraser, op. cit., n. 5, p. 110, n. 24. Fraser's argument in this note accords closely with the general position I want to defend in this paper.

17 See, for example, G. Lloyd, *The Man of Reason: 'Male' and 'Female' in Western Philosophy* (1984).

18 See Young, op. cit., n. 6, ch. 4.

19 See D. Cornell, *Beyond Accommodation* (1991) 92–106, especially p. 95.

20 See, for example, the vision sketched in the final pages of Olsen, op. cit., n. 2.

21 Cornell, op. cit., n. 19, ch. 4.

22 Young, op. cit., n. 6, pp. 169ff. On the danger of deconstruction's re-erecting binary oppositions where our critical thought has begun to escape them, see M. J. Radin and F. Michelman, 'Pragmatist and Poststructuralist Critical Legal Practice' (1991) 139 *Univ. Pennsylvania Law Rev.* 1019, at 1053.

23 Privacy has, of course, been an important strategic counter in certain feminist legal arguments, most notably in the context of abortion rights in the United States of America: *Roe* v *Wade* 410 US 113 (1973). This is not to say that privacy was necessarily the most advantageous conceptual framework for the protection of abortion: see C. A. MacKinnon, *Toward a Feminist Theory of the State* (1989) ch. 10.

24 For a useful discussion of privacy in terms of personhood and in the context of a clear rejection of any public/private *separation*, see M. J. Radin, 'The Pragmatist and the Feminist'. and F. Michelman, 'Private Personal but not Split' (1990) 63 *Southern California Law Rev.* 1699 and 1783 respectively.

25 op. cit., n. 2.

26 op. cit., n. 3, p. 145.

27 See J. Nedelsky, 'Reconceiving Autonomy' (1989) 1 *Yale J. of Law and Feminism* 7.

28 Young, op. cit., n. 6, pp. 119–120.

29 A. Dworkin, *Pornography: Men Possessing Women* (1981). Similar analyses are to be found in C. A. MacKinnon, *Feminism Unmodified* (1987); S. Jeffreys, *Anticlimax* (1990).

30 See S. Kappeler, *The Pornography of Representation* (1986); R. Coward, *Female Desire* (1984). For an analysis of the differences between conceptions of pornography as violence and pornography as representation, see C. Smart, *Feminism and the Power of Law* (1989) ch. 6.

31 Coward, op. cit., n. 30; MacKinnon also makes this point: 'Feminism, Marxism, Method and the State: Toward Feminist Jurisprudence' (1983) 8 *Signs* 635, although in her later work her acceptance of it is less decisive (op. cit., n. 23, pp. 200–201).

32 See A. Dworkin and C. A McKinnon, *Pornography and Civil Rights: A New Day for Women's Equality*, Organizing Against Pornography, Minneapolis (1988). The text of the ordinance is also to be found in R. Graycar and J. Morgan, *The Hidden Gender of Law* (1990) and is discussed in MacKinnon, op. cit., n. 29, Part III. See also Smart, op. cit., n. 30, ch. 6.

33 See *American Booksellers Association, Inc et al.* v *Williams Hudnut III, Mayor, City of Indianapolis, et al.* 771 F 2d 323 (7th Cir 1985). The decision was summarily upheld by the Supreme Court: 475 US (1986).

34 For varied contributions to the debate, see D. Cameron and E. Frazer, *The Lust to Kill: A Feminist Investigation of Sexual Murder* (1987); Coward, op. cit., n. 30; Dworkin, op. cit., n. 29; Jeffreys, op. cit., n. 29; MacKinnon, op. cit., n. 29; A. Rich, *On Lies, Secrets and Silence*

(1977); L. Segal, *Is the Future Female? Troubled Thoughts on Contemporary Feminism* (1987) 105–116.

35 For an assessment of the strengths and weaknesses of the individual enforcement model in sex discrimination law, see K. O'Donovan and E. Szyszczak, *Equality and Sex Discrimination Law* (1988). The limitations of the individual enforcement model are certainly not confined to the United Kingdom; see M. Thornton, *The Liberal Promise: Legislation Against Sex Discrimination in Australia* (1990).

36 See J. Fudge, 'The Effect of Entrenching a Bill of Rights upon Political Discourse: Feminist Demands and Sexual Violence in Canada' (1989) 17 *Int. J. Sociology of Law* 445; J. Fudge and H. Glasbeek, 'The Politics of Rights: A Politics with Little Class' (1992) 1 *Social and Legal Studies* 45. For a contrasting view, see the bulletins of LEAF (Women's Legal Education and Action Fund): cf. *R* v *Butler* [1992] 1 S.C.R. 452.

37 See N. Lacey, 'Legislation Against Sex Discrimination: Questions from a Feminist Perspective' (1987) 14 *J. Law and Society* 410.

38 See N. Roberts, *The Front Line* (1986).

39 Graycar and Morgan, op. cit., n. 32, p. 398.

40 For comment see N. Lacey, C. Wells, and D. Meure, *Reconstructing Criminal Law* (1990) 118–120. See also P. Fitzpatrick, 'Racism and the Innocence of Law' (1987) 14 *J. Law and Society* 119.

41 See L. Segal, *Slow Motion: Changing Masculinities, Changing Men* (1990) 225.

42 In my view, the case of pornography can be distinguished from, for example, current court-centred debates around provocation, diminished responsibility. and 'battered women's syndrome'. Here, the burden of the feminist campaign has been the oppressive way in which the existing legal position fails to recognize arguments which have already attained a degree of acceptance outside the legal sphere. The issue to which the campaign addresses itself is already and unavoidably constituted in legal terms.

43 Young herself wants to draw a distinction between autonomy and empowerment, op. cit., n. 6, p. 251. Her distinction is blurred by my formulation, but the difference between us on this point does not, I believe, affect the way in which I have drawn on her views about public and private.

44 This is not to say that autonomy is the only value which should be of political concern. It is rather to address the influential liberal argument, and show it to be wanting, even in its own terms.

A Brave New World?
Rights Discourse and the Politics of Reproductive Autonomy

New medico-technical knowledges, from *in vitro* fertilization (IVF) to ultrasound, are redrawing the boundaries between the biological and the social. As such, they are located at the centre of struggles over sexuality and gender relations. Medicine has long been used to subject women to a centralized, panoptic mode of containment reducing them to the status of objects of reproduction. However, in recent years, an anti-feminist New Right ideology emerging in Europe and North America has sought to construct rights discourses within law which redefine the interests of foetuses and fathers in the reproductive process. Attempts have been made to attribute to the foetus the status of personhood and patient, thereby asserting control over the bodies and lives of women. Similarly, the quest for genetic parenthood which informs and underpins all new reproductive technologies has found expression in an extension of the legal concept of paternity. In this context, it is hardly surprising that the practice of surrogacy and the possibility of 'virgin births' have attracted great disapprobation. In a patriarchal, phallocentric society the resistance to autonomous motherhood reveals most graphically the problematic, politicized nature of reproduction.

RATIONALITY, OBJECTIVITY, AND MORAL NEUTRALITY?

Headlines proclaimed the birth fourteen years ago of Louise Brown, the world's first test-tube baby, as 'a miracle of science'. In the years that have followed terms such as *in vitro* fertilization, egg donation, and surrogacy have become incorporated into our vocabularies. However, as much as we are fascinated, we are fearful. The elaboration of new reproductive technologies cannot but evoke the apocalyptic nightmare of Aldous Huxley's *Brave New World*. First published in 1932, his fable remains one of the most enduring of anti-utopias in that its chilling prophecy retains a capacity to prefigure current concerns and crises.[1] Huxley offers a vision of a new world order secured by a

*Lecturer in Law, Keele University, Keele, Staffs ST5 5BG, England

I would like to thank Bobbie Farsides, Gillian More, Don Rogers, Suzanne Tyler, and Jenny McEwan for their help and support.

sophisticated technological apparatus of discipline and control. Mass production and scientific management are Huxley's metaphors for debasement and de-humanization. The logic of Fordism is, of course, applied not only to production but also to reproduction.[2] Embryos are gestated in bottles, decanted in hatcheries, and carried on conveyor belts to conditioning centres where hypnosis and behaviourism are used to ascribe to them the fixed identities required by a rigid, hierarchical, scientific/biological caste system. In the brave new panoptic world, science and technology are employed to create docile minds and bodies. Order is bought at the price of a de-humanized, mechanical existence in which diversity and creativity are unthinkable and all emotion is reified and conventionalized.[3]

Brave New World throws out a challenge to science's claim to rationality, objectivity, and moral neutrality remarkably similar to feminism's challenge to law and legal ideology. Huxley questions science's triumphant status as 'father of progress'. He recognizes the relativity of science's claim to truth and, as part of a politics embracing feminism, ecology, and much more besides, scorns its emancipatory potential. Interestingly, his concerns have much in common with feminist critiques of the Enlightenment which start with the insight that science has from its very beginnings embraced a highly partial view of objectivity.[4] Contesting the assumption that science is committed to the ungendered, objective pursuit of the truth, feminism has sought to distinguish the parochial from the universal. Drawing upon the work of Nancy Chodorow and Dorothy Dinnerstein, Evelyn Fox Keller examines the binary divisions between male objectivity and female subjectivity constructed by science, and attempts to reclaim objectivity as a dialectical process.[5] Sandra Harding, however, seeks to deny the very notion of objectivity itself. Knowledge and power, she argues, are inseparable. All knowledge is socially situated, informed by the partial perspective of standpoint, and the standpoint of science is a male one.[6]

The same critique of objectivity has been applied to law. Its shiny ideological adjuncts of equality, neutrality, and universalism are just as vulnerable to charges of epistemological oppression. With its emphasis on rules, rights, and their enforcement, law fosters and privileges a historically and culturally specific form of ordering the world. Rights discourse, its ideological underpinning, speaks of an individualizing, competitive system of values in which the individual is abstracted from her or his social context. Connectedness, mutuality, and reciprocity are systematically effaced. The detached, mechanistic, deterministic view of the world, which is reflected, reinforced, and reproduced by both law and science, in the words of Shulamith Firestone, 'duplicates and exaggerates the catalogue of male vices'.[7] Both discourses are of crucial importance to feminism because they are instruments employed to silence and disempower. By denying the experience of their subject, law and science deny and degrade women's experiences.

This is symbolically revealed in the politics of 'foetal rights'. Law and science are yoked together to produce a chillingly Hobbesian representation of *man* as isolated, atomistic, and egotistical. The technology of ultrasound, for example, allows a visual image of the foetus to be presented which appears free-floating and unconnected. As such, it accords it both the appearance of an objective reality and obscures the contingent nature of its existence. In this reification of pre-natal life, the status of the pregnant woman is reduced to that of reproductive object while the foetus is presented as the personification of abstract individualism. Pro-natalists have juxtaposed images of the rights-bearing foetus with representations of conflict, competition, and distrust appropriate to the battlefield or the marketplace. Keyserlingk, for example seeks to persuade us that 'unless armed with juridical personality as the basis of *his* right to care and protection', the foetus would be 'unable to compete on a more or less equal basis with other parties with whom *his* needs and rights may be in conflict' because they would be legal persons, 'and *he* [the foetus] would remain more or less at the mercy of their ethics, whims or compassion'.[8]

A similar rights discourse, buttressed by the institutions and ideologies of science, has been appropriated by a coalition of right-wing doctors and lawyers in the United States of America to promote campaigns for curbs on abortion and restrictions on the activities of all pregnant women. 'Foetal rights', backed by sanction of criminal and civil penalties for 'foetal abuse', have become an emotive rallying cry. Pregnant women in the United States of America have been compulsorily hospitalized, subjected to non-consensual surgical interventions, and even jailed for disregarding medical advice (see below). Most prominent in this context is the issue of abortion. Mass protests outside clinics, challenges mounted in the Supreme Court, and the drafting of new restrictive legislation all too often evidence an increasing concern for the rights of the foetus at the expense of women's physical and emotional integrity.

THE FOETUS AS A LOCUS OF RIGHTS

The legal status of the foetus in both Britain and the United States of America is bedeviled with anomalies and inconsistencies. The courts have consistently and systematically avoided the question of when life comes into existence and at what point it becomes an appropriate subject of legal protection. Instead, different branches of law have elaborated doctrines of foetal rights tentatively and in isolation, each informed by different sets of assumptions and directed at different objectives. Criminal law, for example, has little interest in the foetus. Coke's classic definition of murder states that its victim must be a 'reasonable creature *in rerum natura*', interpreted in the context of foeticide as meaning totally expelled from the maternal body and capable of an existence independent of it.[9] However, in both the United Kingdom and the United States of America the foetus can be accorded retrospective legal status if it sustains injuries *in utero* but is born alive. Paradoxically, to harm a foetus may attract a criminal sanction, while to destroy it may not. To rectify the anomaly, several states in the United States of America have now amended homicide statutes to include a foetus which dies *in utero*, thereby placing pregnant women within reach of the electric chair.

The principle that a foetus has no independent legal status is similarly recognized in tort. In the United Kingdom there is no cause of action for prenatal death. In *Bagley* v *North Hertfordshire Health Authority* ([1986] N.L.J. Rep. 1014), the defendant's failure to carry out a necessary blood analysis on a pregnant woman resulted in a stillbirth. Simon Brown J, giving judgment, ruled that a claim for grief, sorrow, and loss of society was barred as a *child* had not died.[10] In the United States of America many states permit claims for wrongful death. The concern, however, is with compensating prospective parents for their presumed financial interest in having a healthy child rather than with attributing juridical personality to the foetus. As in criminal law, the legal status of the foetus can in both jurisdictions be recognized retrospectively. In England and Wales, the Congenital Disabilities (Civil Liability) Act 1976, passed to plug a potential loophole highlighted by the thalidomide tragedy, confirms liability for injury sustained *in utero* but protects pregnant women from coercive interventions by creating only a prospective, contingent right. The legislation distinguishes itself by embracing a doctrine of derivative liability serving to frustrate any claim founded on the negligence of the mother. Thus, a tortfeasor will be liable to a child only if also liable to the child's mother.[11] In the United States of America, however, a woman who failed to inform her doctor that she was pregnant and was therefore prescribed drugs which caused damage to her child's teeth was liable for prenatal negligence. The reasonableness of her conduct was judged against an objective, universal standard.[12]

A woman's responsibility for the well-being of her foetus is quite distinct from the responsibility which individuals are generally recognized by the law as having for each other. Thus, a court contemptuously dismissed a leukaemia sufferer's attempt to compel a relative to donate potentially life-saving bone marrow as causing 'revulsion to the judicial mind', yet the 'duty to rescue' is routinely imposed on pregnant women.[13] Moreover, there is a growing body of case law in which rights of custody over a foetus have been conferred on third parties. A recent case in New York bears witness to the extraordinary officiousness of the foetal rights lobby. Hoping to increase her chance of recovery, the partner of a pregnant woman in a coma following an accident sought guardianship in order to have her pregnancy terminated. Claiming to represent the interests of the foetus, third parties intervened in an attempt to have the Supreme Court stay the order.[14] Although the applicants clearly lacked standing (and hence the challenge failed), here and in other contexts the long-established principle that a foetus can have no essential juridical status has been somewhat undermined. By conflating the foetus and the child, and conveniently ignoring the implications for the woman on whom the foetus is dependent, courts have sanctioned both the prenatal incarceration and postnatal prosecution of pregnant women labelled as 'recalcitrant'. Women's perceptions of their best interests have been disdained and overridden by doctors, lawyers, and judges. Surgical procedures including caesarian sections, cervical suturings, and *in utero* blood transfusions have been authorized with little argument, publicity, or protest.[15] Although competent adults are at liberty to refuse medical treatment, pregnant women in the United States of America suspend their constitutional rights and are required to subsume their identity, will, and bodily integrity. The foetal harm laws which are emerging in some jurisdictions render every aspect of women's lives – from work, leisure, diet, sex, and even to movement – a legitimate target of surveillance.

In the United States of America as elsewhere, women's reproductive autonomy has long been regulated. In the nineteenth century contraception and abortion were criminalized, in part to sustain the birth rate among the prosperous, white, Protestant population. In the twentieth century, the attentions of the state have been directed at the underclass. In the early 1900s the state pursued policies of compulsory sterilization, ostensibly as an attempt to eradicate the assumed biological givens of 'criminality' and 'mental retardation'.[16] The 1980s saw a revival of interest in regulating women's reproductive autonomy. However, the policing of the details of the lives of all pregnant women is invasive, expensive, and impracticable. Instead, the state opts for the supervision of a small number of women, invariably those least able to offer resistance. More than eighty per cent of obstetrical interventions ordered by the courts are directed against black, Asian, and Hispanic women.[17] In some states, poor women are forced to use contraception as a condition of receiving welfare benefit.[18]

Notwithstanding these caveats, the American foetus is not as yet a legal subject. The 1973 landmark ruling in *Roe* v *Wade*, enshrining a woman's constitutional right to abortion, remains an authority, undermined but not overturned.[19] Implicit in the fourteenth amendment is a fundamental right to privacy, interpreted broadly enough to include the right to terminate a pregnancy in the first trimester. In *Webster* v *Reproductive Health Services Inc*, a highly politicized challenge in the newly conservative Supreme Court, the legitimate scope for the state regulation of pregnancy was expanded. *Webster* affirmed the right of individual states to pass legislation withdrawing public funding and the use of public facilities for the provision of abortion unless necessary to save the life of the pregnant women and to institute extensive testing for viability after twenty weeks gestation, approving a statute 'finding' life to begin at conception.[20] In June 1992 the Supreme Court delivered the long-awaited decision in *Planned Parenthood of south-eastern Pennsylvania* v *Robert Casey*.[21] The defendant Governor was signatory to a statute which sought to qualify *Roe* by imposing four new conditions: the mandatory provision of literature on the risks and alternatives to abortion; a twenty-four hour waiting period before the operation; limits on its availability to minors; and an obligation on married women to seek the formal consent of their partners. As anticipated, the court struck out only the spouse approval clause and ruled that the state could impose 'reasonable restrictions' upon women's reproductive choice.[22] Similar pieces of legislation which lie on the statute book in Alabama, Idaho, Kansas, Maine, and North Dakota are now likely to be implemented.

Packed with the political appointments of Ronald Reagan and George

Bush, the Supreme Court is engaged in a relentless war of attrition against women's reproductive autonomy. While appearing to adhere to the letter of *Roe* v *Wade*, because it enshrines a general right to privacy which is cherished by interest groups other than women, it has undermined its spirit by introducing conditions and qualifications which have made and will make abortion impossible for many women.[23] Since 1978 the Supreme Court has upheld the prerogative of state and federal government to withhold public funding for 'non-therapeutic' abortion. Every year one quarter of a million pregnant women on Medicare discover that they are denied access to safe, legal abortions. Women in the army, airforce, and marines, and the partners of men employed by the forces are barred by executive decree from having abortions in United States military hospitals. Women entitled to federal government medical insurance and Native American women whose health services are provided by the Bureau of Indian Affairs are similarly expected to find alternative sources of funding.[24] Moreover, the last two Republican administrations have circumscribed the elsewhere much-cherished right to free speech by prohibiting federally funded clinics from even providing abortion advice and counselling.

RIGHTS DISCOURSE, AUTONOMY, AND PATERNALISM

However, the problem is not only the rolling back of *Roe*. Ironically, the very structure of the decision has opened the door to the state regulation of women's bodies and lives. As a direct, albeit not inevitable, consequence of the form in which the right to abortion is articulated, pregnant women in the United States of America who refuse to conform to accepted norms of maternal behaviour suspend fundamental constitutional rights. In founding a right to privacy, the court in *Roe* also claimed that the State had 'an important and legitimate interest in protecting the potentiality of human life'. In the first, heady days it was assumed that the state's interest must necessarily and inevitably be subordinated to a woman's right to reproductive autonomy. But as the political landscape shifted, the content and structure of the decision were distinguished. 'Parties' to a pregnancy were constructed and their respective rights and interests framed in terms of the three trimesters of pregnancy. In the first trimester the right to privacy generally precludes state intervention; in the second, the issue is constructed in terms of maternal health, and in the third the state acquires a compelling interest in safeguarding potential life. Foetal rights campaigners in the United States of America, characterizing a woman's 'freedom to choose' as a 'freedom to *abuse*' have subverted this shifting framework of rights in an attempt to compel the state to protect a viable foetus.

Where doctors have claimed a foetus has little chance of survival without a blood transfusion or a caesarian section, courts in North America have ignored claims to freedom of religion and bodily integrity and have ordered non-consensual obstetrical interventions. As only a handful of cases are reported, the extent of such interventions remains unknown. Some studies suggest, however, that courts are willing to authorize treatment in between seventy-five and eighty-five per cent of cases.[25] In one of the earliest cases, decided prior to *Roe* v *Wade*, the Supreme Court of New Jersey authorized a hospital to administer a blood transfusion to a Jehovah's Witness who was thirty-two weeks pregnant.[26] The reasoning was cursory and confused. The court reviewed cases in which medical treatment could be compelled in order to save a child and cases where recovery was available in tort for injuries sustained *in utero*, and conflated the two only tangentially related sets of issues in a conclusion which asserted a foetus's right to legal protection. No consideration was given to the issue of a woman's right to privacy, autonomy, and bodily integrity. More recently, on similar facts, the Supreme Court of New York declined to distinguish the born and the unborn and assumed it to be entirely unproblematic to exercise a wardship jurisdiction over a foetus, notwithstanding the implications for the pregnant woman.[27] An application to stay a compulsory blood transfusion and caesarian section claimed by doctors to be necessary in order to save a thirty-nine-week-old foetus was refused by the Supreme Court of Georgia. The wishes of the pregnant woman were 'outweighed by the duty of the State to protect a living unborn human being from meeting his or her death'. As in so many of these cases, medical opinion masquerades as incontrovertible fact. The baby was in fact quite uneventfully delivered vaginally.[28] More problematic still was the tragic case of Angela Cardner. Here, a caesarian section was authorized, against the wishes of a terminally-ill pregnant woman and her family, in an attempt to salvage a potentially viable, twenty-six-week-old foetus. The court ruled that the state had an interest in protecting the foetus but could not infringe upon a pregnant woman's right to bodily integrity 'unless to do so will not significantly affect the health of the mother and unless the child has a significant chance of being born alive'.[29] Although all parties agreed that surgery would hasten her death, the operation was performed. Two days later the court offered its condolences to the family for the loss of both mother and baby. A death certificate recorded the caesarian as a contributory cause of death.

Childcare legislation in the United States of America has been expanded retroactively to cover the gestational period. Here the sanction is not obstetrical intervention but preventive detention. In one of the first cases considered by the courts, a social services department sought custody of a foetus carried by a woman with a history of child abuse.[30] In determining whether a child was at risk of neglect or abuse, the court considered it appropriate to examine antenatal conduct. Although it rejected the application, stating that a foetus could not be included in the term 'child' within the meaning of the legislation, the court extended an existing order on somewhat spurious, unrelated grounds. However, when the foetus is clearly at risk, the courts have granted protective jurisdiction. For example, courts in New York have intervened to protect a foetus carried by a woman who was a victim of domestic violence and in a case where a woman's heavy drinking and refusal to seek medical attention put the health of a foetus in jeopardy.[31]

However, increasingly, it is the criminal law which is invoked. The social base from which women targeted for the paternalistic attentions of the state are drawn and the current moral panic about drug abuse in the United States of America combine to rob women of the power to resist. When conviction is unlikely, remand serves the same purposes as sentencing. In 1980 a court in Los Angeles attempted to detain a woman convicted of a minor offence for the duration of her pregnancy, not on the basis of a tariff model of sentencing but in order to prevent potential harm to the foetus. Although the order was reversed on appeal, the woman was still detained for six weeks, awaiting the decision.[32] In 1988 in the District of Columbia a pregnant woman convicted of forgery and found to be using cocaine was jailed for the duration of her pregnancy in order to protect the foetus.[33] More recently, even the avoidance of pregnancy has become the legitimate concern of the criminal law. The first, highly publicized, use of a new implantable contraceptive occurred when a judge in California offered a woman convicted of child abuse a 'choice' between imprisonment and mandatory contraception.[34]

Where antenatal conduct has escaped regulation, the sanction of postnatal prosecution remains. In 1977 a woman in California was prosecuted for felonious child-endangering after giving birth to twins addicted to heroin.[35] At that time, however, the offence could be committed only against a child. In 1986, again in California, Pamela Rae Stewart became the first woman in the United States of America to be prosecuted for antenatal conduct said to contribute to a child's death.[36] It was alleged that she refused to take prescribed medication, failed to alert her doctor to heavy bleeding, and used quantities of amphetamines and cannabis. She was charged with the offence of wilfully omitting to provide a minor child with necessary care, amended by the state to cover a 'child conceived but not yet born'. The case was dismissed and the wisdom of prosecuting under legislation intended to guarantee support for children and pregnant women was pondered by the court. But the very fact that she was charged at all is revealing and begs the question of the appropriateness of using criminal legislation to deal with maternal recalcitrance. Yet, in Florida a woman has recently been convicted of 'delivering' illegal drugs to a child via the umbilical cord. She was charged under a statute intended to be used against dealers, in which the maximum sentence is thirty years imprisonment, and was given a fifteen-year probation order which will include the detailed surveillance of any future pregnancies.[37] In many states, statutes are now being passed to include a foetus as potential victim of homicide. In Massachusetts, South Carolina, and Kansas state penal code provisions have been interpreted to include the foetus. Specific foeticide offences have been enacted in Illinois, Minnesota, Indiana, and Iowa.[38]

In tort, family, and criminal law, the pattern is one of increasing state interference in private lives. Yet no court has examined in detail the constitutional principles which have, in contexts other than pregnancy, been painstakingly elaborated in order to safeguard individual rights. Hearings are often conducted in the delivery room. The women on whose bodies an intended intervention will take place are rarely present or represented. The constraints of a timescale dictated by biology and the social base from which the women forced to be subjected to these invasive and dangerous surgical procedures are drawn combine in such a way as to produce few reported decisions and little scope for public scrutiny or serious debate.

In the United Kingdom the courts have until now declined to exercise a *parens patriae* jurisdiction over a foetus, and the issue has yet to be considered by the House of Lords. In *Re F* (see above, note 29), to date the only direct attempt to seek judicial intervention to protect the unborn, the claim by a local authority for a care and custody order over a foetus carried by a woman whose lifestyle posed a threat to its well-being was rejected. To confer rights on a foetus of a kind capable of overriding a woman's right to self-determination, it was accepted, would serve to construct a conflict of rights which, under a jurisdiction premised on the welfare of the ward of court, would necessarily and inevitably be resolved in favour of a foetus. The court concluded that a change in the law which would impose a rigorous surveillance and subjugation of all pregnant women could only be authorized by Parliament. However, even in the United Kingdom, where the attempt to regulate the pregnant body has not yet demanded its incarceration, the courts in other contexts have been less attentive to encroachments into women's reproductive autonomy and less rigorous in their reasoning. In *Re D* the House of Lords was willing to take into consideration a woman's antenatal conduct when deciding if 'a child's proper development had been avoidably prevented or its health had been avoidably impaired' for the purposes of granting a care order.[39] Although foetal rights only crystallize on birth, the legal construction of a continuum of needs could easily be subverted and expanded to legitimate North American-style prenatal invasions such as forcible caesarian sections, blood trans-fusions, and foetal surgery, admissions to detoxification programmes, and sanctions under criminal law. In October 1992 came Britain's first caesarian section ordered by a court. The family division of the High Court conceded there was little authority for the intervention, but approved it none the less, relying on a misreading of the tragic, now discredited case of Angela Cardner. Ironically, lost to Stephen Brown J, giving judgment, was the fact that after her death the decision was overruled, a victory which marked a turning-point in the United States of America in the struggle for reproductive autonomy. The only comfort in this case is that reasoning is so fatally flawed, it could not survive the scrutiny of the House of Lords.[40]

THE JURIDIFICATION OF PARENTHOOD

Elsewhere, even where the legal decision is to be celebrated the reasoning may be problematic in other respects. In *C v S* a man seeking an injunction to prevent his former partner from having a legal abortion was denied a cause of action as progenitor, putative father, or protector of the unborn.[41] Here, the legal problem of the juridical status of the foetus was sidestepped and, in an attempt to depoliticize it, translated into a medical problem, namely the viability of the foetus. The case was concerned with the status of scientific knowledge, not the allocation of rights. The new conceptive technologies serve even more acutely to crystallize anxieties about the future of gender relations in that they imply a complex, problematic notion of parenthood. IVF, egg donation, and surrogacy mean that motherhood is no longer a self-evident unitary concept. It is fragmented, divisible into its constituent ovarian, uterine, and social functions. The development of the artificial womb could render the whole concept of motherhood, and indeed womanhood, an anachronism. However, these new medico-technical knowledges are in theory capable of posing a much greater threat to fatherhood. It is precisely for this reason that among recent publicized practices in reproduction, it is surrogacy and the availability of IVF to women who are not in stable, heterosexual relationships which have attracted the greatest anxiety, anger, and calls for action. The publicly stated rationalization of the Warnock Committee's unqualified condemnation of surrogacy draws on fears about the commercialization of childbirth. But underlying our concerns about the buying and selling of babies are powerful cultural assumptions about the nature of sex, gender, and the family. Surrogacy exposes the mother/child relationship as fragile and contingent. IVF, however, may reinforce that bond by denying a role to men. Surrogacy and IVF have both become a site for the expression of collective fears about the trend towards autonomous motherhood.

As a powerful symbol of possessive individualism, fathering unites the concerns of the 'New Right' and the men's movement. Although the emphasis on biology is historically and culturally specific, as a symbol of continuity and connection blood ties represent a powerful cultural theme. The paradox of the new reproductive technologies is that the means of permitting a few privileged heterosexual couples to become genetic parents renders the entire concept of genetic parenthood problematic. In vitro fertilization, egg donation, and surrogacy challenge the assumption that genetic parenthood necessarily implies a familial relationship. It is in the context of the disintegration of the trinity of sex, marriage, and the family that fears, particularly male fears, have begun to crystallize. The new-found intensity of interest in fathering has its roots firmly in the tensions in family structures and arrangements. The complexity of new sets of relationships necessarily leads to concern and confusion about the meaning of familial relationships, specifically connections and claims to children. Given the minimal commitment that fathering implies, what is certain is that the weakening or severing of blood ties poses a powerful challenge to the hierarchy of the 'traditional' nuclear family.

Against these currents flow powerful countercurrents. The development of new reproductive technologies has been interpreted as an attempt to appropriate women's difference and unique source of power.[42] Mary O'Brien argues that men's alienation from reproduction underpins their desire to control our bodies. In order to secure biological continuity and political control, historically men have constructed institutions designed to check our autonomy. Drawing heavily on the work of Engels,[43] she explains that in the pre-male, pre-property society of 'primitive communism' both sexes contributed to the fulfilment of common subsistence needs. Even in early property society, no differential status attached to the roles of women and men and all property was inherited through the female line. At some ill-defined point, however, men disposed of this curious social complication and property henceforth was inherited through the male line. The 'world historic defeat of the female sex' heralded the emergence of the public, property-owning male world and its Cartesian 'other', the private non-property-owning female world. Under 'mother-right' succession was self-evident. However, once inheritance was secured through men it became crucial for them to locate their children. Given the fear that one man's child might have had a claim to another man's fortune, there emerged a need to institute a new sexual morality which demanded chastity and monogamy of all women. The market for reproductive technology is underpinned by this desire for a child 'of one's own'. What distinguishes many of the new medico-technical knowledges from anything that has gone before is that they offer men the potential to assert control over women's reproductive capacities, and thereby transform themselves into the fathers of mankind.

The elaboration of these technologies coincides with demands from anti-feminist men's groups to greater access to and control over children. In the United States of America there is a burgeoning literature drawing on Robert Bly's newfound 'father hunger' (*Iron John: A Book about Men* (1990)). In the United Kingdom, groups such as Families Need Fathers and The Campaign for Justice in Divorce have sought to challenge what they claim to be women's privileged position in family law. Women, however, have never had anything approaching the nineteenth-century fathers' absolute rights to children. While some Court of Appeal decisions appear to give weight to the arguments expressed by the men's movement,[44] recent cases, though difficult to reconcile, unite in a retreat from the assumption that women have an exclusive claim to custody of children. Courts retain an absolute discretion which they exercise according to their conception of the best interests of the child. The focus on the child is a leveller not of paternal rights but of parental rights. The welfare principle, vague and ill-defined, operates to the disadvantage of women who do not conform to a narrow stereotype of appropriate maternal conduct. The courts do not so much secure a privileged position for women as mothers as reflect judicial perceptions of the prevailing sexual division of labour.[45] Lesbian or otherwise sexually autonomous women remain vulnerable to a detailed surveillance of their sexual lives.

The focus of the fathers' rights lobby is joint custody. Court orders, however, offer no guarantee of joint parental care and responsibility. The movement embraces the welfarist, child protection ideology and subverts it to legitimate control over women, most powerfully expressed in terms of punishment for sexual transgression. It questions the competence of the courts to determine 'the best interests' of the child by reference to the 'common sense and ordinary humanity' which characterized older judicial homilies. Instead, attempts have been made to import the truth claims of carefully chosen pieces of psychology in order to guarantee unlimited access to fathers. But much more importantly, the movement seeks to use the principle of equality against women by asserting that they are 'having it both ways' by enjoying 'preferential treatment' in the context of child custody. Yet, a gender-neutral approach, premised on the assumption that equality can be secured through assimilation, is clearly inappropriate. It refuses to acknowledge the advantages which accrue to men from the current sexual division of labour. Joint custody orders can be exploited as a lever to gain access to and exercise control over not only children but also women. As Brophy argues, they may be 'a mechanism for the projection and continuation of a power relationship'.[46] Ultimately, men's control over children is control over women.

Custody is an area where feminism has engaged in ultimately futile sameness and difference debates only because it comes to the debate reactively. It is male agendas which have defined the parameters of the debate.[47] The Aristotelian assumption that 'things that are alike should be treated alike, while things that are unalike should be treated unalike in proportion to their unalikeness'[48] dictates that if similarly situated people are treated differently they are discriminated against. If differently situated people are treated differently, they are not discriminated against. However, in the context of pregnancy, this whole sameness/difference debate is circular.[49] It fails to challenge the assumptions of the Aristotelian paradigm of equality. Both strategies judge women against a male referent or comparator. Thus, while the sameness argument only offers a remedy to women whose biographies approximate to their male comparators, the difference argument gives resonance to stereotypes of women as weak and in need of protection.

In the context of custody, men's assertion that women are having it both ways is an artefact of the narrow constraints within which the debate is conducted. The lobby talks of rights but not responsibility. The 'preferential treatment' argument obscures the time, energy, and commitment of women carers. Its curious synthesis of rights and welfarist discourses refuses to engage with the economic and social consequences of pregnancy, childbirth, and childcare. Any position which ignores inequality within marriage because of the overarching principle of formal legal equality will necessarily entrench that inequality. The best interests test, as Klaff so forcefully argues, should be replaced by an evidentiary presumption in favour of the primary carer.[50] As Catharine MacKinnon argues, feminist issues are more appropriately framed in terms of hierarchy and power than equal rights.[51]

FEMINISM, REPRODUCTIVE TECHNOLOGY, AND ANTI-UTOPIA

The reason *Brave New World* has withstood the test of time is not only because its science fiction anticipates social fact. Huxley speaks about 'universals', the primary relations which shape the totality of human existence; production, reproduction, their appropriation, reduction to a mechanical act, and our alienation from them. His concerns are curiously evocative of MacKinnon's tantalizing yet problematic claim that 'sexuality is to feminism what work is to

Marxism; that which is most one's own, yet most taken away'.[52] In an earlier incarnation of radical feminism, Shulamith Firestone similarly substitutes the contradictions of production and reproduction in an attempt to construct what she describes as a 'materialist view of history based on sex itself'.[53] Drawing on the work of Marx and Engels, she argues that the material base of society is constituted by the pre-social reality of biology and that the ideological superstructure, the ideas and institutions which nurture and sustain patriarchy, are, in the final analysis, determined by that biological base. By claiming a woman's body to be not only the site of oppression but ultimately its source, she argues the need to radically redefine our relationship to reproduction. To this end she embraces the promise of embryology within a larger vision of a 'cybernetic' socialism. If women's reproductive capacity and a division of labour based on that capacity necessitates their subordination then emancipation from the tyranny of biology can only be found in a feminist vision of a brave new world.

The construction of mothering as part of an ideological superstructure determined by a biological base was crucial to the task of reclaiming the personal as political. Yet in exploding the myth of the public/private divide, Firestone inadvertently constructs agendas on the basis of many problematic liberal assumptions. Implicit in the elimination of difference is the assimilation of women to a male standard. From the mid 1970s, however, feminism embraced a 'woman-centred' politics. Its celebration of difference, focusing on mothering, sexuality, and subjectivity as sources of value, made Firestone's faith in progress appear not only fanciful but misguided. More importantly, her methodology can be criticized for its uncritical substitution of contradictions.[54] One consequence is that the relationship between reproduction and production can only be addressed at the level of a theory divorced from politics. Paradoxically, any analysis of the detailed relationship between reproductive technologies and the needs of monopoly capitalism is barred. In the late twentieth century, the global distribution of biotechnology is intimately connected to the internationalization of capital. As Monica Sjoo and Barbara Mor argue:

> . . . it is no longer possible to speak of a labour force separate from women workers . . . and by the same token, it is no longer possible to analyse the management of labour production separately from the management of female reproduction.[55]

In the free trade zones of the Third World, national governments collude with multinational corporations, guaranteeing the supply of cheap, docile female labour. The whole biotech industry is driven by the private investment of pharmaceutical and medical supply companies, sometimes augmented by apparently unconnected institutions. Robert Edwards's pioneering research into IVF was, for example, funded by the Ford Foundation. In the 1980s the politics of research science shifted significantly and the relationship between the academy and government laboratories with industrial and military interests became increasingly intimate.[56]

Firestone is not so naïve, however, as to assume that because women's oppression originates in biology that women will necessarily and inevitably be

126

free if that basis is removed. She acknowledges that 'the new technology . . . may be used against them to reinforce the entrenched system of exploit-ation.'[57] The consequences of reproductive technology depend on culture and context. Science is neither monolithic nor determined. Certainly, the rolling back of science cannot guarantee a relinquishing of control to women. Exploitation does not occur only in technological society. In her apocalyptic anti-utopia, *The Handmaid's Tale* (1985), Margaret Atwood takes Andrea Dworkin's 'reproductive brothel' model of regulating women's reproductive lives and applies it to a post-holocaust world ruled by fundamentalist Christians. Fertility is so prized that it has been appropriated as a national resource. Women who possess viable ovaries are forcibly conscripted as handmaids to the households of the powerful. A process of pre-conception resocialization transforms them into docile reproductive vessels. Like cattle, they are penned in together, interchangeable, their individuality effaced, their reproductive capacities commodified. In both Dworkin's account of the medico-technological management of pregnancy and birthing and Atwood's vision of a post-technological future, women are objects in a biological system constructed in the interests of patriarchy. Yet both accounts are limited in failing to acknowledge women's power and ability to resist.

COUNTER HEGEMONIC STRATEGIES

That resistance is at the centre of Calliope Farsides's powerful plea for the creation of a concept of property in the female body.[58] Foetal harm laws in the United States of America render every aspect of women's behaviour a legitimate target of surveillance. Interventions ordered by the courts, which disdain women's decisions about care of the self, reveal women can still be excluded from the ideology of universal rights whenever expedient. Americans, as Purdy says, 'have more say over what happens to their bodies after death than many women do . . . while they are still alive'.[59] Crucial in the political struggle for control and empowerment is the rejection of centralized, panoptic, and male-dominated medico-technical models of surveillance and regulation. Farsides's interest is as much symbolic as instrumental. In a culture in which women are intimately identified with the body there is a 'complex relationship between our experience of ourselves as bodies and the creation of our selves as moral and political agents'.[60] This insight leads her to argue for the need to construct new images and metaphors for women's experiences. This process is already underway. Certainly, women have won partial victories in de-medicalizing childbirth, reasserting control of their bodies through the rediscovery of midwifery.[61] Reproductive technology, however, is central to the attempt to control women by appropriating and imposing new definitions on their bodily experiences. The medical model which it draws upon isolates and alienates. It sees pregnancy and birthing in terms of disease and dysfunction. The definition of infertility as illness provides an opportunity for increased medical control with implications for all women. The new technologies are increasingly used on healthy women, their fertility appropriated to the domain of medical expertise. As Patricia Spallone maintains, 'IVF is not about infertility, but rather is being applied to women in the name of infertility therapy.'[62] Problematically, this precludes discussion of the causes of infertility and imposes on all women the expectation that childlessness is to be equated with failure, that womanhood is capable of being redeemed by science, the father of progress.

Sixty years on, the chilling nightmare of *Brave New World* still has a resonance. Technology, however, is not a monolithic whole. The abstract determinism of Huxley's anti-utopia denies the power and the creativity of women. Our bodies do not determine our social beings. It is the meanings that society ascribes to them that does. Feminism plays a pivotal role in creating and recreating those meanings. Both legal and scientific discourses by their very nature disempower and depoliticize. In the United States of America the framing of the abortion issue in terms of rights has robbed women of the potential to develop any notion of property in their bodies. In the United Kingdom, the absence of a rights discourse in the politics of abortion and the tragedy of Thalidomide have until now spared us the judge in the delivery room. The existence and ethos of the National Health Service raises very different issues of provision and entitlement. Here, resource management has become the unseen, unaccountable, and less obviously political means of denying reproductive choice. The 1967 Abortion Act declines to enact a constitutional right. As Gibson points out, we 'confront a legal miasma'. Therefore, she continues, 'there is no direct legal action in which subjects may enjoin and debate'.[63] Rights discourse, the common sense of liberal legalism, at least provides us with a forum for resistance.[64] In April 1992 three-quarters of a million women marched past the White House, demanding the right to abortion. As either objectives or rhetoric, rights may offer us the opportunity to 'enjoin and debate'. Feminism, however, insists upon the need to redefine conceptual frameworks and agendas. The new medico-technical expertises have politicized sex, parenthood, and the family. To the extent that they are located at the very centre of struggles about sexuality and gender relations, reproductive technologies must be recognized as a key concern of a feminist jurisprudence which gives a voice not to abstract, ungendered rights but to women's experience.

NOTES AND REFERENCES

1 A. Huxley, *Brave New World* (1932).
2 See F. W. Taylor, *The Principles of Scientific Management* (1911).
3 See K. Kumar, *Utopia and Anti-Utopia in Modern Times* (1987).
4 E. Fox Keller, 'Feminism and Science' in *Feminist Theory: A Critique of Ideology*, eds. N. O. Keohane et al. (1982).
5 id.
6 S. Harding, *Whose Science? Whose Knowledge?* (1991) 10.

7 S. Firestone, *The Dialectic of Sex: The Case for a Feminist Revolution* (1970) 206.

8 E. Keyserlingk, 'The Unborn Child's Right to Prenatal Care – A Comparative Perspective' (1984) *McGill Legal Studies* 79 (my italics).

9 *R* v *Poulton* (1832) 5 P. & C. 25; *Sellis* (1837) 7 P. & C. 850; *Handley* (1874) 13 Cox CC 79. In the USA it has been more recently reaffirmed that the foetus must survive outside the womb before a murder charge can be brought. See *Hollis* v *Commonwealth of Kentucky* (1983) SW 2d 61.

10 Damages were available, under two heads, totalling more than the figure of £3,500 payable under similar circumstances to the bereaved parents of a newborn under the Fatal Accidents Act 1976.

11 Under section 2, the legal requirement that drivers hold third-party insurance underpins maternal liability for prenatal injuries in road accidents. See Law Commission, *Injuries to Unborn Children* (1974; Cmnd. 5709) paras. 32–33. A Belfast case recently held a mother liable in negligence in this context. For the common law position on liability for injuries sustained *in utero*, see now *Burton* v *Islington Area Health Authority* [1992] 3 All E.R. 833.

12 *Grodin* v *Grodin* (1981) NW 2d 869 Mich. 14. But in *Stallman* v *Youngquist* 1988) 531 NE 2d 355, to hold a woman liable in this context was held to be a derogation of her constitutional rights to privacy, liberty, and equal protection.

13 *McFall* v *Shimp* (1978) 10 Pa D & C 3d 90.

14 D. Meyers, *The Human Body and the Law* (1990) 13.

15 J. Gallagher, 'Prenatal Invasions and Interventions: What's Wrong with Foetal Rights?' (1987) 10 *Harvard Women's Law J.*; see also E. Sutherland, 'Regulating Pregnancy: Should We and Can We?' in *Family Rights: Family Law and Medical Advance*, eds. E. Sutherland and A. McCall Smith (1988) 107.

16 R. Lee and D. Morgan, 'A Lesser Sacrifice? Sterilization and Mentally Handicapped Women' in *Birthrights: Law and Ethics at the Beginning of Life* (1989) 135.

17 Meyers, op. cit., n. 14, p. 10.

18 In the past year, welfare reform legislation has been enacted in New Jersey and Wisconsin which denies child support payments to women who become pregnant on welfare. Wisconsin's 'Parental and Family Initiative' further penalizes single women who have children. Similar proposals are currently under consideration in California, Virginia, and Maine.

19 (1973) 410 US 113.

20 (1989) US 109 SC 3040.

21 *The Economist*, 4 July 1992.

22 A. Cockburn, 'Almost Free to Choose' *New Statesman*, 3 July 1992, p. 16. The day after *Casey*, perhaps in anticipation of a different outcome, the House Judiciary Committee approved the Freedom of Choice Act which, subject to very minor qualifications, seeks to codify *Roe* as federal law.

23 The Supreme Court is yet to hear appeals on much more restrictive state legislation from Utah and Louisiana, but following *Casey* an outright challenge to *Roe* is unlikely to succeed.

24 (1992) 339 *The Lancet* 1104–5, 2 May 1992.

25 V. Holder et al., 'Court Ordered Obstetrical Intervention' (1987) 316 *The New England J. of Medicine* 1194, 19 May 1987, cited in L. Purdy, 'Are Women Foetal Containers?' (1990) 4 *Bioethics* 273. The campaign is likely to intensify. A recent poll taking in California found that fifty-three per cent of women and forty-three per cent of men favour holding a pregnant woman responsible for harm done to the foetus by smoking and drinking. See Meyers, op. cit., n. 14, p. 13.

26 *Raleigh Fitkin-Paul Memorial Hospital* v *Anderson* (1964) 201 A 2d 537 NJ.

27 *Re Jamaica Hospital* 491 NYS 2d SC (1985).

28 *Jefferson* v *Griffin Spalding County Hospital Authority* (1988) 274 SE 2d 457 Ga, at 460.

29 *Re AC* (1988) 539 A 2d DC. The test was rejected as impossible to quantify by the British courts in *Re F* [1989] 2 F.L.R. 376.

30 *Bay County in re Dittrick, infant* (1977) 263 NW 2d 37 Mich.

31 *Gloria C* v *William C* (1984) NY App 474 NYS 2d 991; *Re Smith* (1985) NY App 492 NYS 2d 331.

32 Cited in (1990) *Harvard Law Rev.* 1573.

33 id.

34 *The Lancet*, op. cit., n. 24.

35 *Reyes* v *Superior Court* (1977) 75 Cal App 2d 214.

36 Meyers, op. cit., n. 14, p. 116.

37 (1990) *Harvard Law Rev.* 1330.

38 A pregnant woman is specifically excluded in the Illinois and Minnesota legislation.

39 *Re D (a minor)* v *Berkshire County Council* [1987] 1 All E.R. 20.

40 *Re S, The Guardian* 20 October 1992.

41 *C* v *S* [1988] Q.B. 135.

42 M. O'Brien, *The Politics of Reproduction* (1981).

43 F. Engels, *The Origins of the Family, Private Property, and the State* (1884).

44 Roxburgh J. in *Re S* [1958] 1 W.L.R. 391 states that 'the prima facie rule . . . is that all things being equal, children . . . should be with their mother'.

45 S. Maidment, 'Women and Childcare: The Paradox of Divorce' in *Gender, Sex, and the Law*, ed. S. Edwards (1985).

46 J. Brophy and C. Smart, *Women in Law: Explorations in Law, Family, and Sexuality* (1985) 108.

47 C. L. Bacchi, *Same Difference: Feminism and Sexual Difference* (1990) 199.

48 Aristotle, *Niomachean Ethics* (1925).

49 See J. Conaghan, 'Pregnancy and the Law: A Question of Strategy?' in this collection.

50 R. L. Klaff, 'The Tender Years Doctrine: A Defence' (1982) 70 *California Law Rev.* 335.

51 C. MacKinnon, *Toward a Feminist Theory of the State* (1989).

52 id.

53 Firestone, op. cit., n. 7, p. 6.

54 MacKinnon, op. cit., n. 51, p. 63.

55 M. Sjoo and B. Mor, *The Great Cosmic Mother* (1987) 358–391.

56 P. Spallone, *Beyond Conception: The New Ethics of Reproduction* (1989) 5. See also D. Nelken, *Science as Intellectual Property: Who Controls Research* (1984).

57 Firestone, op. cit., n. 7, p. 11.

58 C. C. S. Farsides, 'Body Ownership' in *Law, Health, and Medical Regulation*, eds. S. McVeigh and S. Wheeler (1992) 35.

59 L. Purdy, 'Are Women Foetal Containers?' (1990) 4 *Bioethics*.

60 Farsides, op. cit., n. 58, p. 35.

61 The inability of the Royal College of Midwives to resist compliance with the Sex Discrimination Act, however, threatens a shift in the locus of power and a new male agenda: the career progression of Britain's thirty male midwives is startling.

62 Spallone, op. cit., n. 56.

63 S. Gibson, 'Continental Drift: The Question of Context in Feminist Jurisprudence' (1990) 1 *Law and Critique* 173 at 183.

64 A. Hunt, 'Rights and Social Movements: Counter-Hegemonic Strategies' (1990) 17 *J. Law and Society* 309; D. Herman, 'Beyond the Rights Debate' (1993) 2 *Social and Legal Studies* (forthcoming).

Employment Discrimination in the New Europe:
A Litigation Project for Women

FRANCES OLSEN*

INTRODUCTION

Women throughout the world can and should work more closely to help one another. In recent years I have learned much from feminists in Europe, Asia, and Australia. Ideas and insights from these feminists can strengthen the women's movement in the United States of America; I have also learned ways in which Western feminists can and should support women around the world.

As Europe moves toward a closer union, co-operation among women might result in major improvements in the status of women in each country and across Europe. Drawing upon experiences from the civil rights and women's movements in the United States of America, this essay offers a proposal for using law to further such co-operation, by looking at the possibility and advantages of establishing a Women's Antidiscrimination Law Institute to take the lead in co-ordinating a European legal litigation strategy in relation to women's issues. In particular, the essay suggests that such an institute could have an important influence on the development of sex discrimination law in the European Community (hereafter cited as 'EC'). A Women's Antidiscrimination Law Institute could provide institutional support for feminist legal theory and at the same time help to develop effective European law. Such law could help to disrupt the *status quo* and reduce the actual power imbalance between women and men by shifting power towards women. Law in Western industrialized countries has tended to legitimate the *status quo* by embracing mild reforms. Yet there is nothing necessarily conservative about law; legal reforms could contribute to significant improvements in the role and status of women in Europe.

An example from the United States of America, which might suggest some of the advantages of having one institution developing a litigation strategy, is provided by the National Association for the Advancement of Coloured

* *Professor of Law, University of California at Los Angeles, 405 Hilgard Avenue, Los Angeles, California 90024–1476, USA*

Funding for this research was provided by the Council for International Exchange of Scholars–Fulbright and by the UCLA Law Dean's Fund. I wish to thank Joanne Conaghan for helpful comments and suggestions.

People (NAACP) Legal Defence Fund. This organization shepherded through the courts the major cases leading up to the landmark decision in *Brown* v *Board of Education*,[1] which in 1954 overturned more than a half century of bad, pro-segregation law and declared racially segregated public schools to be a violation of the American Constitution. A useful contrasting example, also from the United States of America, is provided by the women's movement. Although important constitutional law changes relating to women's rights began by 1971, legal efforts by women's organizations were splintered and disorganized.[2]

Later in this essay I will suggest that a particularly useful project for a European women's legal institute would be to develop EC law so as to address the massive problems facing women in the newly annexed states of the Federal Republic of Germany (formerly East Germany). Women are bearing the brunt of the economic problems associated with unification.[3] Redundancy is a major problem for men and women, but women are losing their jobs at a much higher rate than men and form a major group of the unemployed. Many middle-aged women realistically doubt that they will ever again find employment.[4] Unless something is done, the likelihood is that German employment policy will do very little to re-employ this group of well-qualified women. Instead, such policy is likely to focus on young men, whose unemployment is seen as a social problem in a way that the unemployment of women, especially middle-aged women, is not. The upsurge in neo-Nazi activity that has followed unification will, I think, encourage this governmental attitude, as the Christian Democrats pursue a policy of accommodation (if not encouragement), willing to use the neo-Nazis in their own political struggles with the Social Democrats, even if, in the process, the government hands dangerous political victories to the neo-Nazis.[5] The German government seems as reluctant as the Weimar judiciary to use criminal sanctions to deter right-wing violence[6] and appears to be more likely to reward violence with jobs for young men, supposedly in the hope of wooing them away from 'extremism' (and perhaps into the Christian Democratic party). As so often happens, women may be the victims who become sacrificed in a dispute among men.

LEGISLATIVE STRATEGY OR LITIGATION STRATEGY?

The Treaty of Rome (1957), the founding instrument of the European Economic Community, establishes the basis for EC law. Article 119 of the treaty provides that there shall be no discrimination in wages between women and men – for equal work, women and men must receive equal pay. This provision was expanded in a 1975 directive (Council Directive No. 75/117 on the approximation of the laws of the member states relating to the application of the principle of equal pay for women and men), to forbid discrimination in wages between women and men when they are doing work of 'equal value'. It was reinforced in 1976 by Council Directive No. 76/207 (on the implementation of the principle of equal treatment for women and men as regards access to employment, vocational training, promotion, and working conditions) requiring that there be no sex discrimination in employment with respect to hiring, firing, promotion, training, and so forth. The directives are addressed to member states and require each member state to enact national legislation to carry out the policies stated in the directive.[7]

Sex discrimination law can be improved either by new secondary legislation or by court decisions interpreting present legislation more broadly. Thus, those seeking change may work through legislation, litigation, or both. In order to understand the advantages and disadvantages of each approach, it is useful to take a closer look at how the EC functions.

Article 189 of the Treaty of Rome enables the European Council and the European Commission to make further, secondary legislation, under limited circumstances. Specifically, Article 100 allows the council, acting unanimously on a commission proposal, to enact directives requiring all member states to pass national legislation in accordance with the directive in order to harmonize the laws of member states and facilitate the functioning of the common market. Article 235 provides a broader authorization to the council to take 'appropriate measures', acting unanimously on a proposal from the commission and after consulting the European Parliament, 'necessary to attain, in the course of the operation of the common market, one of the objectives of the Community'.

The Single European Act 1986 provides in Articles 100A and 118A that under certain circumstances the council can act by a qualified majority vote on a proposal from the commission in co-operation with the European Parliament and after consulting the Economic and Social Committee. The effect of these provisions is that directives relating to the functioning of the internal market or to health and safety can be enacted without unanimity and over objection of an individual member state.

Many improvements in sex discrimination law have been made through EC directives, and more could be made in this manner. Excellent proposals for changes have been put forward.[8] The problem with all such proposals, however, is that they can be blocked or diluted by individual member states. Indeed, the United Kingdom Government has played this game in recent years.[9] A Labour government in Britain might change these policies significantly, but by the time such a government is elected, it is not unlikely that one or other of the member states will have elected a government ready to block or dilute antidiscrimination proposals that might be effective.

Certainly legislation may be enacted that will improve the situation for women, and such action should be supported. But, the limitations of a legislative strategy highlight some of the advantages of litigation. Rather than being blocked by individual hostile governments, litigation may be supported by individual friendly governments. By the time one friendly government is voted out of power, one can hope that another member state will have voted a friendly government into power.

Moreover, EC legislation will be more or less effective depending upon whether it receives a narrow or broad interpretation. The Treaty of Rome created the European Court of Justice (hereafter cited as the 'ECJ'), which is empowered to interpret the provisions of the treaty and secondary legislation. Article 177 authorizes national tribunals, including a country's lower courts, to apply to the ECJ for rulings on the proper interpretation of Community law where such a ruling might be relevant to cases before the national tribunal. If the proper interpretation of Community law may be relevant to a case before the highest court of a member state, or before any national court or tribunal from which no further appeal is allowed, that national court or tribunal must apply to the ECJ for such a ruling on the proper interpretation of European law. In 1963, the ECJ indicated that EC law should prevail over any conflicting national laws and that in certain circumstances individuals could enforce EC law in the courts of member states.[10] Thus, according to the court, the national courts in member states are required to enforce directly effective EC law even when it conflicts with national law. After some initial hesitation, most courts in member states have come to accept these principles.[11]

Cases thus reach the European Court of Justice more quickly and directly than they reach higher courts in the United States of America and most other countries. The fact that any court in an EC member state may refer questions about the proper interpretation of European law to the ECJ whenever it has before it a case in which such interpretation is of relevance to its decision, creates a litigation path untramelled by requirements that domestic/lower court routes first be exhausted.

Previous ECJ decisions have made it clear that European law may be relevant to a great many cases before national courts. A decade and a half ago, the ECJ ruled that Article 119 of the Treaty of Rome, the equal pay provision, was directly applicable in lawsuits in the national courts of the member states.[12] In other words, the national courts must take the equal pay provision into account when they are deciding cases, even if the case is between private parties and regardless of whether or not the government is a party to the suit. Although directives are addressed to governments, they may be directly applicable in a number of cases. First, the government of a member state is not permitted to rely on its failure to fully implement one of the directives in a suit brought against that government itself or against any employer which is an organ or instrument of the state.[13] Further, individual judges have been instructed by the ECJ to interpret their own national law in accordance with the directives.[14]

In a number of member states, including Germany, lower labour court judges and other trial judges tend to be more liberal than the country's appellate judges. While the situation varies from country to country (and even from region to region) and may change from one decade to the next, in comparison with higher court judges lower court judges are generally more likely to be young and female, less likely to be as wealthy, and likely to be more sensitive to issues of sex discrimination. In those EC countries in which this situation exists, these liberal labour and lower court judges can use the European Court of Justice to fight sex discrimination in situations in which their national appellate courts might be less sympathetic.

Suppose that a European Women's Antidiscrimination Law Institute, pursuant to its strategy, were to bring a test case involving European law before such a sensitive or sympathetic judge. That national judge could appeal immediately to the ECJ for a ruling on the issues raised by the test case, which would consider the questions and issue a written opinion. This opinion would then be treated by the court as precedent in subsequent cases.

Meanwhile, once the ECJ has answered the questions posed by the sympathetic national judge, that judge may then resolve any ambiguities in her or his national law to bring it into harmony with the opinion of the ECJ's decision. A creative jurist can often find some way to interpret potential ambiguities in her or his national law and may thus be in a position to decide the case in conformity with the requirements of EC law. Although the lower court's opinion (hopefully in favour of the institute's position) may well be appealed to a higher court with less sympathetic and perhaps more conservative judges, it is less likely to be reversed than an opinion based merely on national law, without reference to an ECJ decision. The higher national court of course has greater authority than the lower court to decide national law and has the power to overturn the lower court decision. Yet, if a national court were to reverse a lower court decision based on EC law, the higher court would in essence be ruling that its own national law was in violation of European law. Thus far, national courts have been reluctant to overturn lower court decisions in such circumstances.

The significance of the legal arrangement just described is that it greatly facilitates the implementation of a litigation strategy. Usually when some group seeks to change and develop law, it must rely on the slow process of appeal from lower decisions, and often the appellate process can move at such different rates of speed in the various courts that it may be difficult for any group to control the order in which cases reach the crucial court (in the United States of America, the Supreme Court). The litigation plan can be stymied at points by an opponent's decision not to appeal an adverse lower court ruling or a supreme court's refusal to accept a discretionary appeal (in the United States of America, a denial of *certiorari*). In the case of a litigation strategy aimed at the ECJ, all a group needs in order to obtain a ruling on a point is to find a suitable plaintiff and a sympathetic lower court judge. Of course, those seeking to develop European law in a manner hostile to women's equality could attempt to use the same approach to shape the law to women's detriment. Perhaps the most a Women's Antidiscrimination Law Institute can hope for is a significant head start in organizing.

THE NEED FOR A LITIGATION STRATEGY IN THE EUROPEAN COMMUNITY

The European Court of Justice is in the process of developing sex discrimination law and will continue to do so regardless of whether or not a Women's Antidiscrimination Law Institute is formed. Without such an organization, however, sex discrimination law is likely to develop in a considerably less satisfactory way. The ECJ appears to function more like a common law court than a civil law court. The concern that it shows for its own precedents is reminiscent of the courts of England and Wales and of the United States of America. Rather than constantly referring back to the wording of the treaty provision or directive, the ECJ builds upon the decisions it has already made interpreting these treaty provisions and directives. While not asserting that it is *making* law, the ECJ's decisions have precedential value. The order in which cases reach the ECJ and the quality of the cases may have a decisive influence on the outcomes of those cases and on the development of legal doctrine. A women's legal institute might well become a major influence on what litigation is brought and what strategies women pursue to try to achieve gender justice throughout the European Community.

There are additional reasons making it advisable to form a Women's Antidiscrimination Law Institute. First, the labour unions are at present a major supporting institution virtually necessary to any sustained litigation in many countries. Yet labour unions are male-dominated and generally insensitive to issues that affect women unless the issue also benefits men in a fairly clear and immediate way.[15]

In addition, throughout much of Europe the universities are so tenaciously dominated by men that it has been difficult for women to influence the decisions regarding what theories will be pursued in academia; the development of legal theory has been inhibited by this male domination.[16] At present there is inadequate institutional support for the development of feminist legal theory in Europe. An institute could provide valuable institutional support.

THE NAACP'S LEGAL DEFENCE FUND AND ITS LITIGATION STRATEGY

The NAACP was organized in 1909 to counter a rising tide of white violence against black Americans. The organization was originally dominated by white liberals, and only one lawyer was active in the group. Until 1930, the NAACP's involvement with law was limited to a few major high-profile cases. In 1930, the NAACP was awarded a $100,000 grant from a foundation that supported socially progressive action. Although the Depression and possibly mismanagement depleted the funds of the foundation after only $20,700 of the grant was paid, this money encouraged the NAACP to embark upon major litigation projects rather than just taking an occasional case.[17] In 1939, the NAACP formed its Legal Defence Fund, which gradually grew in size and developed a degree of independence from the NAACP itself.

When the NAACP Legal Defence Fund decided to launch a legal attack against segregation, it was faced with a difficult task. In 1896 the Supreme Court had considered the constitutionality of state Jim Crow laws – that is, laws requiring segregation – and, in the infamous case of *Plessy* v *Ferguson*,[18] had decided they were constitutional, holding that nothing in the constitution required the races to intermingle and if black people chose to view segregation as a negative statement about their race or as a badge of inferiority, that was their own problem. Although the Supreme Court had specified that facilities were allocated in a fair manner when different races were provided with 'separate but equal' accommodations, the railroad cars at issue in *Plessy* v *Ferguson* were far from equal in quality, appearance, or any other measure.

The project achieved a significant court success in 1938 when the United States Supreme Court ruled in *Missouri ex rel. Gaines* v *Canada*[19] that the State of Missouri violated a black man's constitutional rights when it refused him admission to the state law school (for whites) and offered him the choice between accepting a state scholarship to attend an out-of-state law school or to apply to the state university for black students, which the state said would then create a law school for black students. The Supreme Court left open the question whether a state could constitutionally refuse black students admission to the major state law school if it did create a separate law school for them, but held that 'a mere declaration of purpose [to create a law school for black students], still unfulfilled, is [not] enough'. The scholarship option did not provide 'separate but equal' facilities to Mr Gaines because it would have required him to leave the state of Missouri, and the Supreme Court ruled that the 'equal' provisions had to be established within the state. The possibility of Gaines attending law school in another state might 'mitigate the inconvenience of the discrimination but cannot serve to validate it'.[20]

Ten years later, in *Sipuel* v *Oklahoma State Regents*,[21] the Supreme Court reversed a decision of the Oklahoma state courts denying relief to a black woman seeking admission to the University of Oklahoma Law School. In a short opinion, the court simply reaffirmed the decision in *Gaines*. Oklahoma immediately established a separate law school for black students in three rooms of the state capitol, providing access for students to the state law library and hiring three white attorneys to act as professors. Ms Sipuel attended the black law school for eighteen months; she was its only student. After eighteen months, Oklahoma decided to admit her to the hitherto all-white University of Oklahoma Law School, from which she graduated in 1951.[22]

An additional important victory was achieved in 1950 in the case of *Sweatt* v *Painter*.[23] The state of Texas denied Heman Sweatt admission to the University of Texas Law School on the basis of his race, but established a law school for black students in three rooms across the street from the state capitol; students were to use the state law library and receive instruction from several professors from the University of Texas Law School who would split their time between the two schools. The NAACP Legal Defence Fund challenged the new law school as inferior to the University of Texas Law School. The Supreme Court held that the actual conditions in the law school did not provide blacks students with an education substantially equal to that provided to white students at the University of Texas Law School. Not only was it inferior 'in terms of number of the faculty, variety of courses . . . size of the student body, [and] scope of the library', but more important, the University of Texas 'possesses to a far greater degree those qualities which are incapable of objective measurement but which make for greatness in a law school', such as 'reputation of the faculty, experience of the administration, position and influence of the alumni, standing in the community, traditions and prestige'. Moreover, the Supreme Court asserted that the study of law required 'the interplay of ideas and the exchange of views' and by segregating black students, the state of Texas denied them contact with 'most of the lawyers, witnesses, jurors, judges, and other officials with whom [the students] will inevitably be dealing' as lawyers.[24]

The emphasis in *Sweatt* on intangibles made it relatively easy next to challenge segregation at the elementary school level. The same kind of intangibles certainly denied black children opportunities enjoyed by white children. It has been said that 'organizational control over the sequence and pace of litigation is the cornerstone of successful planned implementation of a law reform policy, the segregation cases being a prime example'.[25]

Brown v *Board of Education*[26] and the litigation that followed it contributed to the rapid growth of the civil rights movement.[27] In addition, by inspiring socially committed young people to look to law for social change, civil rights litigation came to have a profound effect on the composition of the legal profession in the United States of America.

Many factors concurred to make the NAACP's effort successful. The Legal Defence Fund attracted a particularly strong group of lawyers and gave them conditions that were conducive to creative strategizing. These lawyers included Thurgood Marshall (1936–1961), appointed Justice on the United States Supreme Court in 1967, and Derrick Bell (1960–66), who was appointed Professor at Harvard Law School in 1971 and fired in 1992 in a dispute over demands that Harvard add a woman of colour to its law faculty. These NAACP lawyers did not have a great deal of money or other material support, but they were able to focus their attention and concentrate their energies. They worked intensely and had many reasons to be enthusiastic. The people most concerned in the area of law were able to meet together and work out a unified strategy to help improve the legal status of black people. In addition, they had something approaching a monopoly on litigation. To a large extent, they were in a position to pick and choose cases. While they could not simply order up the plaintiffs they wished, they were often able to find very good possible plaintiffs and choose among them. For example, they would generally be able to choose academically well-qualified students to act as plaintiffs to integrate the graduate and professional schools. Some of these factors that made the NAACP's efforts successful were strikingly missing from the women's movement in the United States of America during the 1970s and 1980s.

THE WOMEN'S MOVEMENT AND LAW IN THE UNITED STATES OF AMERICA

Throughout the 1970s and 1980s, the number of women lawyers in the United States of America increased rapidly. Many of the women chose to study law

138

partly because they saw in law a route to significant change in the role and status of women. Nevertheless, the development of the law was haphazard and random. Several cases came before the courts that divided women, with socially conscious women arguing on opposite sides.[28]

The early history of efforts by women in the United States of America to seek constitutional protection resulted in cases about as depressing as *Plessy* v *Ferguson*. In 1872, the Supreme Court had upheld as constitutional a state's decision to bar women from the practice of law;[29] in 1874 it upheld a state's refusal to allow women to vote.[30] In 1908, the Supreme Court upheld protective labour legislation limited to women, while gender-neutral protective labour legislation had been struck down in 1905 as a violation of freedom to contract.[31] (Although this decision was helpful to many women, as it allowed for some useful labour legislation, it also facilitated and legitimated the exclusion of women from many better-paying jobs.)[32] Women charged with crime were often tried by all-male juries, and this practice was reinforced by a 1961 case upholding Florida's jury law that granted an automatic exemption to women and called to jury duty only the very few women who took the trouble to go to the courthouse and volunteer. The Supreme Court justified its decision by the assertion that women were 'still considered the center of home and family'.[33]

The first major break in this pattern came in 1971 with *Reed* v *Reed*.[34] Although the case purported to rule only that it was irrational, and therefore unconstitutional, arbitrarily to prefer men over women as executors of an estate,[35] *Reed* v *Reed* marked the beginning of a closer scrutiny by the court of gender-based discrimination.

The National Organization for Women (NOW) was formed in 1966 and modelled itself on the NAACP. By 1977, it had established a legal defence fund. Other groups, such as the Human Rights for Women (HRW), the Women's Rights Project of the American Civil Liberties Union (ACLU), and Women's Equity Action League (WEAL) also participated in litigation, often adopting different strategic positions from each other. A wide variety of women's groups participated in a few cases each: the National League of Women Voters, the American Association of University Women, Equal Rights Advocates, Federally Employed Women, the National Federation of Business and Professional Women, National Women's Political Caucus, Universalist Unitarian Women, and so forth.

NOW was never able to secure the kind of influence in litigation choices that the NAACP Legal Defence Fund enjoyed. In fact, many more women's rights cases were brought by the American Civil Liberties Union (ACLU) than by NOW or any other women's group. The ACLU has long been sensitive to civil liberties issues, but it has a much shorter history of sensitivity to women's rights issues. Like most organizations associated with law, the ACLU began as a thoroughly male-dominated organization. While women have played increasingly active roles in recent decades, it is still unfortunately quite fair to characterize the organization as male-dominated. The ACLU has played a significant role in dividing women's groups on the issue of pornography, by its decision to characterize the issue to be simply one of free speech and by taking a strong position against any limits on the production, dissemination, or use of pornography.

A 1983 study of sixty-three cases involving gender issues decided by the United States Supreme Court between 1969 and 1980 found that the ACLU participated in sixty-six percent of the cases, more than twice as many as any of the women's groups. Moreover, women's rights groups usually participated only by filing *amicus curiae* briefs,[36] not by initiating the litigation. In only four of the sixty-three cases did a women's rights group participate when the ACLU did not.

NOW participated in more Supreme Court cases than any other women's group during the period 1969–1980, but NOW was still less than half as active in this area as the ACLU. Until 1977, NOW had no lawyer on its staff. During the 1969 to 1977 terms of the Supreme Court, NOW participated in only seven cases, and its participation was largely reactive rather than part of any planned strategy. During the period of the study, 1969–1980, NOW sponsored only two cases (compared with the ACLU's sponsorship of sixteen cases during the same period) and in one of these it entered as co-sponsor at the request of a city attorney already involved in the case and primarily responsible for it.[37]

Many of the cases initiated by the ACLU comprised instances of direct sex discrimination and the use of gender-specific classifications, often involving male plaintiffs seeking equal treatment with women.[38] Generally the ACLU suits sought government neutrality toward gender, or gender-blind decisions. While many of these cases were intended to challenge gender stereotypes and ultimately to benefit women, it is uncertain whether or not this has been the result. The mere fact that gender-specific laws as a whole harm women as a group more than they harm men as a group does not necessarily mean that women benefit from each and every move toward gender neutrality.[39] Nor is there reason to believe that every effort to bring about equal treatment of men and women when such equal treatment happens to benefit men will be followed by efforts that will benefit women. Perhaps men are just more able to take advantage of anything society has to offer, even policies against sex discrimination. The ACLU did not adequately explore these questions before directing equal protection litigation toward a focus on racial or formal discrimination and toward protecting men's rights.

WOMEN IN EASTERN GERMANY

At a conference on sex discrimination in the new Germany held in Bad Homburg in the early spring of 1992, one of the non-lawyer participants, Hortense Hörburger,[40] presented the suggestion that European law be used to protect the jobs of women in the newly-annexed states of Germany. Many of the lawyers at the conference, especially the male lawyers, summarily dismissed the suggestion on the grounds that since whole departments and major employers were being closed down and women were laid off not specifically because they were women, European law simply did not cover the situation. My point of course is not that these lawyers misunderstood European law or the ways in which women were losing their jobs (although this possibility should not be too quickly overlooked), but rather that they were looking narrowly at the present without considering possibilities for developing the law. Viable theories can be developed that would improve chances for women in the newly-annexed states and I believe that a European Women's Antidiscrimination Law Institute would be just the institution to develop the theory and to have a reasonable chance of getting it adopted as European law over time.

There are many different approaches that a Women's Antidiscrimination Law Institute could take to litigation on behalf of women in the European Community. There are a number of reasons why a focus on women in the newly-annexed states of Germany seems appealing.

First, the formal qualifications of the women in the new states of Germany are better relative to their male counterparts than the formal qualifications of women throughout most of Europe.[41] Before unification, the majority of the women in the German Democratic Republic worked full-time most of their lives and they often held relatively important and well-paid jobs. Thus the legal issues may be raised in a particularly crisp manner.

In the absence of a legal litigation strategy, the prospect looks relatively poor. There are some important political developments and there are some wonderful women politicians in Germany, but the general balance of power seems quite depressing and at the moment conditions for women show few prospects for improving.

The German law schools, for example, are particularly retrograde regarding women. The overall number of women law professors is remarkably small. Although accurate statistics seem peculiarly difficult to obtain,[42] estimates of the total number of women full professors of law in Germany range from two to no more than twelve. During a year of interviews, every woman I spoke with believed that for a woman to show any interest in feminist legal theory would have a seriously negative effect on her possibilities for an academic career.

To teach law in a German university, it is virtually required that a person have a 'habilitation' as well as a doctorate degree. Both credentials are available only to students who come to the positive attention of one of the current professors of law in Germany. The professors are under no obligation to accept any particular number of doctorate students or habilitatees, and there appear to be no controls upon the professors to limit sex discrimination. Professors seem to be free to choose upon arbitrary grounds which students they shall support, and most would not even consider supporting a woman interested in feminism. Very few women have the habilitation. German academics acknowledge this shortage but dismiss it as simply due to the long period of study required to receive a habilitation and to the fact that the pursuit of a habilitation is very difficult to co-ordinate with the bearing and raising of children.

141

Under the terms of the unification treaty, the universities in the newly-annexed states, which used to employ respectable numbers of women, have been substantially changed. A great many of the law professors have been fired or pressured out of their jobs in one way or another. Humboldt University in Berlin, for example, has drastically cut the number of women teaching there.

Moreover, the labour unions are not reliable supports for women's equality. One of the unions with the best reputation for supporting women is I.G. Metall. I went to their Frankfurt headquarters to talk with their lawyers most informed about EC matters. One lawyer passed me on to another, then a third, and finally to the women's committee (which had originally set up the appointments for me but itself employs no lawyer), with each lawyer asserting that he really did not know much about sex discrimination. In the short discussion I had with each, I got the impression that their evaluation of their knowledge of European sex discrimination law was accurate – their knowledge was at least as weak as they represented it to be. Unions less pro-woman can only be expected to be worse. Women associated with these unions have suggested, however, that it might be possible for an independent organization to receive financial and other support from the unions, which recognize they should be doing more about sex discrimination and in many cases mean well.

CONCLUSION: ORGANIZATIONAL ALTERNATIVES FOR A WOMEN'S ANTIDISCRIMINATION LITIGATION INSTITUTE

There are many different ways in which one might organize a Women's Antidiscrimination Institute. My own inclination would be to encourage annual membership fees, especially from women and socially-committed lawyers throughout Europe. In addition, grants could be obtained from businesses that wish to show their support for women. I would hope that funds could also be obtained from trades unions, educational institutions, and individual governments.

The ECJ has ruled that European law should take precedence over any conflicting national laws of each member state. Any court in any member state can apply directly to the European Court to obtain a ruling on European law. Cases can thus reach the European Court very quickly and relatively inexpensively. The ruling of the European Court is binding and will be used as precedence in further cases. Gains through the European Court of Justice cannot be so easily defeated by an unsympathetic government in a single individual member state, as legislation has been. An organized litigation strategy, used by the NAACP, is likely to result in better development of the law for women than disorganization or no strategy, as in the case of the women's movement in the United States of America. The establishment of a European Women's Antidiscrimination Litigation Institute, to take the lead in developing a litigation strategy, would be a useful instance of international co-operation by women.

NOTES AND REFERENCES

1   347 US 483 (1954).
2   *Reed* v *Reed* 404 US 71 (1971) was a major landmark applying the equal protection clause to women. On the splintered and disorganized character of the efforts by women's organizations, see K. O'Connor and L. Epstein, 'Beyond Legislative Lobbying: Women's Rights Groups and the Supreme Court' (1983) 67 *Judicature* 134.
3   D. Rosenberg, 'Shock Therapy: GDR Women in Transition from a Socialist Welfare State to a Social Market Economy' (1991) 17 *Signs: J. of Women in Culture and Society* 129, p. 132; C. Klenner, '*Wir wollen unser Recht auf Arbeit*' in *Handbuch Wegweiser für Frauen in den fünf neuen Bundesländern*, ed. K. Rohnstock (1991); C. Schindler, '*Frauenarmut – (K)ein Thema*' (1992) 1 *Weibblick* 26–27; U. Fremerey and P. Kupferschmidt (eds.), *Dokumentation Frauen in den neuen Bundesländern im Prozess der deutschen Einigung* (1992) 1–51.
4   op. cit., n. 3.
5   This view may be becoming more prevalent. See, for example,T. Marshall, 'Political Ploy Led Germany Into Turmoil', *Los Angeles Times*, 1 December 1991, p. 4.
6   Hitler, for his abortive coup attempt that left several people dead, served nine months in jail and was allowed to take his personal secretary with him to work on *Mein Kampf*. For a discussion of the conservativism of the Weimar judiciary, see I. Müller, *Hitler's Justice* (1991) 10–24.
7   See generally F. Olsen, 'Legal Responses to Gender Discrimination in Europe and the USA' in *Collected Courses of the Academy of European Law* (Vol. II) ed. J. Weiler (1992) 207; E. Ellis, *European Community Sex Equality Law* (1991).
8   See, for example, Ellis, op. cit., n. 7, pp. 206–26.
9   Even when a qualified majority procedure applies, a single government can engage in tactics that both delay and dilute implementation, as in the case of the recently agreed Pregnancy Directive. See J. Conaghan, 'Statutory Maternity Pay and the European Dimension' (1991) 20 *Ind. Law J.* 314 and 'Pregnancy and the Law: A Question of Strategy?' in this collection.
10 Case 26/62, *Van Gend en Loos* v *Nederlandse Tariefcommissie* [1963] E.C.R. 1, 12–13.
11 See Ellis, op. cit., n. 7, pp. 8–12. On the question of the 'direct effect' of EC directives, see below.
12 Case 43/75, *Gabrielle Defrenne* v *Societé Anonyme Belge de Navigation Aerienne Sabena* [1976] E.C.R. 455.
13 Case 152/84, *M H Marshall* v *Southampton and South West Hampshire Area Health Authority (Teaching)* [1986] E.C.R. 723; Case 8/81, *Becker* v *Finanzamp* [1982] E.C.R. 53.
14 Case 14/83, *Sabine von Colson and Elisabeth Kamann* v *Land Nordrhein-Westfalen* [1984] E.C.R. 1891, 1909 para. 26. The recent decision in *Marleasing SA* v *La Comercial Internactional de Alimentacion* Case C–106/89 [1990] E.C.R. I–4135, holding that national courts are obliged to interpret domestic legislation in accordance with EC directives, even where the legislation in question was not passed to implement a directive, significantly strengthens the effectiveness of directives in domestic litigation.
15 In relation to the United Kingdom, se R. Townshend-Smith, *Sex Discrimination in Employment* (1989) 110–12, 199–200. See also below.
16 See conclusion below.
17 See R. Rabin, 'Lawyers for Social Change: Perspectives on Public Interest Law' (1976) 28 *Stanford Law Rev.* 207, p. 215.
18 163 US 537 (1896).
19 305 US 337 (1938).
20 Missouri responded to the decision by immediately proceeding to establish Lincoln law school for black students. The NAACP Legal Defence Fund was prepared to argue that the school the state officials established was not 'equal', but the lawyers had to abandon the case when they could not locate Mr Gaines, their plaintiff. See M. Tushnet, *The NAACP's Legal Strategy Against Segregated Education 1925–1950* (1987) 73–75.
21 332 US 631 (1948).
22 See Tushnet, op. cit., n. 20, pp. 122–23.

23 339 US 629 (1950).

24 A similar, companion case ruled that Oklahoma denied constitutional rights to a graduate student of education when it allowed him to attend classes at the state university but required him to sit by himself in an anteroom or alcove away from the rest of the students. The Supreme Court ruled that the restrictions would 'impair and inhibit his ability to study, to engage in discussion and exchange views with other students, and, in general, to learn his profession'. *McLaurin* v *Oklahoma State Regents* 339 US 637 (1950).

25 Rabin, op. cit., n. 17, p. 218.

26 347 US 483 (1954).

27 But see, against, *The Autobiography of Malcolm X* (1965), arguing that *Brown* v *Board of Education* undermined the growing radicalism of African-Americans and contributed to ensuring that the civil rights movement would seek mere integration rather than the empowerment of the African-American peoples.

28 See, for example, *Miller-Wohl* v *Com'r Labor and Industry* 214 Mont. 238, 692 P.2d 1243 (1984) (pregnancy benefits); *EEOC* v *Sears, Roebuck & Co* 839 F.2d 302 (7th Cir 1988) (women's preferences for work); *California Federal* v *Guerra* 479 US 272 (1987) (pregnancy benefits); *American Booksellers Assoc* v *Hudnet* 598 F. Supp. 1316 (SD Ind 1984), aff'd 771 F.2d 323 (7th Cir 1985), aff'd 475 US 1001 (1986) (anti-pornography ordinance).

29 *Bradwell* v *Illinois* 83 US 130 (1872).

30 *Minor* v *Happersett 88 US 162 (1874)*.

31 Muller v *Oregon* 208 US 412 (1908) (upholding maximum-hour labour legislation limited to women); *Lochner* v *New York* 198 US 45 (1905) (invalidating as unconstitutional maximum-hour legislation for bakers).

32 See F. Olsen, 'From False Paternalism to False Equality: Judicial Assaults on Feminist Community, Illinois 1869–1895' (1986) 84 *Mich. Law Rev.* 1518.

33 *Hoyt* v *Florida* 368 US 57, 62 (1961).

34 Above, n. 2.

35 In *Reed* v *Reed* the divorced father and mother of a young man who had committed suicide each applied to be appointed to be the executor of his estate, that is, to handle the financial affairs and other such matters incidental to his death.

36 An *amicus curiae* brief is a legal paper filed with the court by someone who is not a party to the lawsuit but who wishes to make legal arguments that may influence the court's decision.

37 O'Connor and Epstein, op. cit., n. 2.

38 See, for example, *Stanley* v *Illinois* 405 US 645 (1972) (man successfully claims for unwed father rights of unwed mother to hearing before termination of parental rights); *Kahn* v *Shevin* 416 US 351 (1974) (man unsuccessfully challenges tax exemption provided widows but not widowers); *Weinberger* v *Wiesenfeld* 420 US 636 (1975) (man successfully challenges denial to surviving widower with child of benefits routinely awarded to surviving widow with child). See also *Orr* v *Orr* 440 US 268 (1979) (man equally entitled as women to show need for alimony at divorce).

39 For my sceptical view of the possibility of government neutrality, see F. Olsen, 'The Family and the Market: A Study of Ideology and Legal Reform' (1983) 96 *Harvard Law Rev.* 1497; 'The Myth of State Intervention in the Family' (1985) 18 *Univ. Michigan J. Law Reform* 835.

40 Dr Hörgburger has worked as a journalist and in various research projects. She is the author of the book *Europas Frauen Fordern Mehr* (1990) on the social dimension of the European Community, especially as it relates to women. Her most recent book, *Europa – Ratlos Statt Grenzenlos* (Schüren 1992) examines the Maastricht Treaty.

41 See Rosenberg, op. cit., n. 3, p. 135, n. 23.

42 It might seem that some organization in Germany would keep track of such statistics, or that at least an interested person could contact each of the thirty-six German law schools and find out the gender composition of their full professor ranks. The situation was complicated somewhat by unification and the reorganization of the eastern law schools. During the course of nearly a year in the country, I asked a wide variety of government and university officials, most of whom reported having no idea, and the rest of whom presented wildly disparate answers.

144